Education at SAGE

SAGE is a leading international publisher of journals, books, and electronic media for academic, educational, and professional markets.

Our education publishing includes:

- accessible and comprehensive texts for aspiring education professionals and practitioners looking to further their careers through continuing professional development

- inspirational advice and guidance for the classroom

- authoritative state of the art reference from the leading authors in the field

Find out more at: **www.sagepub.co.uk/education**

Formative Asses
for **Teaching** & **Le**

BILL BOYLE & MARIE CHARLES

Formative Assessment *for* Teaching & Learning

Los Angeles | London | New Delhi
Singapore | Washington DC

Los Angeles | London | New Delhi
Singapore | Washington DC

SAGE Publications Ltd
1 Oliver's Yard
55 City Road
London EC1Y 1SP

SAGE Publications Inc.
2455 Teller Road
Thousand Oaks, California 91320

SAGE Publications India Pvt Ltd
B 1/I 1 Mohan Cooperative Industrial Area
Mathura Road
New Delhi 110 044

SAGE Publications Asia-Pacific Pte Ltd
3 Church Street
#10-04 Samsung Hub
Singapore 049483

© Bill Boyle and Marie Charles, 2014

First edition published 2014

Editor: Marianne Lagrange
Assistant editor: Rachael Plant
Production editor: Jeanette Graham
Copyeditor: Rosemary Campbell
Proofreader: Isabel Kirkwood
Indexer: Avril Ehrlich
Marketing manager: Catherine Slinn
Cover design: Wendy Scott
Typeset by: C&M Digitals (P) Ltd, Chennai, India
Printed in Great Britain by Henry Ling Limited, at the Dorset Press, Dorchester, DT1 1HD

Library of Congress Control Number: 2013934399

British Library Cataloguing in Publication data

A catalogue record for this book is available from the British Library

MIX
Paper from
responsible sources
FSC™ C013985
www.fsc.org

ISBN 978-1-4462-7331-9
ISBN 978-1-4462-7332-6 (pbk)

Contents

About the Authors

Professor Bill Boyle holds the Chair of Educational Assessment and is Director of the Centre for Formative Assessment Studies(CFAS) in the School of Education at the University of Manchester, UK. The CFAS is the oldest research centre (founded 1988) in the UK for supporting teachers, teacher trainers, schools and policy makers in using formative teaching, learning and assessment and is involved in supporting the development of formative assessment in the UK and in many countries around the globe. Professor Boyle and his co-author, Marie Charles, publish their research work in academic and practitioner journals, present at international conferences and workshops, and design and support developments in formative teaching, learning and assessment. Currently, they are working with colleagues in Russia, Armenia, Oman, Saudi Arabia and the USA on understanding, training and using formative strategies for more effective teaching and learning.

Marie Charles is a teacher, formative assessment researcher and consultant and an author whose work demonstrates that she believes passionately in the learner (rather than measurement or grading) being at the centre of the education process – a belief that she carries into her classroom practice.

Acknowledgements

We would like to acknowledge the following people and organisations who have kindly made case study and other material available for use in this book:

Robin Alexander

Jodie Hunter

Taylor & Francis (www.tandfonline.com)

Introduction

This book focuses on the recognition of the importance of formative assessment in the process of effective teaching and learning and our aim is to build practitioners' understanding and capacity to use formative assessment in that process. Despite the strategies, myths and gimmicks that have been operationalised in its name, formative assessment is a simple concept. To borrow a quotation from Philippe Perrenoud: 'Any assessment that helps a pupil to learn and develop is formative' (1991, p. 80). It is important that teachers know and understand how formative assessment helps the child to learn and how feedback from assessment supports that learning process.

In 2005, the Organisation for Economic Co-operation and Development (OECD) issued the following Policy Brief (November 2005) which addressed the role of formative assessment in improving learning in classrooms, the issues of what is involved in formative assessment in practice, and how policy can promote formative assessment and hence effective teaching and assessment systems:

> Tests and examinations are a classic way of measuring student progress and are integral to accountability of schools and the education systems. … To be truly effective, assessment should be 'formative' – in other words, identifying and responding to the students' learning needs. In classrooms featuring formative assessment, teachers make frequent, interactive assessments of student understanding. This enables teachers to adjust their teaching to meet individual student needs … Teachers also actively involve students in the process, helping them to develop skills that enable them to learn better (OECD 2005, p. 1).

The OECD Policy Brief further stressed that formative assessment needs to be practised systematically in international education systems and that it should be used as a framework for teaching. Following this approach, teachers would begin to change the ways in which they interacted with pupils, how they set up learning situations and 'scaffolded' pupils towards learning goals and 'even how they define student success' (2005, p. 1) These beliefs are at the heart of this book.

We believe that children's learning needs have to be at the core of successful teaching and learning. Therefore it is important to consider and reflect on definitions of the act of teaching:

Teaching involves a search for meaning in the world. Teaching is a life project, a calling, a vocation that is an organising centre of all other activities. Teaching is past and future as well as present. It is background as well as foreground. It is depth as well as surface. Teaching is pain and humour, joy and anger, dreariness and epiphany. Teaching is world-building, it is architecture and design, it is purpose and moral enterprise. Teaching is a way of being in the world that breaks through the boundaries of a traditional job and in the process re-defines all life and teaching itself. (Ayers 2008, p. 6)

It is within this humanistic framework (Boyle & Charles 2011) that formative assessment has to be located and seen as an integral cog in the cognitive, affective and conative environment of the learner.

Formative assessment through its structural philosophy of evidence elicitation, analysis and action supplies the strategy to make teaching effective and learning deep and sustained. Formative assessment is much more embedded within pedagogy than the simplistic mantra of 'closing the gap' in standards-based measurement which tends to accompany descriptions of its effect on teaching and learning. Formative assessment has to be theorised, understood and practised within the perspective of situated teaching and learning for its full social and cultural effect on the learner as individual to be understood. This is not a statement of rhetoric, it forms the core of our philosophy as teachers and it informed our pedagogical practice in the classroom. This is central to the support and advice we offer to schools and teachers, colleagues and ministries of education all round the globe. We believe that teachers need to have (and constantly revisit, reflect and reinforce) a philosophy of teaching and learning of their own to provide a purpose and rationale for their pedagogy. We are concerned about the misunderstandings that teachers have about the definition or definitions of assessments, and therefore the uses, purposes and practices of assessment. What is formative assessment? How is formative assessment commonly understood? Many times we have heard teachers state in workshops or seminars that formative assessment 'informs next steps'. What are those 'next steps' based on? What types of information (evidence) is the teacher working from to support their pupils through the 'next steps'?

This is not a 'how to do formative assessment' manual in the traditional sense, however. This book shows how an understanding of formative teaching, learning and assessment can enrich normal day-to-day teaching and learning situations. The chapters (which include case studies) are based on observed teaching situations in which the authors have been involved as researchers, and within each case the formative strategies are identified and analysed for the reader.

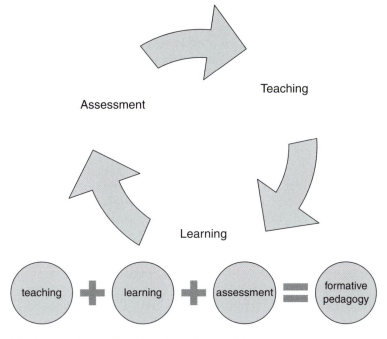

Figure I.1 Integration of Teaching, Learning and Assessment

Structure and content

The structure of the book is based on a sequence of chapters on aspects of formative assessment which are illustrated by case studies of classroom practice or classroom research projects. Each of these chapters shows how to integrate the strategies which the authors (for manageability and coherence) call their 'formative assessment toolkit'. These strategies, although written in isolation for explication purposes in separate chapters of this book, are intended to be combined in classroom practice to comprise a pedagogical formative toolkit. The strategies are: guided group teaching, differentiation, observation and evidence elicitation, analysis and feedback, co-construction, reflective planning, self-regulation and dialogue and dialogic.

Assessment or learning?

What is assessment? What is formative assessment? What does assessment in support of learning really mean? How can teachers use or make use of assessment in their classrooms? What is teacher assessment? What is the purpose of teacher assessment? Teacher assessment is criterion-referenced: a pupil is assessed in relation to a criterion and not in relation to other pupils. The teacher can then share responsibility for the learning with the child by 'feeding back' specific support information to enable the child to move on in his/her next learning steps.

Development of learning depends on many interrelated factors. An assessment that optimises one or more of these factors is formative. 'Anything that influences the working conditions, the meaning of the activity or the pupil's self-image is just as important as the material and cognitive aspects of the teaching situation' (Perrenoud 1991, p. 80). There are many ways to support a pupil to progress his/her learning. These include explaining a concept in more detail or in another way, or setting a different task for the concept. This task may be more motivating or just better matched to his/her ability. The student may need reassurance or a boost to his/her confidence or to be located in a different social learning environment or relationship.

In this book we offer explanations and suggested solutions to explore and extend the readers' discussions and understandings of these pedagogical practices.

Teaching, learning and assessment are interrelated. Assessment should be integrated into teaching and learning activities. The assessment activity should arise from what is going on in the pupils' current learning activity; an assessment task should build on a pupil's previous experience; an assessment task must be clearly introduced to the pupils – they need to understand what is expected of them. Teacher assessment is *not* based on a traditional testing model. Teacher assessment is continuous and classroom life goes on as usual while teaching and learning are modified based on the 'ongoing' assessments carried out by the teacher.

Teachers need to understand how they can change the culture of their classrooms from one in which pupils are being passively prepared against testable curriculum sub-domains. How can teachers move to a situation in which pupils become active learners, with learning deepened and enriched by assessment information? How can this information be gathered from dialogue between teacher and pupil and from pupil working collaboratively with pupil? What makes this assessment 'in support of learning', formative?

There is no entity called 'assessment' which exists on its own and stands alone as a process, independent of teaching and learning. There is the paradigm of 'testing', which is not the same thing as assessment – although the last decade might have made one think otherwise (Hall et al. 2004). The whole and only purpose of assessment is to produce information which is then used to support student and teacher in the learning process. This is assessment as one of an integrated set of processes labelled 'teaching, learning and assessment', which are mutually linked and supportive of assessment. Assessment in support of teaching and learning puts the child and his or her learning needs at the centre of teaching and learning so that the child becomes actively involved in their own learning.

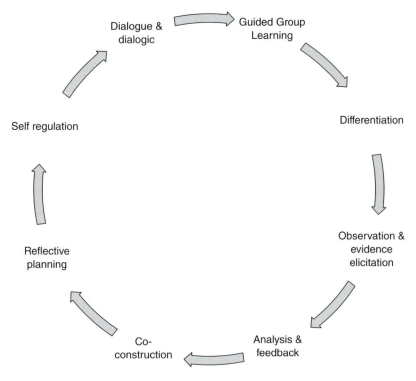

Figure I.2   The inter-connected concepts of formative assessment

That sounds fine as rhetoric but what is it that enables assessment to support learning? One suggested response could be that through formative assessment principles, teachers access specific information on children's learning processes. They then use this information to support their interventions in the pupils' learning processes, actions and activities. The strategies through which teachers access, process, focus and use that information to intervene appropriately in pupil learning are assessment integrated with teaching and learning. In Chapter 2 we explore this aspect through the vehicle of guided group pedagogy. In Chapter 3 we introduce differentiation as a planned but flexible process which is expressed through a guided group methodology supported by analysis and feedback (Chapter 5). The use of a critical lens (observation and evidence elicitation: Chapter 4) is explored. Effective assessment enables teachers to refine their micro observations and to reflect on and revise their planning according to learning needs (Chapter 7: reflective practice).

Concerned that teacher talk is dominating classrooms, we explore the concepts of dialogue and dialogic (Chapter 9) as tools to support the emergence of the learner (self-regulated learning: Chapter 8) and a changing of regulation in the pedagogic transactions (co-construction: Chapter 6) between teacher and pupil.

1

What is Formative Assessment?

> In this chapter we look at different ideas about formative assessment and consider teacher beliefs about formative assessment.

Sharing definitions

We carried out a research survey in UK primary schools in 2008 – five years after assessment for learning had been formally introduced into the national teaching and learning agenda through the Primary strategy: 'Excellence and Enjoyment' (DfES 2003) – to investigate how standardised the definition of formative assessment was across schools. The results were surprising, with a wide range of definitions expressed by teachers. It is essential, therefore, that formative assessment has a clear definition so that its practice can be understood and improved by teachers. The literature in the research field offers several interpretations and definitions. For example, Coffey et al. (2011) suggest that 'formative assessment should be understood and presented as nothing other than genuine engagement with ideas, which includes being responsive to them and using them to inform next moves' (p. 1129), while US researcher James Popham's definition states clearly that 'formative assessment is not a test but a process that produces not so much a score but a qualitative insight into student understanding' (Popham 2008, p. 6). The process and outcomes of formative assessment are the focus for Bennett whose definition links the teaching, learning and assessment activity: 'formative assessment involves a combination of task and instrument and process' (2011, p. 7)

According to socio-constructivist learning theory, individuals assimilate knowledge and concepts after restructuring and reorganising it through negotiation with their surroundings, including fellow learners

(Hager & Hodkinson 2009; Rogoff 1990). All children do not learn all that is taught and teachers cannot know what and how well concepts are understood without using some process to establish pupil understanding. Since each pupil has his/her own unique socially constructed context, ideas, concepts and meanings are not fixed nor standardised across a group or class of pupils. Therefore the individual outcomes of learning situations will be diverse. The word 'assessment' derives from the Latin word 'assidere' meaning 'to sit beside' – this can be taken to imply a close proximity or association between the assessor and the learner in the assessment process (Good 2011).

Criticism of an assessment process which had traditionally been designed to grade and certificate led to the emergence of formative assessment, a concept designed to support pupils' learning processes. 'Beginning in the 1960s researchers and authors from a range of disciplinary backgrounds weighed in against the proliferation of classification practices stemming from the American psychometric current, thus opening the way to prioritising assessments that measured students' learning' (Morrissette 2011, p. 249). These researchers included, in sociology, Becker (1963), Bourdieu and Passeron (1970), Perrenoud (1998, 2004), in anthropology, Rist (1977), in palaeontology, Gould (1981), in philosophy, Foucault (1975), and in evaluation Crooks (1988), Mehan (1971), and Popham (2008) have drawn attention to issues such as the consequences of testing practices on narrowing classroom pedagogy and culture.

> For example the secondary adaptations (plagiarism, cramming) that pupils develop in a context which continually threatens their integrity and self-esteem; the cultural biases of the tests used to assess their learning; the 'instrumental illusion' that is, the ingrained belief that it is possible to exclude all the interpretive processes which are necessarily involved in these practices; and finally the power ascribed to evaluation practices that, on the one hand, contribute to a form of control and standardisation and on the other, perpetuate social disparities. (Morrissette 2011, p. 249)

From these beginnings, there has been an increasing interest in the formative principles and functions of assessment serving to support children's learning rather than to grade pupil outcomes.

Research on formative assessment practices has covered a range of disparate approaches: a focus on the choice of tasks and the context in which they are carried out (Wiggins 1998); formative assessment as a means of modelling, designing and supporting professional development (Ash & Levitt 2003; Boyle et al. 2005); assessment criteria (Torrance & Pryor 2001); the feedback provided to pupils (Hattie & Timperley 2007); and pupils' views about assessment (Cowie 2005).

Linda Allal (1988) has produced a typology of remediation post-assessment of a learning objective for a concept as follows:

- **Retroactive adjustment**: which takes place after a shorter or longer learning sequence, on the basis of micro-summative evaluation
- **Interactive adjustment**: which takes place through the learning process
- **Proactive adjustment**: which takes place when the pupil is set an activity or enters a teaching situation.

These three methods may be combined and none of them are to be associated with a stereotyped procedure. Retroactive adjustment may take the form of a criterion-referenced test followed by remediation. Retroactive adjustment may mean going over much earlier material and temporarily refraining from 'pushing' the child to learn things that may cause him/her problems. It may also entail adjusting other aspects of the teaching situation or even the child's progress through the school.

Enlarged understandings of formative assessment

How assessment links to and is an ongoing inherent aspect of teaching and learning is a perennial issue. In this debate, the definition and role of assessment are crucial. A reductionist definition of assessment with its aim defined as an increase in learner 'performance' measured as test data is too narrow a concept to guide teaching. In England, despite the desire and the recommendation of the Task Group on Assessment and Testing (DES 1988) the reduction of assessment to being viewed as synonymous with 'testing' and a one-dimensional view of 'performance' is exactly the situation that has become reality in the 25 years since TGAT reported.

The TGAT proposed that teachers should assess only that which is observable. Teaching decisions, especially the decision to move on to the next part of the curriculum, should always be based on an assessment, no matter how informal, of the learner's response to the current activity. It is that assessment of current achievement which is the basic building block of any assessment system in the context of a National Curriculum. Assessment in the context of the National Curriculum was not designed to predict how a learner will do in later life, by trying in some way to measure ability or effort. National Curriculum Assessment was intended as a means of demonstrating how children were progressing through the level structure of the entitlement curriculum. However, it has ceased to be criterion-referenced (definition) and now serves as a means of norm-referencing children and schools.

Formative assessment was legitimised and became part of the education policy makers' and teaching fraternity's lexicon through the seminal Task Group on Assessment and Testing report (DES 1988) which developed the assessment system for the National Curriculum encompassed by the 1988 Education Reform Act (DES 1988). However, with the commencement of paper and pencil testing of the National Curriculum (the 'sats') in 1991, soon the only form of 'assessment' which mattered was summative and this was embodied in the end of key stage tests. These quickly became a 'high stakes' priority for schools who felt pressured by both Ofsted (Office for Standards in Education) and the government who used the test results as the principal (often, it appeared to teachers, the sole) measure of national standards and each school's success or failure. This was a very one-dimensional 'standards agenda' as its sole focus was on a school's test scores based on the sub-domains of English and mathematics measured against arbitrarily set national percentage targets.

Officially, summative Teacher Assessment (TA) has 'parity' (Dearing 1994) with the test outcomes – but the school performance 'league' tables use only the test data. The (non-formative) purpose of TA was designed to be the holistic award of a teacher judgement 'level' for each child at the end of the school year. This attainment judgement was based on the child's progression through an 8-level scale, the judgements to be made as a 'best fit' of the child's 'performance' against a prose paragraph describing performance at each level (Boyle 2008; Hall & Harding 2002). This task required standardisation of definitions of quality (at school, regional and national levels) for any judgements to be transferable as reliable and valid. 'Unless teachers come to this understanding and learn how to abstract the qualities that run across cases with different surface features but which are judged equivalent they can hardly be said to appreciate the concept of quality' (Sadler 1989, p. 128). This necessitated dialogue, communication and collaboration by teachers with their colleagues within and essentially across schools and as this strategy was financially unsupported by central government it was soon 'dismissed' by teachers. Their reasons included 'workload', difficulties of communication, administration and logistics of meetings to share understandings and meanings of children's work. Significantly, the 'sats' scores were conveniently received by schools before the date for national returns of TA, enabling schools to avoid disagreement between test and TA and reduce workload by returning as near a match as possible across the two scores (Reeves et al., 2001). The test and TA reported levels were in accord so there appeared to be no need to further investigate a school's performance. The TA process has become even further complicated with the introduction of Assessing Pupil Performance (APP), a government strategy which stresses the making of judgements at sub-levels (2a, 2b, 2c) and then at sub-sub-levels, e.g. high 2c, secure 2c, low 2c.

Both summative and formative approaches to assessment are important. Summative assessments are 'an efficient way to identify students' skills at key transition points such as entry into the world of work or for further education' (OECD 2005, p. 6). Tests and examinations are the traditional ways of measuring student progress and have become integral to the accountability of schools and the education system in many countries. However, internationally assessment has become almost universally equated with high stakes scoring and testing (Hall et al. 2004; Shepard 2000, 2005; Twing et al. 2010) and teaching has consequently been reduced to servicing that metric (Guinier 2003).

Much of the common emphasis on formative assessment has been that it occurs within learning activities rather than subsequent to them. It provides information for the teacher to use to make judgements during a lesson or day-to-day in the planning of matched materials for students in lessons (Ramaprasad 1983; Shepard 2000). Formative assessments are often used synonymously with benchmark or interim assessments and in reference to student performance on test items (Bennett 2011; Popham 2006). Popham defines formative assessment as 'not a test but a process' that, as Shepard adds, can 'inform instructional decision-making' (Shepard 2000).

What is an acceptable definition of formative assessment?

We used a quotation from Perrenoud in the Introduction to this book: 'Any assessment that helps a pupil to learn and develop is formative' (1991, p. 80). However, the statement needs development. The core of formative assessment lies not in what teachers do but in what they see. The teacher has to have awareness and understanding of the pupils' understandings and progress. 'To appreciate the quality of a teacher's awareness, it is essential to consider disciplinary substance: what is happening in the class and of that what does the teacher notice and consider? (Coffey et al. 2011, p. 1128). Do the teachers neglect the disciplinary substance of student thinking? Do they presume only traditional targets of (subject) as the body of information (to be taught and then assessed), selected in advance? Do they treat assessment as strategies and techniques for teachers? It is imperative that teachers consider student thinking not only with respect to its alignment with the 'linear curriculum' but also with respect to the nature of the students' participation. Students' acceptance that 8 squared equals 64 could be seen as alignment with the taught curriculum. However, if students accept that calculation on the teacher's authority, rather than because they experience the problem, design the calculation and see the result supported by evidence and reasoning they become passive recipients of the transmission of knowledge.

'Therefore it is essential that formative assessment – and accounts of it in the literature – consider more than the "gap" between pupil thinking and the correct concepts' (Coffey et al. 2011, p. 1129).

It is attention to pupil thinking that will cause the teacher to abandon his/her original plan for a lesson. Formative assessment will create 'learning objectives' that a teacher will not have had in his/her conceptual planning at the outset – and at two levels. The first level is one of conceptualisation – how the child understands the concept – while the other objective is at the level of how the child approaches the theme/concept. The teacher should be constantly working to move students into engaging with the theme/concept as researchers and away from the 'classroom game' (Lemke 1990) of telling the teacher what they think s/he wants to hear.

In conceptualising assessment as 'learner behavioural analysis', the teacher is formatively assessing student thinking by paying close attention to the demonstrations through behaviours and outcomes of that thinking. S/he wants to understand what the students are thinking and why – as surely would any participant in any meaningful discussion. Formative assessment should be understood and presented as nothing other than genuine engagement with ideas, which includes being responsive to them and using them to inform next moves (Coffey et al. 2011, p. 1129). For example, the teacher is exploring ideas about rainfall with a group of primary children. She originally had set up the dialogue linked to weather in a discussion of words and phrases such as 'wet', 'cloudy' and 'splashing in the puddles'. One child extended the discussion into the related area of her own bath time and used vocabulary related to that experience such as 'the water washes over me'. In this context the formative teacher re-shaped her original idea and teaching concept to the perspective and location of the learners, i.e. the child whose thinking had moved on to 'water' produced a 'water' poem.

A teacher's model of formative assessment in practice should be in close proximity physically and temporally with what the teacher planned that children would learn: the practice of assessing the quality of their own ideas for their fit with their learning objectives. Effective assessment is part of the learning process for children. It is important that they understand, for example, in studying 'forces', what the specific kinds of forces are, but through their own experimentation, for example using concept cartoons such as 'Bottle on the shelf' which open dialogue about the kinds of forces and their actions to move a bottle placed on a shelf (see Figure 1.1). In that case, children are learning to assess ideas as 'nascent scientists' rather than as compliant students. Understanding these discipline-based assessment criteria is part of what educators should help children learn. As children begin to engage in disciplinary assessment, they are learning a fundamental aspect (of their subject) (Coffey et al. 2011, p.1129).

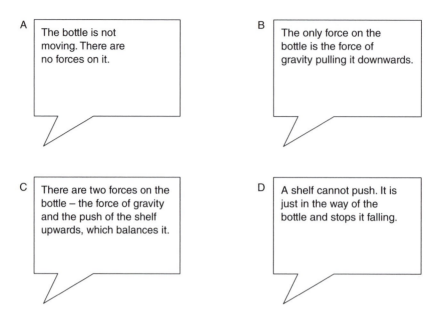

A The bottle is not moving. There are no forces on it.

B The only force on the bottle is the force of gravity pulling it downwards.

C There are two forces on the bottle – the force of gravity and the push of the shelf upwards, which balances it.

D A shelf cannot push. It is just in the way of the bottle and stops it falling.

Figure 1.1 Bottle on the shelf evidencing the force of gravity

Teachers do not need strategies (traffic lights, two stars and a wish) to become aware of and more responsive to children's thinking. This begins with a shift of attention, with a shift of how the teacher frames, and how s/he asks the pupil to frame, what is taking place in the classroom. This orientation towards responsiveness to pupils' ideas and practices resonates with work in teacher education (particularly in mathematics, see Ball et al. 2008; Kazemi et al. 2009) that has pushed for more practice-based accounts of effective preparation. This resonates with learning to teach 'in response to what students do' (Kazemi et al. 2009) and more attention to 'demands of opening up to learners' ideas and practices connected to specific subject matter' (Ball & Forzani 2011, p. 46). By this reasoning, much depends on how teachers frame (plan) what they are doing – and the primary emphasis on strategies (gimmicks) in teacher training may be a part of the problem. Assignments that direct teachers and teachers in training to what they are doing may inhibit their focus on what pupils are thinking. With Coffey et al., we suggest the need for a shift away from the strategies that teachers use as the sole focus of their attention in class, and from that shift a re-framing of what assessment activities entail. We propose that it is essential for teachers to frame what is taking place in class as centred on pupils' ideas and reasoning, nascent in the subject area or domain. Formative assessment then becomes about engaging with and responding to the substance of those ideas and reasoning, assessing with discipline-relevant criteria, and, from ideas, recognising possibilities along the disciplinary horizon. Formative assessment moves out of strategies and into classroom interaction with roots in disciplinary activities and goals (Coffey et al. 2011, p. 1131).

'Formative assessment takes place day by day and allows the teacher and the student to adapt their respective actions to the teaching/learning situation in question. It is thus, for them, a privileged occasion for conscious reflection on their experience' (Audibert 1980, p. 62). As Audibert says, formative assessment is constant analysis of a connected moving picture: if the action taken on the basis of the assessment is effective ('effective' being defined within the iterative nature of learning in which pupils will re-visit concepts several times on their learning journey), the learner has progressed and his/her misconceptions are being supported. Formative assessment is a rich source of information about the pupil. The pupil's knowledge, understanding and skills will have been looked at on many occasions and in many contexts. Assessment cannot be used formatively if it is only intermittent. Learners develop all the time, not just at the end of a term, year or key stage. Just as assessment is a continuous iterative process, so also must the recording of progress be a continuum, an ongoing activity. The formative assessment activity must arise from current classroom practice (*not* externally produced tests, quizzes, work sheets for mass consumption and completion). An assessment task should build on a learner's current experience. The task needs to be clearly, carefully and precisely constructed to enable the learner to demonstrate what he or she knows. Assessment needs to be understood as tightly integrated within teaching and learning. Therefore 'the more the evaluation (assessment) is integrated into situations, it becomes interactive and lasts, the further it distances itself from normative or summative evaluation, the province of tests and exams and their consequences' (Perrenoud 1998, p. 100). For example, if a teacher during a teaching session is assessing a learner's understanding of alphabetic principles (phonemes), we would not expect that teacher to present a worksheet focused on the 26 letters of the alphabet. Rather there would be multiple assessment routes for that concept, for example how the child reads, how the child writes, what form of code the child uses to write. These are all normal teaching activities with which the learner is comfortable (affective and conative domains), however they are also assessments.

The research evidence

First we designed a questionnaire for a representative (based on a random 25% of the total of primary schools) national sample of 4,000 primary schools to collect evidence on each school's prioritisation of formative assessment as a philosophy for teaching and learning; and whether that reported level of prioritisation of formative assessment extended into classroom practice. We visited 43 of the schools to observe formative teaching, learning and assessment. We selected those visits from the responses which, after content analysis, matched most nearly our own construct for formative teaching (based on Allal & Lopez 2005; Perrenoud 1991, 1998; Sadler 1989). Analysis of the observations and transcripts (systematic observation schedule based on Galton et al., (1980) used by Alexander in his 1997 survey of 60 schools) indicated that the observations evidenced a profile of rigid, non-formative teaching, 'the formalism of highly structured lessons, whole class plenaries' (Alexander 2008b, p. 107).

On our visits to schools we asked teachers how they defined their teaching, how they conceptualised their role, what their philosophy of teaching was. 'In terms of her philosophy for teaching and learning – this was something teacher A had not given any thought to. Much of her practice she claimed was based on the modelling of others she felt were worth copying.' We asked teachers if they thought they were 'formative' teachers. To which they replied in the majority, 'what does that mean, I have never heard of that before?' We are wondering if teachers in 2013 need a philosophy. From 207 responses to a survey question 'What is your teaching philosophy based on?', and from 13 case study visits, the typical response was 'That's a really hard one – I've never been asked that before', they certainly don't think they do. They are 'reliant on prescriptive centrally disseminated materials' from which 'politicians and bureaucrats are demanding greater conformity of education offerings which are transparent and superficially testable' (Patrick et al. 2003, p. 239). They have 'strategies' for most of the important things, i.e. numeracy, literacy, Assessment for Learning (AfL), and they have 'frameworks' to plan to and from, and they have centrally supplied schemes of work to save them from having to match teaching materials to developmental or interest levels; in short they have been reduced to technicians. If they follow these formulae they are 'safe' and 'secure' in the accountability and auditing processes conducted internally (by their own Senior Leadership Team) and externally (by Ofsted and the Local Authority). So, in summary, the central purpose for becoming a teacher has been lost. Our belief is that teachers need to understand and to embrace what formative teaching is. It is not disguised within a programme or strategy to improve 'level scores' (although formative teaching and learning does markedly improve the child as a learner) and it should not respond to the summative agenda, but instead to the learning needs of the child, involving the child centrally in the origination and the development of his/her learning. One example from our observations centres on an experienced teacher who expounded widely on her formative practice and then spent the 40 minutes teaching time dictating and controlling language, content, interactions and materials in a closed format which did not enable the children to connect to or be involved in their own learning (Boyle & Charles 2012). In short, the children did not see any relevance to themselves in the theme and content of the lesson (Vygotsky, 1986).

In nearly every case we were handed a formalised lesson plan which was rigidly structured from introduction to plenary and from which the teacher did not deviate to accommodate emerging learning needs. The focus was on the production of summative outcomes for measurement purposes 'just one kind of teaching, traditional direct instruction' (Alexander 2004, p 10). The majority of the teaching time was focused on English and mathematics (Boyle & Bragg 2006), specifically on the types of questions and product which were required for national test success. This raises the question of why teachers are operating from a measurement rather than a developmental pedagogy. Part of the answer is the accountability culture that has prevailed since the introduction of National Curriculum assessment (1989) and has been strengthened by the National Strategies, Ofsted inspections and the setting of national percentage success targets (DfE 2011). 'The Primary Strategy is found to be ambiguous and possibly dishonest, stylistically demeaning, conceptually weak, evidentially inadequate and culpably ignorant of recent education history' (Alexander 2004, p. 7). However, whatever the academic constituency thought and wrote, in classroom terms teachers felt that the route of 'formalism of highly structured lessons [and] whole class plenaries' (Alexander 2004, p. 7) was the pedagogical model which they were being encouraged to follow 'knowing as they do how much hangs on the next round of literacy and numeracy targets' (2004, p. 15). Therefore, 'the imperatives of developmental facilitation and readiness were frustrated by the syllabus and the clock' (Alexander 2005, p. 7). The government has, consciously or unconsciously, engineered a situation in which, by forcing teachers along the route of processing outcomes for accountability purposes, teachers have been left without theoretical underpinning; 'theory matters because without it education is just hit and miss ... we risk misunderstanding not only the nature of our pedagogy but the epistemic foundations of our discipline' (Carlile & Jordan 2005, p. 11). In this climate of accountability it is difficult to agree with Brown's statement that 'teachers' pedagogy is influenced by their beliefs about teaching, learning and assessment' (Brown, 2004 in Winterbottom et al. 2008, p. 15).

Analysis of questionnaire data

On being asked what importance they gave to formative assessment in their planning, over two-thirds of respondents said that they gave it a very high priority (90% responded that they gave it a 'high' or 'very high' priority). However, on being asked to elaborate on 'why' they had assigned such a high level of priority, the schools supplied a range of responses. Some of these did not show a strong relationship between assigning a priority and the supplementary question 'why' (see Figure 1.2).

The main classifications of response on this question emerged as follows: approximately 40% of the sample reported that they had given a very high importance to formative assessment because it 'informs next steps' or 'it informs the next teaching plan', both of these responses were considered and counted in the same category. The next most reported categories were: 12% of schools reported that formative assessment 'informs all our planning', 8% stated that they gave a very high priority to formative assessment because it 'helped them assess where children are'. We felt this was vague, but in the context of an open-ended questionnaire without telephone interview follow-up, it was as good a category description as possible for this aspect of formative assessment. Eleven per cent of the sample reported that formative assessment enabled 'personalised learning' and this justified the high priority they gave to formative assessment.

Six per cent of respondents stated that formative assessment supplied 'an accurate way to set targets'. The only other significantly reported reason for the high priority given to formative assessment in planning was that 'it supports the identification of pupil needs, enabling the setting of differentiated targets for lessons', this from 6% of the sample – a clear indicator that the notion of differentiated planning for teaching is not seen as a pre-requisite for formative assessment by the majority of teachers.

There was then a wide range of low frequency responses across the schools, which we have tabulated in Figure 1.3 as 'other'. In summary these included: 'child's personal next steps'; 'informs pace and value added'; 'targeted activities'; 'effective comments for the child'; 'generates flexible teaching groups'; 'change planning to cater for pupils' needs'; 'match work to pupils' needs'; 'enjoyment'; 'accurate picture of what children are learning'; 'recommended by Ofsted'; and 'a requirement says the SIP'. Equally low frequency but possibly more valid representations of what formative assessment means for the respondents were seen in, 'teachers to be highly responsive to child's needs/adapt and adjust daily'; 'update plans on a daily basis for each child'; 'instant feedback to children', and more of the same.

As can be seen from the above, despite the very high percentage reporting prioritisation of formative assessment, schools clearly have very different definitions of what it is and what its purpose is. The correlations between Q1a: 'What importance do you give to formative

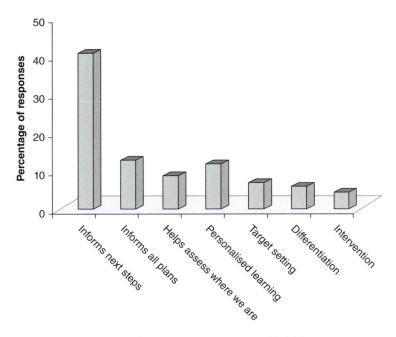

Figure 1.2 Why do you rate formative assessment so highly?

assessment' and Q1b: 'What is the reason for that prioritisation', showed no significant relationship.

In Question 2, schools were asked which key aspects of formative assessment they used. As there was no 'supplied' list this gave an opportunity to note and analyse what schools would determine as key aspects of formative assessment (see Figure 1.3). The most highly reported aspect, by almost one in four schools (24%), was 'pupil self-evaluation/self-assessment'. The definitions of this category varied, for example 'self assessment – checking off against given success criteria'; 'self-evaluation (traffic light system)'; 'self-assessment against targets'; 'self- and peer-assessment is used to assess understanding' and 'identify individual pupil targets which are used by the pupils to assess their own performance'. The second highest reported key aspect of formative assessment was 'providing feedback to the learner' (20%) with the definitions of that feedback including 'regular marking and feedback'; 'feedback on completed work'; 'feedback during lessons'; 'formative feedback when marking books' and 'feedback on targets set'. Sixteen per cent of the responses reported 'gimmicks' related to their key practice of formative assessment, for example 'two stars and a wish'; 'WALT, WILF and TIB' and 'traffic lights/thumbs up'. Twelve per cent of schools reported 'targeted questioning', 12% 'sharing success criteria' and one in 9 schools (11%) reported 'analysis of product' as key aspects of formative assessment which they used.

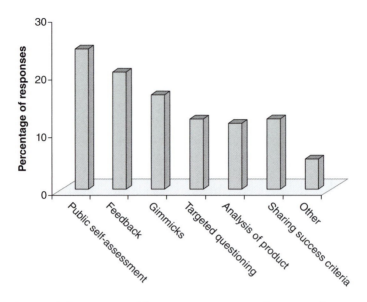

Figure 1.3 Which key aspects of formative assessment do you use?

One in 20 schools reported their key approach as 'sharing learning objectives/success criteria with children'. In terms of numbers, these were the most significant responses in identifying key aspects of formative assessment; there was also a scattering of individual reports demonstrating the breadth of interpretation, for example 'working alongside children', 'levelling/moderation of work', 'teacher and pupil setting targets together', 'checking children against targets', 'promoting children's learning', 'key questions: what do we know? what do we want to find out?' and 'APP/single level tests'. These responses led the authors to believe that formative assessment has no common understanding across teachers, in definition, components or aspects of practice.

Question 3 asked teachers to report how formative assessment supported learning outcomes in their schools. The responses (as with Questions 1 and 2) indicated a range of understandings, not only of what formative assessment is but of what learning outcomes are now classified as ('achieving targets') and the link between assessment and learning ('enables additional support when not achieving targets'). The most popular response to the question,[6] 'How does formative assessment support learning in your school?' was 'next steps identified by both teacher and pupils' (21%) and that was regarded as both positive (teacher and pupil described as working together to identify next steps in learning) and formative (see Figure 1.4). The other significantly (in numeric terms) reported responses were 'informs next day's planning'

(18%), which was at least formative, 'planned to match differentiated objectives and targets', which hinted that it might or might not be formative and then 'identifies targets and ability groups' (18%), 'standards raising/achieving targets' (9%) and 'enables additional support/not achieving targets' (8%), all of which were not, in the authors' view, either formative or supporting learning. There was a range of low frequency responses covering the possibly formative, for example 'individualise assessment for each pupil' and 'small steps which are reviewed and adjusted' to the unspecific, for example 'central to learning process', 'pupils empowered', 'helps pace of lessons' and the summative, for example 'enables teachers to make predictions', 'children's individual half term targets', 'grouping of children relative to academic progress' and 'analysis of data allows appropriate targets to be set'.

Survey Question 4 probed the schools' views of the links between formative assessment and learning. The responses ranged in specificity from the generalisation of 'they are inextricably linked' to 'children need to know how to continue to improve' (16%). The most reported response was 'involves children in measuring their own learning/increases confidence' (26%) which the authors felt summed up two positive aspects of

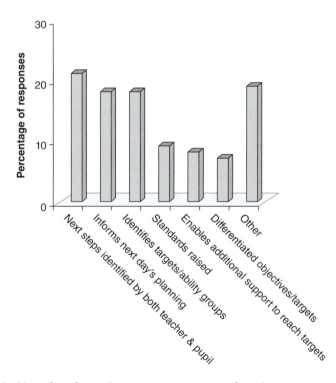

Figure 1.4 How does formative assessment support learning outcomes in your school?

formative assessment and supplied a link between the assessment and learning. Other responses which had some numerical support were 'children cannot move in learning unless AfL is in place' (10%), 'teaching must be driven by what children already know' (11%) and 'learning has to have formative assessment to move it forward' (9%), all of which we thought were too general to detail any specific link between formative assessment and learning (Figure 1.5).

There was the usual range of low frequency responses which we have encapsulated in the 'other' classification column (19%). These included the esoteric and unspecific, for example 'it's a continued cycle, teacher challenges children and keeps them motivated', 'so we all have the same philosophy' and 'the greater the quality of the formative assessment the deeper the learning process'. We also received responses that were vaguely formative, but at least linked to learning, for example 'if pupils do not understand a concept this must be returned to', 'assessment is seen as an integral part of teaching and learning', 'quality feedback to signpost areas of work they need to concentrate on' and 'involves children in

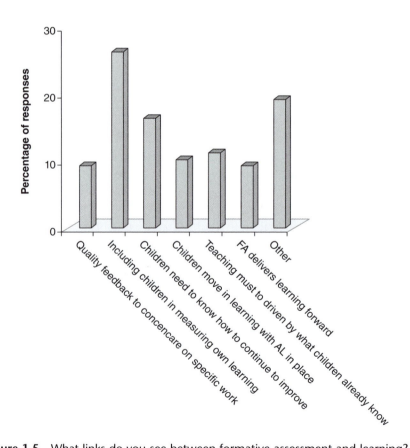

Figure 1.5 What links do you see between formative assessment and learning?

actively monitoring what they have to do next'. The latter signalled both the active involvement of the child in the process (a crucial component of formative assessment) and gave the authors hope that the 'next' referred to was actually a specific micro-learning step rather than a generalised statement of intent. The hope was soon dampened by a school response which 'formatively' stated the link between formative assessment and learning as 'only as a means of testing'.

Survey Question 5 specifically focused on the AfL principle of actively involving children in their own learning and asked how this was being done in practice. The highest supported response (29%) stated that children were involved in their own learning through 'self-reflection/self-evaluation' which seemed ambiguous to the authors as it was not clear (until we observed the teaching sessions) when, how or if this self-reflection took place, or whether the results of the self-reflection transferred into active involvement in learning. One in five schools (20%) identified 'setting own targets/reaching own targets' as an active involvement while 10% of schools reported 'learning styles/what they like to learn and how'. Twelve per cent of respondents reported 'gimmicks' as the route to actively involving pupils in their own learning, for example 'thumbs up/down/sideways', 'WALT, WILF', 'star checkers', 'two stars and a wish', and of course the ubiquitous 'traffic lights' (Figure 1.6). The wide range of individual responses to using formative assessment covered the bold but unspecific 'HOW COULD YOU NOT!' (sic) through 'enthusiasm', 'circle time' and 'good plenary sessions', to the summatively oriented 'revision topics'.

Already AfL has collected too much 'clutter' of terminology; it is dominated by gimmicks (WILFs, WALTs, TIBs and OLIs) rather than focusing on the specific understanding and practical application of formative assessment (FA), assessment for learning (AfL), continuous assessment (CA) and teacher assessment (TA). Just as the Education Reform Act in 1988 ushered in a plethora of abbreviations – SAT, AT, SoA, etc. – similarly, as our previous sentence illustrates, assessment now has its own potential for confusion through abbreviations. This confusion over terminology derives from a scant understanding of the works of the original formative assessment theorists, misrepresented or 'popularised' by the travelling consultants who see money to be made from the centre-periphery training model for AfL. 'Is there a formative assessment pack?' we were asked by one teacher, misunderstanding both the purpose of our visit and the purpose of formative assessment. If there isn't a 'pack', a download from the internet, do not expect it to be done, because that demands experimentation with pedagogy (frowned upon by School Leadership Teams and School Improvement Partners), and then inevitably deviation, which,

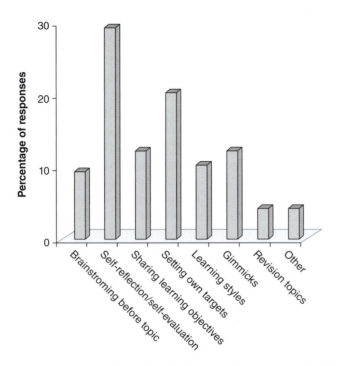

Figure 1.6 How do you actively involve children in their own learning?

contrary to the cynics, produces successful (and deep) formative teaching and learning.

Sadly, none of the above sample responses matched the research literature on understanding the involvement of children as co-constructors, self-regulated learners and negotiators of their own learning (see the work of Vygotsky, Perry & Thaulberger, Schunk & Zimmerman, Myhill, Wyse).

Discussion and implications

Following those varied definitions and understandings we have still to see a formative classroom or a teacher whose pedagogy is based on formative principles in any of our 43 observation visits to schools, despite these visits being based on the most 'formative' responses to our survey. We are, however, seeing a succession of teachers following a formula of planned predictability, controlling the content of the 'three part menu' which is being delivered to passive children. This rigidity has its pedagogical roots firmly planted in the National Numeracy and Literacy Strategies with 'the formalism of highly structured lessons, whole class plenaries' (Alexander 2008b, p. 107). Among the concessions to AfL, from our observations, are the 'solitary' learning objective on the inter-active whiteboard (how can one learning objective be adequate for the range of learning needs present in every class?). Our classroom inter-views provided some informative responses from the teachers on that theme, such as 'But I have the top set [for literacy]' indicating that some teachers believed that they did not need to differentiate within a class which had been streamed (Boaler 2005; Dunne et al. 2007). We observed and were treated to rhetoric about 'doing' self and peer assessment and the free scattering of terms such as 'open questions', 'feedback', etc. There was no evidence of any of these strategies in place.

A typology

Differentiation

'If formative assessment is carried out on a fairly regular basis, the result is pressure to differentiate' (Perrenoud 1991, p.89).

The evidence from our sample indicates the notion of differentiated planning for teaching is not seen as a pre-requisite for formative assessment by the majority of teachers (only 7% of our sample states that formative assessment enabled the setting of differentiated targets for lessons. This is a still-strong legacy from the National Numeracy Strategy with its discouragement of differentiated teaching 'we are concerned that children should not continue to work at many levels, with the teacher placing them in a wide range of differentiated groups' (DfEE 1998, p.54) and' its format as a fixed curriculum to be taught to all pupils regardless of attainment indicates that very little curricular differentia-tion is recommended' (Brown et al. 1998). So strong that five years after Excellence and Enjoyment: The Primary Strategy we are observing a majority of lessons in which differentiation is totally absent. Why are we observing lessons with one static learning objective which embraces the whole extent of a class's learning? This signals two things. The pedagogi-cal messages of the National Literacy and Numeracy Strategies in which differentiation was frowned upon and the absence of teacher under-standing of the need for a differentiated menu to match the range of learning needs and the presence of a 'one size fits all' mentality are prov-ing difficult to shift.

In conversation with teachers during our 43 school visits we raise the word 'differentiation' and the vagueness of the responses begins. We are told 'I set one task and then I differentiate by what they produce' or 'I have an extension task ready for those who finish'. Our observations indicate that this is what AfL in practice has been reduced to. The responses demonstrate misconceptions of the basic principles of how children learn and the sacrifice of developmental learning on the altar of 'coverage', 'pace', 'moving the cohort on' and 'getting through the pre-planned package'. Clearly our initial teacher training programmes need to return to the conceptualisers and theorists of formative assessment to change technicians back to pedagogists. Principal amongst these theorists is Philippe Perrenoud whose philosophy is based on 'to the extent that pupils do not have the same abilities nor the same needs nor the same way of working, an optimal situation for one pupil will not be optimal for another… one can write a simple equation: diversity in people + appropriate treatment for each = diversity in approach' (Perrenoud 1998, p.93–4). In even simpler terms, 'good teaching forces differentiation' (Perrenoud 1998) is called for. Linda Allal reinforces the point, 'differentiation of instruction is planned rather than just being added on after observing difficulties' (Allal 2005, p.246).

Divergence

'So in the face of pace, objectives, targets and tables that have become part of the dominant linguistic and conceptual discourse of education reform in England, we might wonder how confident good divergent teachers will be to stray from pre-set paths for better pastures. We might wonder what the absence of divergent thinking will mean, in the longer term, for children's motivation and interest in their learning experiences' (Dadds 2001, p.53).

Dadds in 2001 described a scenario which has further deteriorated by 2009. In our classroom observations we keep looking for the first teacher who 'diverges' from the norm of the pre-packaged lesson. This is delivered (usually script perfect) around a sole common learning objective (or alternatively in some cases a 'whole class task') to the class who are then invited either (i) to talk to their partner, or (ii) to complete a common task, or (iii) indulge in an 'AfL professional development day' gimmick ('snowball', 'traffic lights', etc) or (iv) to wake from their lethargy induced by this format being repeated day after day, to recall some of the detail from the teacher's (lengthy) contextualising or introductory remarks. We see teachers 'covering' work at pace, we see teachers 'controlling' and imposing the narrowness of the learning agenda and forgetting that the learning is not in the tidiness of the schema but in the response, the involvement, the energy, the interest of the child as participant learner; learning is a 'messy' and complex process not a neat and tidy one. Therefore their misinterpretation of divergence as inevitably resulting in chaos and reduction in quality must be challenged. We need to see but are not, teachers having the confidence to relax that control, to allow children to be involved in the 'why?' am I doing this, 'what if?' and in the 'how?' can it best be done, and encouraging collaboration and conversation and children setting personal progressive targets.

In the classroom example below children were consciously or sub-consciously connecting prior learning to a present theme and they were re-drafting openly and orally their developing conceptualisation of counting in tens in a non-rigidly controlled classroom environment. This is an example, rare in our observations, of co-construction between the teacher and the child enabling the children's dialogue to expand by non-intervention from the teacher at the point of the first child's question, thus enabling the children to 'drive' the learning direction.

Mathematics lesson Year 1 children

Learning focus: counting in tens (10 more/10 less)

Context: The previous week the children had explored the concept of odd and even numbers. In this lesson the whole class was on the carpet exploring counting. The teacher recorded the following dialogue which took place as the children worked on grouping as part of the process of understanding the concept.

Teacher (T); Let's count to 100 in tens.

Burhan: Three sets of ten make 30 but it is an odd number.

Mohammed: Is it an odd number?

Burhan: Yes, it is odd.

T: Well is it an odd number?

Burhan: If you had three people, one would get 10, one would get 10 and one would get 10.

T: What about two people?

Reem: One person would get 5, 5 and 5.

T: How many is that?

Reem: 15.

T: What is that doubled?

Reem: 30.

T: Burhan, you can share 30 as 15 and 15.

In this formative classroom situation the children were demonstrating the following: they were consciously or sub-consciously connecting prior learning to the present theme and they were re-drafting orally and collaboratively their developing conceptualisation of 'counting in tens' in an open classroom culture. This is a genuine example of co-construction between the teacher and the group of children (through enabling the children's dialogue to expand and by non-intervention at the first child's question) and of divergence from a planned format to enable the children to 'drive' the learning direction.

The misconception that the digit 3 makes 30 into an odd number is explored and rectified in group discussion. The teacher, by not closing the learning agenda by responding with an answer to the first child's question, has enabled the children to orally work through two concepts, ie multiples of 10 and odds and evens.

In conversation the teacher reflectively observed 'I should have given Burhan, Reem and Mohammed a task outside the main group to explore their own numbers'.

However, unlike the above example the norm is that far from the formative principles of involving children in their own learning, teachers are controlling the learning agenda even more firmly. 'Many schools give the impression of having implemented AfL when in reality the change in pedagogy that it requires has not taken place. This may happen when teachers feel constrained by external tests over which they have no control. As a result they are unlikely to give pupils a greater role in directing their (own) learning.' (ARG 2007, p.9)

Definition

'Formative assessment takes place day by day and allows the teacher and the student to adapt their respective actions to the teaching/learning situation in question. It is thus, for them, a privileged occasion for conscious reflection on their experience' (Audibert 1980, p.62).

On our visits to schools we ask teachers how they define their teaching, how they conceptualise their role, what their philosophy of teaching is. 'In terms of her philosophy for teaching and learning – this was something teacher F had not given any thought to. Much of her practice she claimed was based on the modelling of others she felt were worth copying.' (Case study school 5). We ask teachers if they think they are 'formative' teachers. To which they have replied in the majority, 'what does that mean, I have never heard of that before?'. We are wondering if teachers in 2009 need a philosophy. From 207 responses to a survey question 'what is your teaching philosophy based on?' and from 13 case study visits the typical response was 'that's a really hard one – I've never been asked that before' (school X), they certainly don't think they do. They are 'reliant on prescriptive centrally disseminated materials' from which 'politiicans and bureaucrats are demanding greater conformity of education offerings which are transparent and superficially testable' (Patrick, Forde & McPhee 2003, p.239). They have 'Strategies' for most of the important things, ie numeracy, literacy, AfL, and 'Frameworks' to plan to and from and they have centrally supplied schemes of work to save the need for matching teaching material to developmental or interest levels; in short they have been reduced to technicians. If they follow these formulae they are 'safe' and 'secure' in the accountability and auditing processes conducted by their own Senior Leadership Team. So, in summary, the central purpose for becoming a teacher has been lost. Our belief is that teachers need to understand and to embrace what formative teaching is. It is not disguised within a programme or strategy to improve 'level scores' and it should not respond to the summative bell but instead to the learning needs of the child, involving the child centrally in the origination and the development of his/her learning. One example from our observations centres on an experienced teacher who expounded widely on her formative practice, her current studying for a further degree and then spent the 40 minutes teaching time dictating language, content, control and materials in a closed format which did not enable the children to connect to or be involved in their own learning. In short, they did not see the relevance of the lesson (Vygotsky 1986).

Depth

'Teachers bring skills in devising and constructing tasks to elicit revealing and pertinent responses from children.' (Sadler 1989, p.80)

Depth of learning: this equates with the immersion of the teacher and the child in the teaching and learning process. Our search is to identify through our observations of teaching and in conversations with children, teachers and LA officers their priorities in planning for teaching and learning. How is an independent and lifelong learner developed? Is there a relationship between the intrinsic development of engagement, self-motivation, interest and research skills at an early stage of a child's education and current pedagogical practice? Is the current observed paradigm of controlling teacher/passive recipient moving at pace through a prescribed programme going to develop a generation of 'deep and reflective thinkers' and lifelong learners? From our recent classroom observations the authors' response is that in the current summative framework the chances of developing reflective children involved in self-motivated research activities is negligible. A missing component is the acknowledgement of the child as learner within the affective domain, in short acknowledging that social development is equally important as and a primary factor in cognitive development – but the latter is the area on which curriculum and assessment and therefore pedagogy focuses in a summative Standards agenda. The importance of a nurturing pedagogy is recognised by Reeves (1993) who argues that 'if we are to take quality seriously we have to get closer to our learners, their needs, their learning styles and their motivation' (Dadds 2001, p.53). The evidence of our observations across the 43 schools justifies the necessity of reminding the teacher that he/she is working with discrete individuals, all with emotional and learning needs, not just delivering a centrally devolved teacher-controlled subject diet. Wink suggests that pedagogy involves human interaction and joy, of playing with new ideas and '[to] challenge all educators to look beyond the complexities and familiarities of their own teaching' (Wink 2005, in Graziano 2008, p.162). Within the current climate this position seems both irrelevant and unobtainable as the dominant discourse is one of controlling pedagogy and performativity.

Demythologising

'The search for theoretical frameworks could lead to an increasingly abstract vision of formative assessment cut off from the realities of classroom practice. This is why it is essential to articulate theoretical work with the study of how assessment is actually practised in the classroom' (Allal 2005, p.251).

Already AfL has collected too much 'clutter' of terminology; it is dominated by gimmicks (WILFs, WALTs, TIBs and OLIs) rather than focusing on the specific understanding and practical application of formative assessment (FA), assessment for learning (AfL), continuous assessment (CA) and teacher assessment (TA). Just as the Education Reform Act in 1988 ushered in a plethora of abbreviations, ie SAT, AT, SoA, etc, similarly, as our previous sentence illustrates, assessment now has its own potential for confusion through abbreviation. This confusion over terminology derives from a scant understanding of the works of the original formative assessment theorists, misrepresented or 'popularised' by the travelling consultants who see money to be made from the centre-periphery training model for AfL. 'Is there a pack?' we were asked by one teacher, misunderstanding both the purpose of our visit and the purpose of formative assessment. If there isn't a 'pack' do not expect it to be done because that demands experimentation with pedagogy (to be frowned upon by School Leadership Teams and School Improvement Partners), then inevitably deviation (to be frowned on by everybody!) which, contrary to the cynics, produces successful (and deep) formative teaching and learning.

Our anticipation was that after six years of a national AfL strategy we would not just see the isolated individual formatively teaching but there would be in a majority of schools a shared learning community of formative teachers working collaboratively with children at the centre of the whole school's teaching and learning ethos and culture (Allal & Lopez 2005). From our survey responses and our observations in the classroom, the typology of five issues described above has emerged. Teachers for whatever legacy or conceptual reasons clearly have problems with differentiation: 'differentiation implies the imposition of different curricula for different groups of pupils – or it means nothing' (Simon 1985, p. 126). The following of a formulaic 'lesson plan' seems to be the sole pedagogical model and there is no 'divergence':

> so in the face of pace, objectives, targets, tables that have become part of the dominant linguistic and conceptual discourse of educational reform in England, we might wonder how confident good divergent teachers will be to stray from pre-set paths for better pastures. We might wonder what the absence of divergent thinking will mean in the longer term for children's motivation and interest in their learning experiences. (Dadds 2001, p. 53)

Understanding of formative assessment (or its synonym, AfL) in practical operation is poor so there is no clarity of definition: 'formative assessment takes place day by day and allows the teacher and the student to adapt their respective actions to the teaching/learning situation in question. It is thus for them a privileged occasion, conscious reflection on their experience' (Audibert 1980, p. 62). In terms of depth: 'teachers bring skills in devising and constructing tasks to elicit revealing and pertinent responses from children' (Sadler 1989, p. 80), 'coverage' has precedence over depth and security in learning, and the associated 'jargon' around the simple truth of formative teaching needs demythologising: 'the search for theoretical frameworks could lead to an increasingly abstract vision of formative assessment cut off from the realities of classroom practice. This is why it is essential to articulate theoretical work with the study of how assessment is actually practised in the classroom' (Allal & Lopez 2005, p. 251). These issues are itemised below with an introduction to each supplied by a theorist in the field.

Formative assessment: the learner, the teacher, the process

Formative assessment is synonymous with 'assessment for learning'. It is an intrinsic and essential part of teaching and learning and provides the specific information (elicitation of evidence) that enables teachers to support learning progress matched to the individual and complex needs of pupils. Pupils' learning needs have to be located at the centre of planning teaching and learning. This focus on identifying where pupils are in their learning (elicitation of evidence: formative assessment) and understanding how to support those learning needs with matched instructional strategies, will lead to improved teaching and learning (Allal & Lopez 2005; Perrenoud 1998).

Formative assessment requires the empowering of pupils to have more involvement in the learning process through co-construction of learning with the teacher. The teacher needs to understand that assessment is a continuous process not a summative measure. The information (evidence) that the teacher elicits from formative assessment has to be planned into support for the pupil while the pupil is still involved (self motivated) in the learning activity. Professional development issues for teachers include introducing a 'formative toolkit' to support teachers in developing their formative teaching and learning awareness and strategies.

Conclusion

Formative teaching, learning and assessment is best summarised by Perrenoud as:

> pupils do not have the same abilities nor the same needs nor the same way of working, an optimal situation for one pupil will not be optimal for another ... one can write a simple equation: diversity in people + appropriate treatment for each = diversity in approach (Perrenoud 1998, p. 86)

Pryor and Croussouard extend this definition of Perrenoud's and his philosophy of a change in the relationship or 'regulation' between teacher and child in the classroom: 'The educator teaches different definitions of him/herself to the students and develops different relationships with the students through them ... to become teacher, assessor, subject expert and learner, all involving different division of labour and rules shaping their interaction with students' (2008, p. 10). This is problematic to some teachers who have become used to the neatly planned rigidity and conformity of whole class teaching and the preparation of pupils to solve problems in specific ways to obtain good test marks. This is not teaching for learning because 'learning is messy and takes time' (Martin et al. 2005, p. 235).

Changes in classroom practice are central to the effectiveness of formative assessment. One of the focuses of professional development must be on the changing of roles between teacher and pupil. There is a need, therefore, to raise teacher awareness of what formative assessment is, the important role that children have in it, through negotiation, self-regulation and co-construction, and why formative assessment is important and how it can be incorporated into teaching.

For formative assessment to be effective in supporting and improving teaching and learning, both the teachers and the children must understand what they are doing. This raises the question of how well teachers are trained pedagogically as formative teachers. Teaching learning and assessment is very demanding and difficult as teachers are required to make continuous assessments and incorporate the information they gain into their teaching and learning strategies.

Changes to classroom practice are central to the effectiveness of formative assessment. One of the focal points of teacher training must be an awareness of the changing role for teacher and pupil in the learning context (see Perrenoud quote above).

Formative assessment implies empowering the pupil to have more control over his/her learning, to understand the adjustments to his/her learning behaviours and thinking that are required, and is a continuous process not a summative measure.

Perrenoud establishes the model for the optimum state of pedagogy to be achieved by a well-trained teacher who understands that formative assessment supports the learner within a de-regulated classroom. Perrenoud insists that:

> in the absolute an ideal teaching approach would do without all formative assessment. All the feedback necessary for learning would be incorporated in the situation, without it being necessary for a teacher to observe and intervene in order to bring about learning progress. In other words it would be absurd to proceed with formative assessment without first calling into question the teaching methods and without seeking, as a priority, to make the teaching situations more interactive and richer in spontaneous feedback. (Perrenoud 1991, pp. 94)

Perrenoud is boldly contesting the 'one size fits all' testocracy, the teaching to the test pedagogy which dominates so many schools' practices. His message to teachers is that differentiation is essential but differentiated teaching has to be based on teachers 'knowing' their pupils and where those pupils are in their individual learning trajectories. This is not the faux differentiation of allocating to groups and handing out 'differentiated' worksheets.

> When one is thinking in terms of formative assessment, it is necessary to break with this egalitarian approach. There is no need to give all the pupils the same dose of formative assessment. The differentiation begins with the amount that goes into the observation and interpretation of the processes and acquisitions of each pupil. There is an analogy with medical diagnosis: it is not a case of carrying out the same tests, analyses and examinations on all patients. The important thing is to make a correct diagnosis and identify a disease and, if possible, its causes. In some cases the diagnosis is glaringly obvious and no particular analysis is required. In others, it entails a succession of hypotheses and checks which require specialists. Like medical diagnosis, formative assessment requires differential investment. (Perrenoud 1991, p. 96)

The reason for teachers coming under pressure to restrict the learning experience to testable domains has been made clear in the literature: 'Under pressure from bureaucrats to demonstrate achievement, schools which desperately need to cater to their pupils' diverse learning requirements are having to tailor teaching to the test' (de Waal 2006).

This has the inevitable consequence of a reduction in the learning content of children's taught experience: 'This has resulted in a huge distortion in primary school teaching and learning activity skewed towards the tested subjects and reducing teaching time for the non-tested subjects' (Boyle & Bragg 2006, p. 578).

Our research survey data reinforced that:

> to enable a change to take place from an auditing to a teaching and learning culture in our schools, we need to accept that some professional development in 'using assessment to support learning' will have to take place – basically because after over a decade in which summative assessment (testing) has dominated pedagogy, teachers have either forgotten how to or lost confidence to incorporate rigorous teacher assessment into their planning for teaching and learning. (Boyle 2008, p. 21)

Another factor in the above is the change in the pre-service teacher training model which for the last 15 years has focused on the model of teaching for grading rather than preparing newly qualified teachers to support the learner and learning.

Research by Gipps et al. (1995) identified three broad categories of teachers in their approaches to classroom assessment: intuitives, evidence gatherers and systematic planners.

> For intuitives, assessment is a kind of 'gut reaction'. They rely upon their memory of what children can do and so it was difficult for us to observe any ongoing teacher assessment or describe the processes they were using. Evidence gatherers particularly like written evidence, 'trying to get as much evidence as I can' is the aim of many of these teachers, one of whom described herself as a 'hoarder' who 'keeps everything'. Systematic planners plan for assessment on a systematic basis and this has become part of their practice. (Gipps et al. 1995, p. 36)

Torrance and Pryor (1998) investigated the practice of formative assessment in key stage 1 classrooms and reported on detailed classroom observations of 'assessment events', i.e. teacher–child interaction in the context of assessment, the act of teachers making judgements about children's achievement and how children understood those judgements. They conclude that young children have very little understanding of what it is that teachers want them to do or to achieve in curricular terms. They concluded that teachers need to be clear about their curriculum goals, shorter-term learning intentions and the purpose of classroom tasks in relation to those learning intentions. They need to communicate those intentions and the purpose of tasks to pupils – i.e. communicate task criteria – as well as communicating what it means to do tasks well – i.e. quality criteria. Teachers also need to give feedback relating to those criteria, indicating positive achievement as well as what and how to improve, while being equally alert to unanticipated learning outcomes and encouraging them when encountered, i.e. be alert to the possibilities for divergent as well as convergent assessment (Torrance & Pryor 2007, pp. 616–18).

2

The Guided Group Strategy

In this chapter we explore guided group pedagogy as an organising strategy; as an opportunity for focused teaching and tightly-planned learning; and as an opportunity for the teacher to focus on observing learning behaviours.

What is a guided group?

A guided group is a form of guided, co-operative learning featuring a collaborative learning environment of learning leaders and listeners. It requires expert scaffolding by a teacher and direct instruction, modelling and practice in the use of the four simple strategies (questioning, clarifying, summarising and predicting) that serve to prop up an emergent dialogue structure (Brown 1998, p. 443). Sadler emphasises that 'Teachers [must] bring some skills in devising and constructing tasks to elicit revealing and pertinent responses from children' (Sadler 1989, p. 80).

The primary importance of a guided group pedagogy is to establish reciprocal roles within the classroom in which all participants feel valued (affective domain) and there is mutual respect. The traditional view of grouping pupils for independent/self-supported learning in classrooms is that this form of working has the potential to improve learning but in reality many 'of these groupings inhibit learning and the motivation to learn' (Blatchford et al. 2007, p. 1). Galton et al. (1980, 1999, 2009) point out that children often spend up to 80% of their classroom time seated in small groups being assigned individual tasks and the quality of talk within the groups is at a low cognitive level (in Blatchford et al. 2007, p. 4). Cowie and Ruddock's (1988) research demonstrated that many children, as well as their teachers, do not like working in groups. Many children often feel insecure and threatened when told to work in groups and respond by withdrawal from participation. The SPRinG project (Blatchford et al. 2007) observed that the main problems identified about group work are 'the limited coordination between the size of groups, the composition, pedagogic purpose of learning tasks and interactions among group members' (p. 5). In summary, the SPRinG data reveal that there is little awareness of social pedagogical relationships or approaches in the group teaching context. The SPRinG report further reveals the limitations in training pupils for effective group work: 'only a quarter of the two hundred teachers in the study reported that they prepared their classes for group working and the majority of these teachers cited 'circle time' as their only form of preparation for group work' (Blatchford et al. 2007, p. 6). In the main, the SPRinG data described small groups as likely to be composed of same-sex and same-ability pupils, 'providing contexts of social exclusion rather than inclusion in the classroom' (Blatchford et al. 2007, p. 6). The majority of learning tasks described pupil groups assigned practice tasks which in fact required children to work alone. Similarly, teacher or adult support was present in 'virtually all of the observations within which new knowledge/cognition was presented to pupils.Therefore, not allowing opportunities for pupils to co-construct and further develop their own new knowledge' (Blatchford et al. 2007, p. 6). Many teachers do not seem to understand their need to have multiple roles/functions within group work – not always to view themselves as the sole transmitters of knowledge. A key reported finding of the SPRinG programme and one shared strongly by these authors is that group work skills have to be developed.

Goals of a guided group pedagogy

It is important that group learning is not analysed 'independently of the curriculum and the culture of the classroom' and that 'collaborative learning tasks are set up in a way that is conducive to working together and not to independent work' (Blatchford et al. 2007, p. 9). We agree in part with this finding of SPRinG, but teachers do need to identify in their planning for group work whether learning tasks are intended to be for collaborative or independent working. For Vygotsky, pupils learn by solving problems with people more capable than themselves, who take them through their zone of proximal (or potential) development (Vygotsky 1986). Indeed, Vygotsky saw social interaction as the essential factor (Smith 1996). In our current research, we stress that teachers need to develop approaches which enable them to explore pupils' thinking and problem-solving strategies by seeking explanations of why the group did certain things in certain ways. This requires an understanding by teachers of the necessary role of socio-cognitive apprenticeships, for example in writing. As part of this developmental process, Englert et al. (2006) discuss the establishment of communities of practice in which pupils 'participate in inquiry-based conversations about texts, learning to treat printed words as thinking devices' (p. 211). When pupils interact on a frequent basis they have a greater opportunity to understand and internalise, 'thereby laying the foundation for the development of dialogical skills that support text production' (Rijlaarsdam et al. 2008, p. 60). In brief, talk is an essential component of learning – whether that learning is in the domain of creativity or numeracy.

The Williams report (2008) stated that 'guided group work offers an organisational approach where attention can be given to particular children who may require additional support or challenge to ensure that they continue to progress in learning' (p. 67). The DCSF (2007) also recognised the importance of these 'organisational and instructional changes' as a move away from the dominance of whole class teaching. However, our definition and use of guided group pedagogy is more formative.

The guided group is focused on 'the importance of inquiry, construction and collaboration rather than the delivery of outcomes' (Wells 2001, p. 2). The teacher is trying to identify strengths and misconceptions, and to do that s/he has to facilitate opportunities for all the children in the guided group to demonstrate their learning in an open, equitable and trusting context. In the guided group context, integration of the cognitive, affective and conative domains are optimal (Allal & Ducrey 2000). Therefore the teacher needs to understand that s/he needs to be flexible enough to deviate from his/her planned lesson if s/he notices that learning is not taking place. With five pupils (rather than 25–30 pupils) to observe in their learning, s/he has much more opportunity to register the need to change his/her teaching strategies *during* the course of the session. Planning is essential, for pupils' emerging needs often require that planning is changed *during* a teaching session.

We agree with Williams in part but we see a guided group as offering four things:

(i) a strategic organisational device
(ii) an optimal opportunity for specific and focused teaching
(iii) the small group situation enables learning to be planned tightly and offers ready accessibility for the child to the teacher
(iv) it is the optimal opportunity for the teacher to focus his/her observations of learning behaviours with a group size of five pupils.

The theoretical underpinning of guided group work is encapsulated in Hayes's (2008) recognition that 'child centred teaching included behaviour that actively involves pupils in guiding the learning process, such as offering choices, encouraging activity and suggesting solutions' (p. 433). The authors propose that teaching 'is not a one way process from the teacher to the pupil, it is a fluid, dynamic and often seemingly effortless dance between teacher and pupil' (Matthews 1999, p. 162). Makin and Whiteman (2006) support this view, stating that teachers and pupils 'are partners in teaching and learning transactions. We need to find ways of interacting with pupils to co-construct shared meanings in ways we cannot do if the children themselves are not active participants in exploring this situation' (p. 35).

Conditions for effective guided group pedagogy

In inquiry-based classroom settings, the bearer and receiver of authority are more fluid roles and are taken on by both teacher and pupil at different times (Hamm & Perry 2002). Authority in a classroom hinges on three major concepts: 'authority relation, legitimacy and change. We define legitimacy of authority as the knowledge, skills position or experiences that influence a person or group within an authority relationship' (Gerson & Bateman 2010 p. 195), and these three aspects rotate fluidly and authentically between teacher and pupils.

Guided group teaching is applicable for all age groups (and key stages) in early years, primary and even secondary schools. It needs to be planned *for* and planned *into* the teaching timetable. It is an optimum technique for the integration of teaching, learning and assessment and provides specific assessment information to support learning in 'real time'.

Just as children do not have to know the full cultural analysis of a 'tool' (technique, strategy, technical language or discourse) to begin using it, the teacher does not need to have the complete analysis of the pupils' understanding of the situation to start using their actions in the larger system.

> [In an instructional dialogue] the participants can act as if their understandings are the same. At first this systemic vagueness about what an object really is may appear to make cognitive analysis impossible. However, it now appears that this looseness is just what is needed to allow change to happen when people with different analyses interact. (Newman et al. 1989, p. 62)

Modelling desirable behaviours – developing social norms

It is important that teachers model active listening by focusing on non-verbal communication, such as good eye contact, interest by facial expression, gesture, posture, nodding, touching, emotions and feelings and other aspects of paralanguage elements, all better known as kinesics (Birdwhistell 1970). Teachers should understand the power and effects of paralanguage within their teaching, learning and assessment contexts. All of the desirable social norms being modelled by the teacher are for the purpose of demonstrating and 'handing over' desirable behaviours for good teaching and learning models. These 'desirable behaviours' become internalised by the pupils as ways of interacting with their peers and adults. Neglecting this aspect of modelling will lead to pupil negativity. The teacher's look of disinterest or boredom (albeit unintentional) will inevitably alienate pupils, rather than creating the intended inclusive learning environment in the classroom. For example, most classifications divide paralanguage into three kinds of vocalisations:

1. Vocal characterisers (laughing, crying, yelling, moaning, whining, yawning)
2. Vocal qualifiers (volume, pitch, rhythm, tempo, resonance, tone)
3. Vocal segregates (un-huh; ssh; uh-; oooh; mmmh)

Many inferences about content and character can be formed first from the sounds people produce, therefore paralanguage may indicate one's emotional state, represent one's demographic traits and reveal one's personality and characteristics (Jiaoqian 2004, p. 2).

Teachers need to reflect and respond carefully to the ideas of others and lead pupils into 'in-depth' discussions, conversations and investigations. Teachers need to be disciplined in terms of refraining from completing sentences or phrases for pupils because 'I knew what she was going to say ... '. Similarly, they should display constant and consistent modelling of oral situations such as 'Tell me again why and how ... '. Individual learners need to be coached to give space for their peers to tender and complete their ideas and interjections. Roles should always be fluid across who leads in dialogue and who responds. From the macro to the micro, the intention is for pupils to replicate those desirable behaviours in small group collaborations. For example, the teacher has to decide what the task will support in terms of those behaviours. Is the task an active problem-solving one or is the desired behaviour demonstrated by the pupils' individual/collaborative actions/interactions? Is the task interactive? Is it more independent? In the SPrinG project, only a quarter of the 200 teachers in the study reported that they prepared their classes for group working, and most of these teachers cited 'circle time' as their only form of preparation for group work (Blatchford et al. 2007, p. 6).

Group working

Teachers establish social norms so that pupils can work and learn together. As one example, active listening is critical to group work and class discussions. Many social norms support learning in a variety of subjects. Yackel and Cobb (1996, pp. 458–77) have found that teachers who work to establish socio-mathematical norms (norms that specifically support mathematical thinking) create a classroom climate that supports problem solving and inquiry. Figure 2.1 illustrates the key differences between general social norms and socio-mathematical norms.

Social norm	Socio-mathematical norm
Students question each other's thinking.	Students ask each other questions that press for mathematical reasoning, justification and understanding.
Students explain their ways of thinking.	Students explain their solutions using mathematical arguments.
Students work together to solve problems.	Students reach consensus using mathematical reasoning and proof.
Students solve problems using a variety of approaches.	Students compare their strategies looking for mathematically important similarities and differences.
Students see making mistakes as a natural part of learning.	Students use mistakes as an opportunity to rethink their conceptions of mathematical ideas and to examine contradictions. Mistakes support new learning about mathematics.

Figure 2.1   The key differences between social norms and socio-mathematical norms

The opening to this chapter stressed the importance of 'a guided co-operative learning structure … that serve[s] to prop up an emergent dialogue structure'. This focus on developing pupils' language requires an analysis of the types of language being used within group work to develop higher order discourse for richer, deeper learning experiences. The important work of Mercer (2000) investigated pupil talk when working in small groups.

Examples: Disputational talk

Disputational and cumulative talk are characterised as disruptive (Hunter 2009). These types of talk focus on self-defence and keeping control rather than trying to reach joint agreement. The following examples are taken from Hunter (2009).

When questioned about his solution strategy a pupil responded with:

Peter: Because I felt like it.

In another instance a group is examining 'True and false' number sentences and failed to reach consensus:

Rani: If you plus 3 to equal that.

Matthew: No, you can't do that.

Rachel: Why?

Matthew: Because if you do then it's changing the whole thing.

Zhou: I am getting even more confused.

It is clear from the above examples that the pupils had not internalised the social norms needed for effective collaborative learning as defined by guided group learning.

In the following example, active listening and questioning were emphasised as the norms by the teacher in her modelling of guided group behaviour:

Teacher: You have to help and you have to understand, everyone in your group needs to understand the strategy. It is not good enough if it is only one person, you need to try and help the rest of your group understand it.

Ruby: You have to ask questions if you don't understand.

Teacher: Exactly you don't just sit there and hope that others will explain it to you. You need to ask questions.

In another example, the teacher models how to disagree in discussions.

Teacher: What if you don't agree?

Mike: If you don't agree ask them why ... why did you do that?

Teacher: You can say 'I am not sure about that'...or 'I am not convinced about that part there. Can you convince me?' It's not just about sitting there while other people are talking. You actually need to be involved and engaged in what is happening. So if you disagree and are not sure of that part, you actually need to say that.

With formative assessment, the teacher learns what at least some of the pupils understand about the lesson topic. Members of the group also have the benefit of hearing a range of views and pupils are offered models of questions for eliciting reasons and those who contribute undertake a useful exercise of having to try to express their ideas clearly. (Mercer 2008, p. 11)

Teacher:	Keighley, would you read out number 9 for us.
Keighley [reads]:	'The moon changes shape because it is in the shadow of the earth'.
Teacher:	Right, now, what does your group think about that?
Keighley:	True.
Teacher:	What? Why do you think that?
Keighley:	Erm, because it's because when earth is dark then, erm, not quite sure but we think it was true.
Teacher:	Right, people with hands up [to Keighley] who would you want to contribute?
Keighley:	Sadie.
Sadie:	I think it is false because when the moon moves around the earth it shines on the moon which projects down to the earth
Teacher [to Sadie]:	Do you want to choose somebody else. That sounds good.
Sadie:	Matthew.
Matthew:	Well, we weren't actually sure because we were thinking that the actual moon changes which it never does or if it is our point of view from earth which puts us in the shadow.
Teacher:	That is a good point isn't it? It doesn't actually change, it looks as if it changes shape to us. That is a really good point.

The teacher engages the pupils in a series of questions. On one hand this is archetypal classroom dialogue but the questions are not the usual closed 'tests'. The teacher does not make a critical assessment of these ideas as right or wrong (making only one evaluative comment at the end) but rather takes account of them and allows the dialogue to continue (Mercer 2008, p. 11).

Implementing a guided group strategy

Research on classroom talk and interaction has typically focused on either whole class teacher-led sessions or on collaborative group work when children work without the teacher. Links have been made between these two types of interaction. For example, it has been shown that the ways in which pupils interact in groups can be strongly influenced by the ways in which teachers interact with the whole class or in teacher-led groups. One other way a teacher might influence group work is by joining a small group, either spontaneously or at the request of pupils and making an active contribution to the group dynamic or output. Ruthven et al.'s data (2011, p. 81) suggest that while group work has been encouraged in schools for a long time it is not obvious to teachers how to enable high-quality talk among pupils. Teachers often 'take over' group tasks, leading pupils (or often an individual pupil in a group) through the task in small steps until a solution is achieved. This undermines the autonomous problem-solving activity of the group. Alternatively, in trying to avoid doing this, teachers may leave groups altogether to their own devices, even though they may not work nor talk effectively. Other teachers do seem able to 'scaffold' group activity without disrupting it. Those teachers establish new ways of mediating small group talk and collaborative problem solving through modelling discussion and exploratory talk, and scaffolding groups' work on a problem. There are some implications for the initial training and professional development of teachers in their ability to develop their own awareness and that of their pupils in the use of talk in the classroom (Ruthven et al. 2011).

Our experience of teaching and research in this field has led us to an understanding that 'if you are teaching pupils as a whole class group, rather than planning your teaching and learning around individual learning needs, then you cannot be teaching formatively. If you teach without using differentiation, then how can you be matching learning to each child's developmental needs?' (Boyle & Charles 2008, p. 22). This has led to a commitment to the principle that group work has to be modelled and understood as teaching and learning through collaboration and co-construction (Allal & Ducrey 2000; Perrenoud 1998) rather than through imposition 'from without' (Vygotsky 1978). The authors feel that using a guided group strategy in a differentiated classroom 'balances learning needs common to all students with more specific needs tagged to individual learners' (Tomlinson 2001, p. 4). For McAdamis (2001) 'Differentiation allows the teacher to focus on the same key principles for all students, however the instructional process, the pace and rate towards understanding these concepts varies' (p. 3). The authors define a guided group (Boyle & Charles 2012) as always operating within a whole class teaching structure, that is, a movement from homogeneity to heterogeneity. The guided session will be focused on new learning or on consolidating a concept which the teacher feels that the children have not internalised in their learning, or on pursuing a learning sequence of carefully planned stepped activities. The teacher will have planned for a number of differentiated learning activities within a teaching theme. Three out of the four groups will work independently (or with Teaching Assistant support) on those activities; the fourth group remaining with the teacher and continuing to be taught is the guided group. The duration of that focused uninterrupted teaching session for each guided group is around 20 minutes. The teacher plans a rota of guided group sessions to match, nurture and challenge the pupils' learning needs throughout the day and the rest of the week and onwards (Blatchford et al. 2007; Boyle & Charles 2012).

The importance of a nurturing pedagogy is recognised by Reeves who argues that 'if we are to take quality seriously we have to get closer to our learners, their needs, their learning styles and their motivation' (Reeves (1993) in Dadds 2001, p. 53). The evidence of our observations across 43 schools justifies the necessity of reminding the teacher that he/she is working with discrete individuals, all with emotional and learning needs, not just delivering a centrally devolved teacher-controlled subject diet. Wink suggests that pedagogy involves human interaction and joy, playing with new ideas and '[challenging] all educators to look beyond the complexities and familiarities of their own teaching' (Wink 2005, in Graziano 2008, p. 162). Within the current climate, this position seems both irrelevant and unobtainable as the dominant discourse is one of controlling pedagogy and performativity.

Example 1

In one Nursery class phonics session observed by the authors, the teacher dealt with the class en masse. All the children were taught the shape, sound and directionality of the letter P. The children were then all required to trace the directionality of the letter P. Therefore, the teacher made the assumption that all the children were at the same stage in their learning and their conceptualisation of the letter P was the same. If the teacher had used distributed practice (Solity 2003) which includes a guided group approach s/he would have immediately recognised the variations in understanding of the letter P across the small group. She would then have differentiated her teaching to accommodate the following:

   (i) A percentage of the class would have been constructing whole words using the letter P

  (ii) A percentage of the class would not have understood the abstract nature of the letter P and would still need aural and oral work to identify phonemes

 (iii) A percentage of the class would not yet be ready for the fine motor requirements (visual tracking) of this concept

 (iv) A percentage of the class could not yet distinguish between a letter and a numeral

  (v) A percentage of the class disengaged because they were not involved in the learning as their location in the learning activity had been ignored – 'one size fits all'.

Example 2

A teacher with a Year 1 class is exploring number bonds with the whole class using a dice to encourage the children to provide the next number by counting on to make 10. Similarly to the previous example s/he assumed that no children in the class could count beyond 10 and conversely below 10. S/he did not know the children well enough as learners. S/he was asking questions of children who were struggling with combining two sets of numbers while some children could not retain the number in their head and then count on. Some children felt that the task was beyond them and 'froze' while other children were conceptually beyond the task demand – these became bored and disengaged.

   A more formative teacher using a guided group strategy would have:

   (i) understood the learning capability of the children in the group and 'scaffolded' the learning experience accordingly through differentiating the questions being asked

  (ii) integrated the visual computations alongside the mental calculations required

 (iii) asked the children to generate their own number bond problems for the other children to solve

 (iv) had high expectations and exposed the children to more/less complex number combinations

  (v) addressed the abstract nature of the + sign and technical mathematical language demands ('more', 'all together', 'count on').

Case study   Guided group working on a Design & Technology theme

Dennis's Design & Technology session with his group of Year 1 children aged 5–6 years shows clear evidence of his understanding of using assessment in support of children's learning in a guided group situation. Careful questioning by the teacher to establish (assess) the children's current understanding of the problem-solving aspect of what they are doing runs throughout this activity. Dennis's cognitive questioning reveals the initial design problem of: 'How are the ear pieces going to stay on Mr Bear's head?' The children are clearly choosing their own materials and Dennis is carefully timing his questions and interventions to help their thinking through of their designs. Dennis uses individualised questions and is able to use the information given by the children in their responses and through their behaviours, to reveal assessment evidence. He can then support the children's developing understanding of the structural elements of their design pieces and the suitability of their chosen materials, for example some materials don't bend, some will not stick with glue, etc. His formative pedagogy encourages the children to drive their own investigations and nurtures their independence and decision-making capabilities.

Dennis's use of the interrogatives, i.e. questioning 'how' and 'why', has a triple function:

(i)   It enables him to learn more about the children's understanding of the suitability/durability of certain materials

(ii) He is establishing a fluidity of roles (Perrenoud 1998) so that the children do not develop a construct of an adult dominance over their ideas

(iii) Finally, he maintains a successful balance in supporting the children's cognitive and affective domain development in which the children's motivation, enthusiasm and ownership of the design are in harmony with their cognitive design thinking.

Dennis is acutely aware of individuals and individual learning needs within the group working on the activity. He observes a child who has not chosen her own materials and has not made selective independent decisions in constructing her design piece. He encourages the child to actively problem solve and observes the child choosing the suitably shaped materials for ear-pieces, i.e. the circular lid.

Dennis perceptively weaves the developmental differences that the children exhibit through the design and technology activity. He uses assessment information successfully to support individual design ideas. The children are allowed space and time to reflect and think and to demonstrate what they understand about materials, construction, assembly, suitability, perseverance and design requirements. This pedagogical style of teaching in which learning and assessment are integral allows the teacher to gather relevant information about the individual child, their strengths, skills and areas for development and to use that information when it is timely to support the learning development of each individual.

The guided group session began with the teacher introducing the D&T theme through a read-aloud story (focused on Mr Bear, a story well known and well liked by the children). He involved the children in participating and talked through the purpose of the activity with all the children in a whole class session. The class was organised into differentiated working groups and the guided group Dennis had with him worked out design solutions to the D&T problem in their own individual ways. The teacher was being carefully diverse as he had selected the composition of the guided group based on the children's problem-solving abilities. He deliberately selected a group which demonstrated a range of physical dexterities, confident oral contributions and high levels of creativity.

Dennis's intention was to demonstrate focused assessment questioning based on identifying individual understanding of design problems. He wanted to strategically intervene to support each individual's thinking and his aim was that his formative pedagogy would encourage individuals to become independent learners. The authors were interested to see if Dennis could carefully manage a balance of affective and cognitive development for the children. The opening of Dennis's lesson is transcribed below.

Dennis explored design ideas with the group to make headwear for Mr Bear to enable him to sleep through noise. He begins with the key design question: 'How are the ear pieces going to stay on Mr Bear's head?'

Dennis: Asafa have a look round here and see what you could use from here to take back.

[Asafa is busy exploring the materials box and emerges with some small plastic lids and places them over and around both his ears.]

Dennis: Now you still need something to go over your head with the idea you have. Are you going to use flat ones like that?

[Asafa nods in agreement 'Yeah'.]

Dennis: Now what are you going to use for the head part?

[Asafa continues to search in the materials box and picks up a used margarine container.]

Dennis: Right you decide, you choose then.

Asafa: I'll pick this one...

Dennis: Right you have got some ideas then.

[Dennis turns to another child who is holding up two empty yoghurt pots.]

Dennis: Amina, now how are you going to get these to stay on your ears?

Amina: Erm, I, I...

Dennis: Could we not make it easier for him? How can we make it easier for him? How are we going to get them onto his head without falling off? Sellotape them onto his head or sellotape them onto something else.'

Amina: I know, I know. We could sellotape on here

[Asafa points to his set of materials including yoghurt pots, cardboard tube, glue...]

Dennis: Right, are you telling me, Amina that he's going to have to spend all night holding them onto his head like this.

Asafa: No

Dennis: Right then

[Dennis holds up the plastic pots.] How are we going to fix them onto something?

Amina: Glue.

Maryam: Like this sir.

[Maryam holds up yoghurt pots on either end of a cardboard tube].

Dennis: [ignoring Maryam] I don't think he'd like glue on his head Amina. Gluing them onto his head, I don't think he'd like that.

(Continued)

(Continued)

[Maryam holds up her suggestion again.]

Dennis: Now how is that going to work Maryam? How is that going to keep the noise out of his ears? Those ear muffs that I brought into school, how did they work?

Maryam: You could put the tube on top of it.

Dennis: Show me how that is going to work.

[Maryam now changes position of pots from end of tube to underneath the tube.]

Dennis: 'Mmmm. How is that going to work Maryam? How did my ear muffs work? How did they stay on my head?'

Analysis and discussion

We can see that Dennis has recognised the importance of these 'organisational and instructional changes' as a move away from the dominance of whole class teaching (DCSF 2007). He understands that a guided group is not as Williams states (2008) 'an organisational approach where attention is given to children who require additional support' (p. 67), i.e. it is *not* a Special Needs support strategy.

Dennis also demonstrates 'that if you are teaching children as a whole class group, rather than planning your teaching and learning around individual learning needs, then you cannot be teaching formatively. If you teach without differentiation then how can you be matching learning to each child's developmental need?' (Boyle & Charles 2008, p. 22). The children were sufficiently motivated by Dennis to enable them to produce individual design ideas and subsequently products in a move away from a 'one size fits all' homogeneity.

Key teaching, learning and assessment from the guided group

  (i) The teacher demonstrates focused assessment questioning based on identifying individual understanding of design problems.
 (ii) Note the careful timings of the teacher's interventions to support each individual child's thinking.
(iii) The teacher's formative pedagogy encourages individuals to become independent learners.
 (iv) Note how the teacher carefully manages a balance of affective and cognitive development for the children.

(v)   The teacher has created a working culture in the classroom based on fluidity and role self-definition.

(vi) The teacher demonstrates his use of observation as an assessment tool.

(vii) Note the teacher's allowance of time and reflection to integrate assessment to scaffold learning for the children – there is no sense of 'rushing' through for coverage and completion here.

Elaborated code/restricted code in teaching and learning

However through Bernstein's perspective (1962, 1973), closer analysis of Dennis's language code evidenced by the transcript suggests his pedagogy is that of the restricted code rather than the elaborated code. Analysis of Dennis's control of the language transactions, almost monologic, and certainly not dialogic in any shape or form, indicated to us that Dennis's perception of his pupils and their abilities is firmly rooted in the Ofsted analysis. One can note the labelling language used in the report: 'a school with very high levels of social deprivation, Free School Meals (FSM) and with 90% English Additional Language' (Ofsted Report, School A, March 2009). We felt that Dennis's confused attempt to introduce guided group philosophy offered some insights into Bernstein's socio-linguistic code theory. How could the guided group with whom Dennis is working and which is being labelled as Bernstein's 'restricted code' population, benefit from the treatment of a 'pedagogy of plenty' (Haberman 1981) to enable them to attain 'elaborated code' status? (Bernstein 1962b, 1973). First, Dennis has failed to change the regulation (Perrenoud 1998) in the learning process between himself and his pupils. He has assumed the traditional role of power (Bernstein 1970) in which he asks the questions and hence structures the children's thinking. The illusion of formativeness is maintained through the group set-up and the free movement of the children to and from the materials. However, from analysis of the transcript of the working session, it is evident, even from the representative section printed below, that Dennis controls the materials selection by challenging the pupils' choices of materials and design, for example see the opening section of the transcript for the continual uninterrupted question sequences from Dennis. There is not one question framed by a child in this section of the transcript. Dennis is taking the position of control and indicating to the children that he is the problem solver and the architect and they are merely the recipients of instructions which they then carry out to produce quite firmly controlled outcomes.

The children are struggling to find a solution, that is a band to connect the ear-pieces, so Dennis pursues this with:

Dennis: How did my ear muffs work? How did they stay on my head? How did my ear muffs stay on that I was using? I did not have to hold them on with my hands like that.

Safia: No, no ...

Dennis: But why did they not fall off?

Safia: Because you have a big head.

Dennis: I have got a very big head Safia but it was not just my big head that kept my ear muffs on was it?

Safia: No.

Dennis: How did they stay on my head?

Amina [interjects and replies]:   I know. You had a band on your head.

Dennis: That's right I had a big pink band across my head to keep it on my head.

Dennis: Right Safia, you have got plenty of feathers there. I want you to tell me how it is going to stay on my head first.

[Maryam comes over with a large straw and hands it to Dennis.]

Dennis: How is that going to work? Go on and show me.

[Hands the straw back to Maryam. Maryam turns yoghurt pot upside down and places straw across bottom.]

Dennis: Mmm. Is that going to be strong enough Maryam or is that going to break? Do you think we need something stronger?

[Maryam bends the straw to see if it does break. It doesn't.]

Dennis: It is going to break isn't it? Go and see if there is something stronger. Maryam, what can we use to make a band? What can we use to make a band go round your head?

Maryam: A bubble ... a bubble.

It is even more noticeable from the full transcript that Dennis's style of interaction has limited rather than enhanced the children's responses. In fact, his pedagogical style has put limits on the children's colloborative learning, preventing any dialogic inquiry or cooperative exploration. His questions 'do not cognitively challenge the child' (Siraj-Blatchford & Manni 2008, p. 13) and his questions dominate the session in quantity rather than quality, 'demanding only simple recall' (ibid, p. 13). Maryam's response – by gesture – is typical of the group, for example Maryam bends the straw but does not say anything in response. Inadvertently, Dennis is embodying the 'restricted code' in full. He expects no language in response to his constant questions and is rewarded by getting none. He does not self-evaluate and modify his own behaviour, for example the sequence of questions without pause to Maryam played out as follows:

> Dennis: Have you ever made one from that [points to a piece of leather] in school? Maybe we could have a look for some? [Maryam runs off to resource area to find some leather.] Do you want to come and look for some because you are going to have to put it around your head? [Dennis is addressing the rest of the group.] That won't break, come and have a look. [Motions again to the rest of the group to put down the materials they are working with. Children continue working.] Maryam come over here. [Maryam returns empty handed.] Now I think Amina's [model] might work, let's go and find something that you are going to need Asafa that will keep it on his head otherwise it will fall off. Safia, I want you to leave ... come on, put those feathers on [Maryam and Asafa go off with Dennis to the resource area.] What about things like this then? [Dennis holds up a long strip of material.] Which way does it go? [Asafa demonstrates long pieces hanging down like ears.]

Analysis of the full transcript reveals that of the 107 oral transactions in the 21-minute session, Dennis made 60 of these. This approximates to teacher-speak every 20 seconds of the session. Even at this level the balance of transactions between one voice (teacher) and four children (Asafa, Maryam, Safia and Amina) is inequitable. However, on closer inspection, Dennis's 60 contributions actually contain 112 questions or direct instructions, a dominance of the session which shuts down the 'principal means by which pupils actively engage and constructively intervene through talk' (Alexander 2004). The four children respond as follows: Asafa makes nine responses, Amina 11, Maryam 15 and Safia 7; without exception these responses are all short, do not engage in exploration of problem solving in the design and technology context and are very limited in terms of cognitive interrogatives. In plain statistical terms, the children only respond to about a third of Dennis's questions – in many cases, because he either does not allow them sufficient time to respond or because they are used to his pedagogical style of the discourse in which the teacher is dominant at the centre (Alexander 2008; Allal & Ducrey 2000; Freire 1970). In short, Dennis has 'restricted' not just the opportunities for dialogue and dialogic (Wells 2001) but the potential for collaborative exploration of the design and technology process. Dennis's low percentage (5%) of open questions compares 'poorly with the 9.9% of open questions used by key stage 2 teachers in the ORACLE primary school study, already disappointingly low' (Galton et al. 1999, p. 29). Dennis's percentage correlates closely with Siraj-Blatchford and Manni's REPEY Study (2008) which 'found that 94.5% of all the questions asked by staff were closed questions that required a recall of fact, experience or expected behaviour, decision between a limited selection of choices or no response at all' (p. 5).

Implications of assessing group participation

Six children had been on a visit to the airport as part of a project on flight. They were asked to present an oral report to the class. As the group planned and carried out the presentation, the teacher observed them and recorded her observations on a checklist which included the features which had previously been identified as indicating achievement (criteria).

From the teacher's observations it became clear that one member of the group dominated both the planning and presenting, while another remained passive, contributing little to the group discussion during planning, and being content to participate as directed by the others. The teacher expressed concern about the observations for these two individual children, because in designing the checklist such issues had not been taken into account. Furthermore, the teacher was unclear as to how to relate the performance of these children to the interpretation of the criteria. Both children had been involved in planning and participating but their degree of involvement was suspect and open to question in terms of interpersonal skills and group interaction. On the other hand, they had planned and participated in a presentation and so if the criteria were interpreted in a narrow sense then they had satisfied the criteria for attainment. This example demonstrates the need for a clear focus on the task, its demands and its relation to the criteria for assessment. While assessment tasks should be clearly planned and structured it is necessary that teachers are adaptable in order to respond to pupil performance and behaviour which is not anticipated.

Depth of learning

Deep learning is achieved if both teacher and child are immersed in the teaching and learning process. Our search is to identify, through our observations of teaching and in conversations with children, teachers and Local Authority Education officers their priorities in planning for teaching and learning. How is an independent and lifelong learner developed? Is there a relationship between the intrinsic development of engagement, self-motivation, interest and research skills at an early stage of a child's education and current pedagogical practice? Is the current observed paradigm of controlling teacher/passive recipient moving at pace through a prescribed programme going to develop a generation of 'deep and reflective thinkers' and lifelong learners? From our recent classroom observations our response is that in the current summative framework the chances of developing reflective children involved in self-motivated research activities is negligible. A missing component is the acknowledgement of the child as learner within the affective domain, in short acknowledging that social development is equally important as, and a primary factor in, cognitive development – but testing the latter is the area on which curriculum and assessment and therefore pedagogy focuses in a summative Standards agenda.

3

Differentiation

In this chapter we introduce differentiation as a planned, flexible process. We consider various misconceptions about differentiation, and set out alternatives.

Differentiation, although the key strategy of formative teaching, learning and assessment, is as much misunderstood as is formative assessment itself. Differentiation is synonymous with 'setting' in many teachers' practices (the 'locking' of pupils into sets from the cradle to the grave – see Boaler 2005) or with the school of thought which differentiates by 'outcome' or 'has something extra' for the 'fast finishers' to 'do'. The research literature offers some solutions to unlocking this pedagogical principle – although many teachers still require exposure to modelling in their specific pre-service and in-service training on the technique. Allal & Lopez (2005) remind us that 'Differentiation of instruction is planned rather than just being added on after observing difficulties' (p. 246), while Perrenoud is clear that 'If formative assessment is carried out on a fairly regular basis, the result is pressure to differentiate' (Perrenoud 1991, p. 89).

In the mid 1960s there was a greater understanding and insistence on individual pupils' interests and needs. The current thinking of that time favoured systematic differentiation in teaching: 'Teachers will have to adapt their methods to individuals within a class or a school. Only in this way can the needs of gifted and slow learning children and all those between the extremes be met' (Central Advisory Council for Education 1967, p. 460). Since 1988 (Education Reform Act – introduction of the National Curriculum in England and Wales) government reforms have shifted the focus towards achievement and standards. These aims are linked in official documents with particular pedagogic practices, namely with whole class teaching, and with various forms of ability grouping, for example setting: 'Unless a school can demonstrate that it is getting better than expected results through a different approach, we do make the presumption that setting should be the norm in secondary schools. In some cases, it is worth considering in primary schools' (Department for Education 2011, p. 38). Differentiation is understood here as the process by which teachers adapt curriculum objectives, teaching methods, learning activities, resources and assessment to match the educational needs of individual pupils. Learning can be differentiated in many ways: by curriculum structure, course content, learning tasks, teaching approach, pace of learning, support, outcome and assessment. (See Figure 3.1 below)

Differentiation of Instruction:

Is a teacher's response to learner's needs

Guided by general principles of differentiation, such as:

| Respectful tasks | Flexible grouping | On-going assessment & adjustment |

Teachers can differentiate

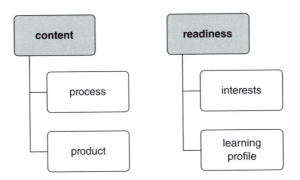

Figure 3.1   Differentiation of instruction

In any class, children are confronted with situations intended to make them learn: some do, some do not and others do to an extent. The classic approaches to difficulties in learning and failure in school look for a solution in the make-up of the child: the level of development, cultural and linguistic capital, knowledge previously acquired, motivation, ambition, attitude towards knowledge, family background, etc. In summary, schools provide standard learning situations, which, sadly are fruitful only for those children who have a specific profile which includes all the prerequisites for learning. For example, the teaching of reading at the beginning of a pupil's school life is designed for children with a normal intellectual, perceptual and motor development who wish to learn to read and whose family background encourages the written word and has almost certainly begun the pre-school reading process with the child. It should not therefore be surprising that a year or two later those children know how to read well enough to make 'the expected' progress through a primary school curriculum. The other pupils, not within the above socio-economic profile, proceed more falteringly, with weaknesses. These weaknesses in one discipline or domain will have an effect on all their learning as the curricular programmes assume that pupils know how to read from the second year of compulsory education onwards. 'Difficulties in schooling can be explained in the differences between pupils often described as failings or shortcomings in pupils who do not reach the norm: socio-cultural handicap, linguistic poverty, poor family background and lack of motivation and support, so many expressions which stigmatise pupils in difficulty' (Perrenoud 1998, p. 93). Bourdieu (1966) demonstrated that these difficulties do not explain inequality. 'Rather it is because the school ignored them in accordance with an indifference to difference which is embedded in the structure of teaching programmes as well as in the culture and practices of teachers' (Perrenoud 1998, p. 93). Bloom (1988) stated that 80% of pupils could manage the programmes if they were placed in learning situations which were optimal for them.

The question becomes, given the diversity of 6-year-old children in terms of level of development, relation to the written word or development of language, how do teachers lead them to an adequate reading level a year or so later? Differentiated teaching is an answer to the question. It is achieved through a diversified approach, that is, daily in learning situations with which the children are confronted, not just by noting differences, 'diversity of approach at the service of equality in the face of knowledge' (Perrenoud 1998, p. 93). Avoiding all pupils doing the same learning at the same time is not an aim in itself; it is only a consequence of differentiated teaching which attempts to locate each pupil in a learning situation which is optimal for her/him. 'To the extent that all pupils do not have the same abilities nor the same needs nor the same way of working, an optimal situation for one pupil will not be optimal for another' (Perrenoud 1998, p. 94).

The diversification of approaches has to be matched and fit for each particular case.

> In a hospital one does not attempt differentiated treatment for its own sake; one only attempts to give each person what suits them best and the inevitable result is a differentiation in therapy. One can write a simple equation: diversity in people + appropriate treatment for each = diversity in approach. (Perrenoud 1998, p. 94)

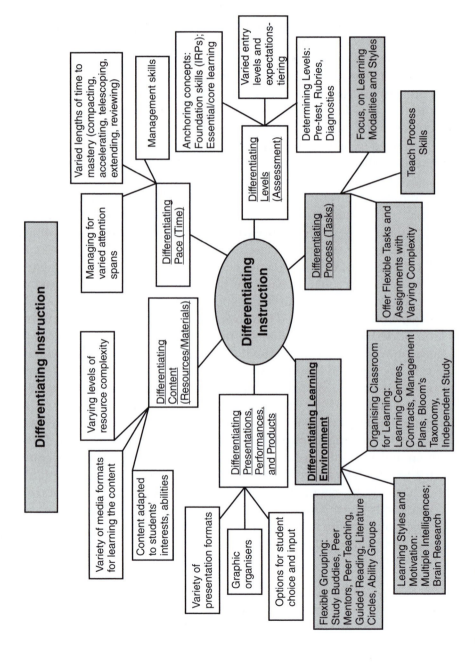

Figure 3.2 Differentiating instruction

Differentiation is simply the adjustment of didactic treatment to suit the individual pupil's needs. It has a simple premise – that there is no point locating children in a situation where the teacher knows in advance that the child will not learn very much.

The skills involved in regulation depend as much on the capacities of observation and dialogue of the teacher as the way he or she understands the cognitive obstacle in the mind of the child and subsequently analyses what prevents the child from overcoming the obstacle. The teacher requires the ability and the motivation to put him/herself in the place of the person who does not know, does not understand and sees no solution. These skills involve formative assessment in the richest sense of the term. These skills 'can only be enriched by a didactic culture based on experience as well as research which allows the teacher to mould not only the understanding to be developed but the way it will develop in the pupil's mind' (Bain 1988). In simpler terms, formative assessment furnishes the intention of regulating the learning process, whereas the didactic approach furnishes the terms of reference appropriate to the discipline and the knowledge in question.

How does a teacher organise the parallel teaching of 30 pupils within the constraints of school programmes and timetables?

Optimising the learning situation for each child must not be confused with the isolation of each child in individual tasks. Differentiated teaching does not consist of a succession of individual lessons nor is it a permanent arrangement of individualised learning, with each child being occupied with his/her own activities. The problem then becomes based on the reconciling of the individualisation of the learning trajectory, a condition of the optimisation of the learning situations for each child. On the other hand, the collective and interactive character of a significant number of the tasks is likely to produce interesting learning situations.

Undertaking differentiated teaching in schools involves the breaking up of levels and classes and the creation of broader areas of instruction in time and space, entrusted to teaching teams who will collectively take in hand for a period of at least two years, a group of children equivalent in number to two whole classes. 'Classroom management' is replaced by a complex organisation of work in which monitoring individual progress and didactic input poses difficult problems. Increasing the complexity and size of the input is vital to achieve a critical mass large enough to differentiate usefully; at the same time this development can cause a crisis in professional skills, routines, organisation, the familiar groupings and trappings of the class situation, which could cause less learning and greater inequality if the teacher does not control for its negative effects. All of which makes it imperative to consider 'new tools' for collective development of the mechanisms of teaching programmes which presuppose different ways of organising schools and new forms of professional co-operation (Perrenoud 1997, 1998).

Case study

This study focused on 12 socially disadvantaged English and French classrooms and was based on two weeks of observations in each class (Raveaud 2005).

Context: Every one of the English teachers systematically provided differentiated tasks for written work, whereas not a single one of their French colleagues did so. All the English classes were mixed-ability classes. There was no streaming nor setting observed and the main form of grouping was within-class grouping of same-ability pupils. There were four or five such same-ability groups per class. Research based on wider samples indicates that these observations are typical of English classroom practice, with within-class ability grouping in the majority of classes (Blatchford et al. 2001; Galton et al. 1999; Hallam et al. 2004; Kutnick et al. 2002). In the French schools there was barely any differentiation: pupils were given identical tasks to complete and most work was undertaken either in the guise of whole class instruction or as individual work from a set book or worksheet handed out to each pupil. Depending on the class, pupils were seated in rows facing the whiteboard or grouped around tables. But in either case they worked individually and simultaneously on the same task (Alexander 2001). Though there were inevitably differences in the outcomes produced by the pupils, very rarely did teachers allocate pupils tasks tailored to their individual needs.

Example: Mathematics tasks were given to 5-year-old pupils in both countries. The French exercise consisted of a worksheet focused on the 'number 6', written by the teacher and handed out to the whole class at the same time. Interestingly, the class teacher referred to this task as 'differentiation' – yet there were no differences in the task required to be completed by all the pupils, regardless of their knowledge and understanding of number. In the class in England, the pupils were divided into four groups – Group 1 being the lowest attainers – and each group was supplied with a task that the teacher considered to match the pupils' level of understanding. Therefore the work was differentiated for four same-ability groups of pupils.

The research indicated a range of differentiation strategies used in the classes in England. These were based on the quantity, complexity and degree of abstraction of tasks. Quantitative differentiation is the basic form of differentiation: it concerns the length of a task or the number of times children are to repeat it. In this example, Group 1 (i.e. the lowest attainers) had a drawing of two ladybirds to complete, compared to the requirement of four ladybirds in the other groups in the class. For writing tasks, the teacher indicated the differing quantities of writing required by each pupil/group by the drawing of a different number of lines in pupils' writing books. Tasks can be differentiated by their complexity. Depending on which group they are in, pupils may need to count up to 6, 8 or 10. Also, Groups 3 and 4 were adding two lots of 'spots' corresponding to the wings drawn on the ladybirds while their peers in Groups 1 and 2 only counted one lot of spots. Variation in the degree of abstraction reflects the fact that 5-year-olds are still in the process of acquiring symbolical codes of representation such as words and

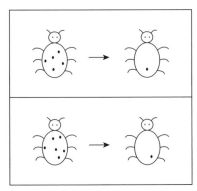

Group 1: children are to add spots to the ladybird on the right so that it contains the same number of dots as the one on the left

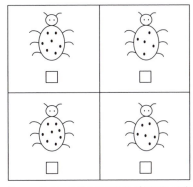

Group 2: count the number of spots and write it in the box

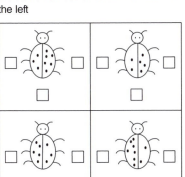

Group 3: count the number of spots on each wing, write the number in the box on the side, and the total number of spots in the box underneath

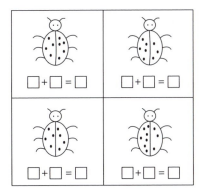

Group 4: count the number of spots on each wing, write the number in the box and add up the total

Figure 3.3 Differentiated tasks

numbers. In Group 1, pupils do not need to resort to numbers: they only need to identify a quantity and to reproduce it. Group 2 represents the next step up in the teacher's learning hierarchy, linking a quantity and its symbolical representation – the corresponding number. Groups 3 and 4 are progressing towards the formalised presentation of 'sums' as types of calculations. In a writing exercise this type of differentiation leads to some young pupils telling a story (narrative) by drawing a picture – while other pupils will have advanced to writing text.

The interviews with the French and English teachers suggest that the strong contrasts observed regarding the use or non-use of differentiation are not experienced as pedagogical choices but as necessities. The systematic creation of same-ability groups in England reflects a widely held assumption that it is absurd to expect all children to address the same levels of difficulty. The need to differentiate seemed to require no justification in the minds of the English teachers. In contrasting her situation with that of her French colleagues one teacher stated that it would be easy for her simply to provide all her pupils with the same task but that would be unrealistic and unfair on the pupils. 'It's just got to be differentiated'. French teachers rarely or never adapted tasks to cater for the range of attainment in the class. Some forms of support for pupils with special educational needs exist but these take place outside the classroom with specialised staff. In the course of the daily teaching programme, French teachers gave all pupils identical tasks to fulfil – only one of the teachers in the sample claimed to use differentiated pedagogy. However, in the course of the fortnight of observation, she did not once adapt tasks to the perceived ability or needs of a particular pupil or group of pupils. She explained her view of differentiation:

> I differentiate work because I have children who say 'I don't know, I can't do it'. So I make the situation less threatening to them. I don't let them get bogged down in their mistakes. I sit down beside them if they need help and we go over it until they have understood. If they need to have it explained three times, then that is what happens. (Raveaud 2005, p. 469)

This teacher differentiated the means – by giving the 'weakest' more support – to maintain the same ends for all. Differentiating means rather than ends appeared to be the dominant way in which French teachers dealt with the diversity in the pupils' learning needs. There were great differences in the time French pupils took to complete identical tasks. 'The hares had finished before the tortoises had settled down to work' (Raveaud 2005, p. 469). This led to problems which the teachers in this study resolved through two strategies: timing and extra support. Egalitarian ideals meant that setting the 'faster' pupils extra work was not an option, as this would be seen as widening the attainment gap inside the class. Instead, teachers usually proposed gap-fillers such as silent reading, colouring-in or playing, until all the other pupils had finished the set task. Secondly, although most work was individual, weaker pupils got support from their teacher or their peers. Much peer support was observed as involuntary on the part of other pupils, particularly in the cases where a pupil copied the work of the pupil sitting next to him/her. This mechanism has some beneficial effects as one French teacher pointed out: 'Those who are lost latch on to the others. If they have not understood the task, they can see what their neighbour is doing and then off they go' (Raveaud 2005, p. 469). The absence of differentiation in tasks in French classes meant that some pupils were under more pressure than their peers in England, but teachers in France compensated for this lack of flexibility (to some extent) by introducing some forms of support. Although the French teachers agreed that it might be necessary to take special measures for one pupil exceptionally, their explicit aim was for differences to be smoothed out. Although French teachers were willing to give individual children extra support, time and explanations, differentiation appeared as a last resort, in contrast to England where it is used more regularly (with a range of definitions). French teachers were reluctant to set different tasks and targets for different pupils, viewing differentiation with a degree of suspicion as a means of perpetuating social inequalities. French debates around the topic of differentiation tend to focus on issues of social equality, rather than its effects on academic achievements or on pupil disaffection. Promoters and opponents of differentiation both claim that their approach is the one that best contributes to democracy at school and in society (Zakhartchouk 2001, p. 34). This reflects the core values of the French education system. Schools are expected to strive to erase, as far as possible, differences that stem from social background, that is, middle-class pupils will arrive at school with greater cultural capital in the form of more developed vocabulary, more familiarity with books, more abstract notions than their working-class peers (Bourdieu & Passeron 1970a). Critics of differentiation argue that teachers following this approach would be promoting a self-fulfilling prophecy, leading to the reproduction of social inequalities in society (Rosenthal & Jacobson 1968). Alexander cautions that:

> We should be alert to the power of pedagogy to deliver messages which may or may not be consistent with the educational goals which we espouse, just as we should understand that in importing teaching methods which we find admirable we may also import values with which we feel less comfortable. (1997, p. 25)

Choosing whether or not to differentiate rests on pedagogical concerns but also on wider views of pupils' social, cultural, developmental and learning needs and of the school's educational aims. In summary, differentiation is NOT 'setting', in which pupils are consigned to a 'high' or 'low' ability group for a sustained period of the school year – or even longer. The teacher will review each pupil's learning situation (i.e., did today's guided group work for that pupil) and then make a fresh decision on group composition for the following day/subsequent lesson. The authors are not advocating in any way the 'locking-in' of pupils to permanent labelling or learning situations: group compositions will always be case or subject specific. However, the French position leads to the transmission of a highly valued body of knowledge and culture and to the development of citizens. The English ideal for differentiation in practice rests on respect for the individual and the needs of the pupil. Through the experiences of social construction which the pupils participate in and internalise, schools participate in a wider process of meaning making, shaping pupils' views of their society and their place in it (Raveaud 2005).

What is the relationship between differentiation and 'good' pedagogy?

Alexander posits a dynamic, evolving definition of pedagogy:

> Pedagogy is the observable act of teaching together with its attendant discourse of educational theories, values, evidence and justifications. It is what one needs to know, and the skills one needs to command in order to make and justify the many different kinds of decisions of which teaching is constituted. (Alexander 2008, p. 29)

Similarly Alexander's definition is likened to Edwards's (2001) in that it has as its core ideas about learners, learning and teaching, and these are shaped and modified by context, policy and culture (Alexander 2008).

The complexity of the subject is such that within the literature there is a range of definitions. However, any discussion on pedagogy 'cannot be just a matter of disembodied technique it reflects and manifests values. In turn these are not merely the personal predilections of individual teachers, but the shared and/or disputed values of the wider culture' (Alexander 2008, p.19). Rowsell, Kosnik and Beck (2008) suggest that 'pedagogy refers to an educational position or approach that includes both theory and practice' (p. 110). This definition clearly focuses on the strength or weakness of the connection between theory and practice in the teacher's pedagogical development. In short, there should be no end point in the teacher's development as a practitioner, and for that development to produce a truly reflective formative practitioner there has to be a synthesis between theory and practice. However, Edwards (2001) develops this further as 'teaching is using informed interpretations of learners, knowledge and environments in order to manipulate [those] environments in ways that help learners make sense of the knowledge available to them' (p. 163). For Edwards the pupil is located at the centre of not only the curriculum, but of what that unique individual brings to those environments; the teaching is then informed, which leads to a differentiated pedagogy.

However, another missing component from both of these definitions is the failure to acknowledge the pupil within the affective domain, in short acknowledging that social development is equally important as, and a primary factor in, cognitive development, but the latter is the area on which curriculum and assessment and therefore pedagogy currently focuses. Alexander (2008) cautions against a simplistic interpretation and states that: 'For children then the preferred indicators are affective as much as cognitive and instrumental … focussing on affectivity alone is as conceptually and empirically restrictive as is the treating of mathematical test scores and educational outcomes as synonymous' (Alexander 2008, p. 3). In support of this Hayes (2008) suggests that 'pedagogy captures the multi-layered and dynamic practice necessary to support children's holistic development' (p. 436). The importance of a nurturing pedagogy is recognised by Reeves (1993) who argues that 'if we are to take quality seriously we have to get closer to our learners, their needs, their learning styles and their motivation' (in Dadds 2001, p. 53). This clearly identifies the importance of the teacher understanding that s/he is working with 25 discrete individuals all with learning and emotional needs, not just delivering an atomised subject menu as centrally devolved. Going beyond Rowsell et al. (2008), Wink suggests that the word pedagogy involves human interaction and joy, and playing with new ideas, challenging 'all educators to look beyond the complexities and familiarities of their own teaching' (Wink 2005, in Graziano 2008, p. 162). Within the current climate this position seems unobtainable, as the dominant discourse is one of controlling pedagogy and performativity.

The teaching paradigm: 'Knowledge rich – knowledge poor'

To start with a simple question about something as complex and multi-layered as the science of teaching: why do some teachers have a strong pedagogical base while others do not? Through our questionnaire survey and the resultant school visits to observe teaching, we have evidence of a profile of teachers without a learner-centred pedagogy (Boyle & Charles, 2010), reliant on prescriptive, centrally disseminated materials through which, 'politicians and bureaucrats are demanding greater conformity of education offerings which are transparent and superficially testable' (Patrick et al. 2003, p. 239). This period of change in the pre- and post-Education Reform Act (DES 1988) years is illustrated in Barber's (2002) 'knowledge poor – knowledge rich, prescription – judgement' matrix, as shown in Figure 3.4.

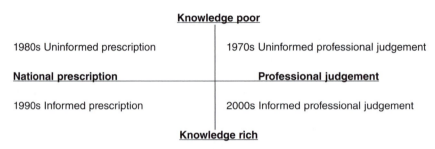

Figure 3.4 The knowledge/poor, knowledge/rich matrix of teacher development

Barber's matrix (he was then Director of the Ministry of Education's Standards and Effectiveness Unit) provides a model of the dominant political influence of successive UK governments on teachers' pedagogy, and his advice to the government on how to improve 'standards' was based on the belief that 'the education system will never be world class unless virtually all children learn to read, write and calculate to high standards before they leave primary school' and that 'at the time of the 1997 election the national data showed how far we were from achieving this goal' (Barber 2001, p. 23). He also suggested that the initial stages of such government-imposed top-down change would challenge teacher ownership of such change:

> winning hearts and minds is not the best first step in any process of urgent change … sometimes it is necessary to mandate the change, implement it well, consciously challenge the prevailing culture … the driving force at this critical juncture is leadership … it is the vocation of leaders to take people where they have never been before and to show them a new world from which they do not want to return. (Barber quoted in Mahoney et al. 2004, p. 452)

This emphasises that 'the teacher is no longer the autonomous self-directed individual, but rather someone who interacts at the boundaries of expertise, knowledge specialism and state control' (Eraut 1994, in

Patrick et al. 2003, p. 243). The dominant pedagogical model throughout the period has been and still is that of substantial whole class teaching, which Myhill (2006) suggests causes 'an orientation towards coverage and elicitation of facts rather than the creation and co-construction of interconnected learning' (p. 34) and evidences no 'substantial use of progressive child centred methods' (Gammage 1986, p. 107). As Alexander stated in his critique of the government's research which underpinned the National Strategies and the adherence to whole class teaching: 'direct instruction through whole class teaching is the commonest teaching approach world-wide so it is as strongly associated with low educational standards as with high' (Alexander, 2004, p. 17).

Origins of a teacher-centred pedagogy

Galton, in his follow-up to the ORACLE studies of the 1970s, found that teacher-centred pedagogy had increased between 1976 and 1996 (Galton et al. 1999, p. 24). If teachers are, according to Eraut (1994, p. 243), no longer 'autonomous self-directed individuals', this suggests a movement from a position when teachers were autonomous. The next question then has to be: how was that autonomy eroded and ultimately dismantled? The basis for the government intervention, which began in the mid-1980s with the legislation of a prescribed National Curriculum (1988 Education Reform Act (ERA)), the introduction of national testing (1991) and regular inspection of schools (1992), and resulted in a standards-driven agenda (DfE 2011), was a developing understanding of the importance of being seen to be intervening effectively in education as a political message to the electorate. Throughout this process teachers' autonomy was being reduced and they were being pushed towards performativity (Patrick et al. 2003), becoming more compliant in utilising the centrally developed materials which focused on the production of test outcomes (Alexander 2004; Brehony 2005; Hall & Harding 2002; Patrick et al. 2003; Topping 2001; Wyse et al. 2007) at the expense of child-centred pedagogy.

In 1991 Kenneth Clarke, then Education Minister, defended the government's position with an attack on his perceived critics, 'the British pedagogue's hostility to written examinations of any kind can be taken to ludicrous extremes. The British Left believe that paper and pencil examinations impose stress on pupils and demotivate them' (Clarke 1991, in Ball 1994, p. 40). Clarke here uses the word 'pedagogue' as a term of abuse (Edwards 2001, p. 164) to reinforce the philosophy of the right, that is that testing is the sole way of measuring children's learning and the only way forward. That message of central government became the dominant discourse throughout the 1990s. Clearly there was a shift of emphasis in pedagogy as the centrally imposed methodologies eroded and marginalised child-centred education. The newly instituted Office for Standards in Education (Ofsted) was now used by central government to support their version of pedagogy. Ofsted's review of school inspection data for the years 1994–99, 'remarked with approval on the revival of the more traditional whole-class, brisk, subject-specific, directly-focused method of teaching' (Ofsted 1999, paras 4.1 and 4.5). This is reinforced by research evidence (Kutnick et al. 2002) which reported that teachers in the 1990s experienced pressure towards an increased amount of whole class teaching 'at the expense of a more interactive pedagogy' (in Osborn et al. 2000, p. 140). In summary the reforms of the 1990s introduced 'performative regimes into English primary schools. Legislated changes, the stated purpose of which is to raise standards by supporting and improving teachers have resulted in the introduction of assessment regimes linked to accountability systems' with 'each teacher being set measurable performance objectives which are systematically reviewed' (Troman et al. 2007, pp. 549–50).

In 1997 the Labour government replaced 18 years of Conservative administration, announcing its arrival with a renewed focus on 'education, education, education' (Blair 1997, BBC News), but with the retention of Conservative initiatives such as national testing and the piloting of literacy and numeracy strategies. Ofsted oversaw the arrangements for raising standards and it did so with clear calls for explicit, direct, whole-class teaching. 'The grip which Ofsted exerted on the teachers and teacher educators was formal and bureaucratic' (Hartley 2002, p. 90). For the Labour government 'the raising of standards has become something of a clarion call. League tables abound. Performance – and its measurement – has become the watchword. There has been a pedagogical drift back to basics, back to whole-class, direct teaching' (Hartley, 2002, p. 90). Teachers 'play safe, even though some remain committed to individualised work' (Pollard et al. 1994, in Hartley 2002, p. 90). The National Literacy Strategy (1998) and National Numeracy Strategy (1999) were formally introduced and strongly influenced pedagogy with recommendations such as 'a daily mathematics lesson to all pupils, lasting between 45 and 60 minutes depending on pupils' ages. Teachers should teach the whole class together for a high proportion of the lesson … ' (DfEE 1998, p. 2, in Brown 1998, p. 362). Hamilton asserts that 'good practice cannot be handed over ready-made, like … technical operatives to receive packages of pedagogy from the outside which can be "read off" and "read in"' (Hamilton 1994, in Dadds 2001, p. 48). However, performance management systems are in place throughout all phases of the schooling system to ensure that these technicians can be evaluated for surface accountability (Strathern 2002; Troman et al. 2007).

What was all this doing to pedagogy?

'Education can either socialise students into critical thought or into dependence on authority' that is, according to Shor (1992), 'into autonomous habits of mind or into passive habits of following authority, waiting to be told what to do and what things mean. Unfortunately in traditional schooling the latter often occurs' (in Graziano 2008, p. 153). According to this definition the teacher's pedagogical positioning is at the centre of the 'how' and 'what' of teaching and learning. In short, pedagogy is dichotomous, it can encourage and support growth for children, locate and empower children at the centre of learning, or it can stultify and reduce the process to following externally prescribed schema (Dadds 2001; Dunphy 2008; Edwards 2001; Macleod & Golby 2003).

However, the 'how' and 'what' of teaching for Edwards (2001) is 'an intense, complex and discursive act which demands considerable expertise' (p. 163); for Siraj-Blatchford (2004), 'it is the practice (or the art, the science, or the craft) of teaching … it refers to the interactive process between teaching and learning and the learning environment (which includes family and community)' (in Dunphy 2008, p. 56). For McFarland (1999) 'teachers shift from control of knowledge to creation of processes whereby students take ownership of their learning and take risks to understand and apply their knowledge' (in Graziano 2008, p. 154). Makin and Whiteman (2006) state that 'teachers and children are partners in teaching and learning transactions. We need to find ways of interacting with children to co-construct shared meanings in ways we cannot do if the children themselves are not active participants in exploring the situation' (p. 35). However, Hayes (2008) recognises that, 'child centred teaching includes behaviours that actively involve the children in guiding the learning process, such as offering choices, encouraging activity and suggesting solutions' (p. 433). This pedagogy is operationalised in, for example, Northern Italy and New Zealand. In New Zealand the National Curriculum Framework for early childhood is called Te Whāriki (Ministry of Education 1996). Written in both English and Maori and originating from Maori epistemology (Carr 2001), it has an holistic approach based on a socio-cultural view of the child as expressed by Vygotsky (Soler & Miller 2003, p. 63). This model envisages the curriculum as a web or woven mat rather than a set of stairs; Eisner (1985) contrasts the step model of the English national curriculum with the spider's web of the New Zealand system:

> The step or staircase model conjures up the image of a series of independent steps that lead to a platform from which the child exits and at which point measurable outcomes can be identified … Te Whariki emphasises a

model of knowledge and understanding for young children as a tapestry of increasing complexity and richness. (Carr & May 1996, in Soler & Miller 2003, p. 63)

The New Zealand model recognises the intricacies and complexities that children develop in a non-linear way. The metaphors used in both models provide an interesting representation of how children learn, the 'woven mat' representing the ever-expanding development of children's learning in a horizontal rather than a vertical linear 'stepped' way. Similarly to New Zealand, in Northern Italy the teachers of Reggio Emilia 'have challenged the dominating discourse and accepted practices of early childhood pedagogy by "deconstructing" the dominant ideas and theories that have shaped our conceptions and images of children and childhood' (Dahlberg 2000, in Soler & Miller 2003, p. 65). Reggio Emilia has many similarities to the Te Whāriki model but the main difference is that 'Reggio Emilia is not a compromise between a national curriculum framework and a learner-centred curriculum' (Soler & Miller 2003, p. 64). What is unique about the Northern Italian school concept is that its core philosophy of child-centredness has been accepted, maintained and strengthened since its 1967 inception. A criticism levelled at the schools is based on their absence of a written curriculum leading to a perception of a lack of measurable accountability. Reggio Emilia's philosophy is based on 'opposition to a focus on standardisation and outcomes' (ibid., p. 65).Its authenticity has enabled it to retain its child-centred philosophy because of the absence of any rigid accountability as experienced in many other countries (ibid., p. 65).

However, current pedagogy in the UK is represented by a philosophy in which 'the teacher (rather than the child) has greater control of the content' (Hayes 2008, p. 439). This control has led to the situation which Dadds (2001) describes as '... the potential consequences for teaching and learning when teacher professional judgement is dislodged by government in favour of centralist prescription of curricula and pedagogy' (p. 44). How did teaching and learning, and consequently teachers' pedagogy, become so reduced? This was mainly caused by the focus of the government's education agenda on the testing of the sub-domains of three subjects to the virtual curriculum exclusion of the remainder (Boyle & Bragg 2006). This Standards agenda (Brehony 2005), reinforced by the National Strategies (NLS 1998; NNS 1999a; DfEE 1998a & 1999a), was strengthened by the introduction of percentage success targets for schools, which became the sole measurement tool for a school's perceived success or failure. As a result, in the time-honoured 'teaching to the test' tradition, pedagogy became reduced to the acquisition of facts rather than focusing on meaning and learning (McNaughton & Williams 1998, in Dunphy 2008, p. 57). Research observation evidence (Boyle & Charles 2010, p. 295) indicates that children 'become dependent rather than independent, passive rather than active and powerless rather than powerful' (Dunphy 2008, p. 66). Despite the criticisms by teachers of the Strategies, many teachers obviously welcomed the changes in teaching approaches, especially at key stage 2, which saw 'more changes in teaching approaches than in the previous two decades' (Webb & Vulliamy 2007, p. 561). The Ontario Institute's School of Education's (2003) evaluation report stated that 'many teachers report that their own learning has been positively affected' (in Barkham et al. 2008, p. 5). Beard's (2000) evidence suggests that the teaching of literacy methodologically improved after the introduction of the National Literacy Strategy (NLS), as 'direct teaching of literacy skills was surprisingly rare' before the introduction of the NLS (in Jolliffe 2004, p. 2). However, according to Burkard (2004) 'since the Literacy hour was launched in 1998 over a million children have left primary school with poor literacy skills' (p. 2). This is a significant level of failure. Have teachers failed to transfer learning across learning situations? Do teachers have 'strong pedagogical content knowledge and high levels of pedagogical skills?' (Dunphy 2008, p. 66). Despite the dissemination of strategies, frameworks and policy documents, our evidenced view of current teaching practice (pedagogy) would be that it is uninformed and lacks a focus on the learning needs of the individual child. Why do teachers not have an understanding that to have a child-centred pedagogy requires them to have a philosophy shaped by learning theory and its practice? Why is there not a theoretical construct underpinning their practice? Rowsell et al. (2008) suggest that 'pedagogy refers to an educational position or approach that includes both theory and practice' (p. 115). This definition focuses on the strengths or weaknesses of the connection between theory and practice in the teachers' pedagogical development. There should be no endpoint in the teacher's development as a practitioner, and for that development to produce a truly reflective formative practitioner there has to be a synthesis between theory and practice.

Despite the evidence to the contrary in the current practice as reported and observed, our hypothesis is that a knowledgeable basis of theories of learning leads to the natural evolution of an informed personal teaching philosophy, that is, a philosophy which locates the child at the centre of learning, involved in the co-construction and self-regulation of that learning with the teacher, and therefore, independent of an over-reliance on centrally devolved one-size-fits-all strategies. However, while an outcomes-based teaching and measurement of learning culture exists, teachers can only verbalise their philosophy of pedagogy in the concrete terms of using a traffic light system as a learning strategy 'to close the gap'– at best a highly dubious self-assessment tool used for a misunderstood aim – and trade in the language of cohort and population targets for level accretion and effect size predictions.

Studies on learner-centredness and restricted pedagogies

At the beginning of this chapter, Rowsell et al. (2008), Hayes (2008) and Edwards (2001) described theoretical aspects of a definition for pedagogy. In practice, Siraj-Blatchford (2004), through her Effective Pedagogy of Pre-School Education (EPPE) study of effective settings from ages 3–7, highlighted the importance of 'the presence of a "good" pedagogue who is seen to orchestrate a pedagogy by making interventions that were suitable to children's potential level of learning or to the concept or skill being taught' (Dunphy 2008, p. 59). Related to that definition she identified three salient features for a 'good' setting: (i) adult–child verbal interactions; (ii) differentiation; and (iii) formative assessment. The related Researching Effective Pedagogy in the Early Years (REPEY) report (Siraj-Blatchford 2002) supported the findings of EPPE (these studies are best understood as one continuous sequential explanatory mixed-method study (Creswell 2003; Siraj-Blatchford et al. 2006)) and revealed that 'the excellent settings encouraged relatively more "sustained shared thinking"' (Siraj-Blatchford, in Dunphy 2008, p.60). 'Sustained shared thinking' can be defined as: 'an episode in which two or more individuals "work together" in an intellectual way to solve a problem, clarify a concept, evaluate activities, extend a narrative, etc. Both parties must contribute to the thinking and it must develop and extend thinking' (Sylva et al. 2004, in Dunphy 2008, p. 60).

Significant points to consider from REPEY are the importance of the practitioner's role in balancing adult-led and child-initiated activities, the need to engage in 'sustained shared thinking' and the kind of interactions that will guide but not dominate pupils' thinking (DfES 2005, p. 10). Even more significantly, 'Sustained Shared Thinking' (Section 4c) has now been included as one of the core 'Principles of Learning and Development' of the Early Years Foundation Stage Guidance (DCSF 2008) applied to all schools from September 2008. However, in their report, Siraj-Blatchford and Manni (2008) stated that:

> It was found that 94.5% of all the questions asked by the early childhood staff were closed questions that required a recall of fact, experience or expected behaviour, or a decision between a limited selection of choices or no response at all. Only 5.5% were open-ended questions. (Siraj-Blatchford & Manni 2008, p. 5)

Edwards's (2001) statement that 'teaching is informed interpretations of learners, knowledge and environments' (p. 163) is congruent with Allal & Lopez (2005) and Perrenoud's (1998) formative or self-regulative philosophy of the co-construction of learning between teacher, learner and environment. Similarly, Alexander (2008) supports a model of pedagogy that includes 'teacher formative experiences' and 'pupil formative experiences' (p. 27). Unfortunately, the REPEY (Sylva et al. 2002) findings indicate that this positive profile is optimum and does not occur very frequently (Dunphy 2008, p. 60). Of particular importance is Siraj-Blatchford et al.'s (2004) profile of 'good' settings in which she describes three pedagogical features – differentiation, formative assessment and adult–child verbal interactions – which have been positively discouraged in the post-Strategy period. On this theme, Alexander states that: 'This rigidity has its pedagogical roots firmly in the National Numeracy and Literacy Strategies with the formalism of highly structured lessons, whole class plenaries' (Alexander 2008b, p. 107). However, 10 years before the Strategies, Tharp and Gallimore (1988) in their classroom observations based on whole class teaching reported that 'all stages of schooling were dominated by the "recitation script"' (in Smith et al. 2004, p. 396). Earlier research by Sinclair and Coulthard (1975) originated the notion of the three-part exchange of teacher recitation – Initiation, Response, Feedback, shorthanded as IRF – demonstrated as 'directive forms of teaching' and consisting of 'a series of teacher questions that require convergent factual answers and pupil display of known information' (in Smith et al. 2004, p. 396). Significantly, Williams's (2008) *Review of Mathematics Teaching in Early Years Settings and Primary Schools* strongly asserted that 'first and foremost pedagogy must be learner-centred in the sense that it is responsive to the needs of the particular children being taught' (para. 234, p. 64). This scenario is diametrically opposite to the current national profile of pedagogy reported by Alexander (2004, 2005) and Boyle & Charles (2010). Williams comments that the National Strategies do not explicitly state a pedagogical model related to pupils' learning (2008, para. 232, p. 63). This provokes several questions: how can a pupil's voice be heard within this structure? How can a teacher differentiate within a system predicated upon a whole class approach? How can formative teaching flourish when the target is to move whole cohorts at pace through units of work?

The Organisation for Economic and Cultural Development (OECD) study (2004) provided data from a survey of 15 classrooms to respond to these questions. It found that 'in general the pedagogy was not focused on the observed interests of the children but sought to interest them in the concerns of the teacher'. In short, what the OECD team observed was a teacher-centred rather than a learner-centred pedagogy

(OECD 2004, p. 59), characterised by 'a focus on literacy and numeracy related activities, with evaluation criteria narrowly focused on cognitive outcomes, and the early introduction of written symbolisation' (ibid, p. 59). Moyles et al. (2002) studied nine early years settings. They reported that:

> the pedagogy observed was inappropriately 'formal' and seen to be domi-
> nated by lessons, subjects, timetables and tightly defined learning objec-
> tives, the daily rhythm of classroom life generally observed was described
> as being made up of long, inactive plenary sessions working through a list
> of learning intentions, an overriding emphasis on literacy and numeracy.
> (Adams et al. 2004, p. 105)

In 2008, Hayes reported on findings from classroom observations of 400 primary school children that they 'have limited choice in or control over the activities they engage in and although teachers are recorded as pro- posing active participation the findings did not show children actively participating in their learning' (p. 434) and the 'children mainly observed worked silently' (p. 433).

There was movement towards offering an alternative menu in 2003 when the DfES 'called for a rich, varied and exciting curriculum' (Troman et al. 2007, p. 551). Entitled *Excellence and Enjoyment: A Strategy for Primary Schools* (DFES 2003), this document stated that teachers could achieve excellence in performativity allied to a more creative teaching and learning agenda. However, Brehony (2005) responded that in the context of the current Standards agenda 'there is an irresolvable contra- diction in excellence and enjoyment' (p. 31). While Webb and Vulliamy (2006) point out 'that much of the text of "Excellence and Enjoyment" is devoted to reiterating the familiar messages of the Standards agenda because "testing, targets and tables" are here to stay' (p. 20). The ten- sions and the contradictions between pedagogy and performativity would seem, as Brehony (2005) states, to be irresolvable within this sum- mative measurement agenda (p. 31).

The evidence discussed above strongly suggests that because of the focus on whole class teaching, the concept of the individual as the focal point of planning for teaching and learning and of pedagogy has been reduced, replaced by the provision of centrally devolved test materials and pre-planned packages delivered at pace to cover the maximum amount of material regardless of depth of learning. Issues of the pace of teaching in the current outcomes-based climate have concerned research- ers with regard to the opportunities available for the development of critical language and reasoning capabilities for the individual (Eke & Lee 2004, p. 220). The National Literacy Strategy's legacy of lists of learning outcomes by term and by year still holds sway in many schools and produces a requirement for strong pacing of 'teaching as coverage'.

Ofsted has exacerbated this situation as its inspectors' 'concern to sharpen pace in teaching has led to the pursuit of pace at all costs, regardless of the fact that pace without attention to [children's] understanding leaves all but the fastest learners stranded' (Alexander 2008, p. 18). Following Bernstein's research into elaborated and restricted codes of language (1973) this has two consequences '... since time is at a premium what counts as appropriate talk, in both length and form, will reduce pupil speech and increase teacher talk' (Eke & Lee 2004, p. 220). Myhill's (2006) research found that

> contrary to the advocacy of the National Literacy and Numeracy Strategies much whole class teaching involved relatively little interaction which supported and scaffolded children in their learning. Teacher talk dominated whole class teaching ... the child's answer served to end an interaction sequence and rarely to begin or initiate it. (p. 24)

Despite evidence that the teachers had a strong sense of cognitive concepts and skills 'which they hoped would be addressed through their teaching' (p. 34), this cognitive and conceptual understanding in principle was not realised in the practicalities of the classroom learning situation. As Myhill stated:

> The low percentage of questions making links between prior knowledge and present learning and the relative paucity of process questions giving children opportunities to reflect and articulate their learning points to whole class discourse more oriented to teachers' curriculum delivery goals than to guiding pupils towards greater understanding. (p. 35).

In support of this finding, Eke & Lee's (2004) research revealed that in one class of 30 children 'over half of pupil utterances were less than six words' (p. 222). This unbalanced relationship is even recognised in current government policy statements: 'Teacher talk continues to dominate pupil talk despite efforts to the contrary' (DCSF 2008, p. 9). Inevitably the individual is diminished as the focus for teaching and learning and pedagogy sits within a contradiction – the 'closed recitation script' (Alexander 2004) with its basic assumption that all children learn in the same manner. That manner or pedagogical style is the predominance of whole class teaching as espoused by the Strategies, while by contrast, for the formative teacher it is a given that

> ... pupils do not have the same abilities nor the same needs or the same way of working, an optimal situation for one pupil will not be optimal for another ... one can write a simple equation: diversity in people + appropriate treatment for each = diversity in approach. (Perrenoud 1998, pp. 93–4)

Deregulation defines differentiation

Pryor and Crossouard (2008) extend this definition of Perrenoud's of differentiated teaching and his philosophy of the changing relationship or 'regulation' between teacher and pupil (Perrenoud 1991, 1998) to its inevitable conclusion. In that 'the educator teaches different definitions of themselves to the students and develops different relationships with the students through them' (Pryor & Crossouard 2008, p. 10). Those identities include 'teacher, assessor, subject expert and learner' and all 'involve different division of labour and rules shaping their interaction with students' (p. 10). This is problematic to some teachers who have become used to the neatly planned rigidity and conformity of whole class teaching, but as Martin et al. (2005) recognised 'Learning is *messy* and *takes time*' (p. 235, italics in original).

The evidence from our 2010 sample (Boyle & Charles 2010) indicates the notion of differentiated planning for teaching is not seen as a pre-requisite for formative assessment by the majority of teachers (only 7% of our sample stated that formative assessment enabled the setting of differentiated targets for lessons). This is a still-strong legacy from the National Numeracy Strategy with its discouragement of differentiated teaching; 'we are concerned that children should not continue to work at many levels, with the teacher placing them in a wide range of differentiated groups' (DfEE 1998a, p. 54) and 'its format as a fixed curriculum to be taught to all pupils regardless of attainment indicates that very little curricular differentiation is recommended' (Brown et al. 1998). This legacy is so strong that five years after *Excellence and Enjoyment* (DfES 2003) we are observing a majority of lessons in which differentiation is totally absent. Why are we observing lessons with one static learning objective which embraces the whole extent of a class's learning? This signals that the pedagogical messages of the National Literacy and Numeracy Strategies in which differentiation was frowned upon and the absence of teacher understanding of the need for a differentiated menu to match the range of learning needs, as well as the presence of a 'one size fits all' paradigm, is proving difficult to shift.

In conversation with teachers during our 43 school visits we raised the word 'differentiation' and there was vagueness in the responses. We were told 'I set one task and then I differentiate by what they produce' or 'I have an extension task ready for those who finish'. Our observations indicated that this is what AfL in practice has been reduced to. The responses demonstrate misconceptions of the basic principles of how pupils learn and the sacrifice of developmental learning on the altar of 'coverage', 'pace', 'moving the cohort on' and 'getting through the pre-planned package'. Clearly our initial teacher training programmes need to return to the conceptualisers and theorists of formative assessment to change technicians back to pedagogues. Principal amongst these theorists is Philippe Perrenoud whose philosophy is based on the principle that

> to the extent that pupils do not have the same abilities nor the same needs or the same way of working, an optimal situation for one pupil will not be optimal for another ... one can write a simple equation: diversity in people + appropriate treatment for each = diversity in approach (Perrenoud 1998, pp. 93–4).

In even simpler terms, 'good teaching forces differentiation' (Perrenoud 1998). Linda Allal reinforces the point, 'differentiation of instruction is planned rather than just being added on after observing difficulties' (Allal & Lopez 2005, p. 246).

Is this because the complexity inherent in pedagogy, as outlined by Flower (the requirement forced on the pupil to 'juggle' often conflicting learning themes and concepts, for example in one lesson a pupil may be required to 'juggle' visual/graphemic elements of a letter, the spelling of a word, character development, sentence organisation, coherence, etc.) and Perrenoud (the need to differentiate your teaching and learning pro-grammes), may cause 'a perceived crisis in teachers' professional skills, routine and organisation'? (Perrenoud 1998, p. 98). Has the summative agenda of the last twenty years reduced the capacity of the teacher so that 'juggling' and differentiating is now beyond them? In short, has the teach-er been reduced to the technician who has been trained to deliver the whole class menu but cannot diverge in his/her pedagogy to meet the learning needs of the individuals in their classrooms?

Differentiation is an essential element of teaching for learning rather than for coverage. It is based around the theory of pupil individual learning differences and the resultant complexity of learning therefore requires different treatments, that is, differentiated teaching.

Perrenoud's definition seems very obvious and difficult to dispute if one reflects on the differences in learning behaviours in any class of pupils. However, many teachers need support to change from the com-mon pedagogical model of 'one size fits all' conformity of planning for whole class 'movement' through a set of learning objectives. Teaching in many countries has been reduced to preparing pupils to solve problems/ questions in specific ways to obtain test marks/levels. Learning is not linear, however; it is messy and involves regressions as well as progression – it takes time and different pace and routes for different pupils, hence the need for differentiation. As we quoted from Perrenoud at the beginning of this chapter, formative assessment and differentiation are integrally linked chains, implicitly synonymous: 'If formative assessment is carried out on a fairly regular basis, the result is pressure to differentiate' (Perrenoud 1991, p. 89).

Case study 1   Elaine's reading lesson

Context: Snowy day; Elaine has a class of six children in Reception (ages 4–5). She had prepared sentences about a snowman. The sentences were differentiated by the teacher but the sentences were not matched to the reading ability of the pupils. The teacher asked the pupils to read each word to complete the sentence and then to cut up the words to demonstrate understanding.

The teacher reads: 'A hat on a snowman'. She asks Ismail to read the sentence aloud to the group, holding the sentence in a position which visually is upside down for the child. The child manages to read the sentence, but only with lots of phoneme prompting from the teacher.

Teacher:	We are going to chop the words up and make the sentence again. Do you think you can do that?
[Ismail:	Nods]
Teacher:	If I make a line here [she sections off each word so that the child can cut off each word from the sentence], you cut them out and put them in the right order. Then draw me your picture.
Teacher [moving on to address Rebecca, sitting next to Ismail]:	Are we all looking? [Teacher motions to the other four children to pay attention.]

[Teacher then points to first word on the child's sentence which reads: I am a snowman.]

[Rebecca voices phoneme 'i' sound for the word 'I'.]

Teacher:	It says 'I' [she points to the next word, 'am']. [Teacher voices] a … m. What does it make?

[Rebecca looks up with no response.]

Ismail [shouts]:	and.
Teacher:	No, not and but am. [Rebecca is struggling with the strategy of blending phonemes.]
Teacher:	You help each other. [Teacher points with pen to the words 'I am'. She shouts] Are you practising with yours? [motioning to the other four children. Teacher sounds out] a … mmm. It says am … we practised this on the carpet didn't we?
Rebecca:	[No answer.]

Teacher [moves on through sentence and reads]:	I am a snowman. Now I want you to cut these words up. [Teacher sections off each word and asks Rebecca to cut them out and put them in the right order.]
Teacher: Peter [reads]:	Let us see if Peter can read this one ['a pin on a tin']. A pin... [then struggles with the word 'on'. Peter does a return sweep as reading strategy and returns to the beginning of the sentence for meaning, before reading on successfully. The teacher ignores the successful reading strategy which Peter has just used.]
Teacher:	Cut up your sentence and stick it in your book.
Teacher:	Are you ready for your word? [Reem's sentence is: Pat the snowman.]

[Reem reads 'Pat', struggles with 'the'.]

Teacher:	Now this is one of our tricky words, now if it is a trick word we cannot sound it out can we?
Reem:	Mmm.
Teacher:	We have to look at this word, point to it and say it [points at 'the'].

[Reem: Says 't'. Looks at teacher for response.]

Teacher:	I will tell you today and we will see if you can remember it tomorrow. Pat the, the...Just look at it because a 't' and a 'h' doesn't make 'the' ... 'Pat the...' What is the big word we have been looking at today? [Reem is rocking back and forth in chair.]
Reem:	Snowman.
Teacher:	Right, read it again...
Reem:	Snowman.
Teacher:	Right read it again.
Reem:	Pat... [Child struggles with 'the' and looks at teacher for help.]
Teacher:	the ... ssss...
Reem:	Snowman.
Teacher:	Now I will draw the lines down and let's see if you can make this sentence again.

[Teacher moves on to Sultan, who, already with his fingers over his mouth, is looking at the teacher with confusion.]

(Continued)

(Continued)

Teacher: What's that word? [Covers up the rest of the sentence] OK, let's see if we can read this word [Snowman].

Sultan: Snowman.

Teacher: OK, we have got snowman. Now on to the next word [big].

[Sultan sounds out 'b']

[Teacher sounds out and isolates the three phonemes, 'b','i','g'.]

Teacher: Now put them together.

[Sultan points to 'b' but skips back to the beginning of the sentence and voices 'a'.]

Teacher: No, no, not that one, this one 'b'.

[Sultan points to 'big' and voices 'b' 'i' 'g' 'g']

Teacher: Now, what word does that make?

Sultan: 'g' [then puts his fingers over his mouth].

Teacher: No, not 'g'. What does 'b','i','g' make?

Sultan: Big.

Teacher: Big [motions with her finger to the beginning of her sentence and reads 'a' 'b...]

[Sultan looks confused.]

Teacher: Now what did we just say?

[Sultan looks at the teacher and then looks at the word the teacher is pointing to.]

[Teacher points to the word 'snowman']

Sultan: Snowman [child continues to rock back and forth in chair with his fingers in his mouth].

Teacher: I want you to cut out the words and put them in the right order again.

[Sultan is left to cut out a big snowman.]

[Teacher returns to talk to Reem. The child has cut out the words and appears confused.]

Teacher: Now, can you find the word 'pat'?

[Reem places the word 'pat' on the table. Teacher replaces it at the beginning, left hand side of the paper. Child is silent throughout, rocking back and forth.]

Teacher:	Right … Pat … the
Sultan [shouts]:	Snowman.
Reem [voices]:	'Pat the snowman'.
Teacher:	No, yours does not say 'Pat the snowman'. Remember, we are not copying are we? [Reem is looking at Sultan's sentence]
Teacher [reads and points out to Reem]:	I am the snowman [using her fingers to point at each word.]

[Peter finds 'I' and glues it down. Peter says 'I am a snowman'.]

Teacher:	Let's find the glue … I asked Ismail to put them in the right order before he put them on. Did you?
Teacher:	Have a look for 'pin'.

[Rebecca locates and places in order 'a pin on a snowman'.]

Teacher:	What is that big word?
Rebecca:	Snowman.
Teacher:	Let's read it all together.
Peter:	A 'p', 'i', 'n' 'o' 'n' a snowman.
Teacher:	Now, I want you to read that without saying 'p', 'i', 'n' [isolating each phoneme].
Peter [reads]:	A pin, 'o', 'n' a snowman [isolates two phonemes 'o', 'n'].
Teacher:	Stick them on now and draw your picture.
Reem [shouts]:	I like to play snowballs.
Teacher [taking the word 'snowman' from his hand]:	Now come on, we have got the words and I know you know this big word here, 'snowman'.
Teacher:	What is the first word of your sentence? [A big snowman. Points to word 'A' to prompt Joanne to read the word. Child looks confused.]
Teacher:	What was your snowman? [Gestures with hands to make a big shape.]

(Continued)

(Continued)

Joanne:	Bigger.
Teacher:	Yes [Points to the word 'A']. Now what does this say?
Joanne:	Big.
Teacher:	No, A big snowman. [Places the sentence in order for the child.] Now stick them on.
Teacher [turns: round and asks Ismail]	What did your snowman have on?
Ismail:	A hat.
Teacher:	Where is it?
Ismail:	I am doing it. [Teacher then gives pencils out to the group and the children continue to glue words and draw their pictures in silence.]

Analysis

A more formative teacher would have understood that:

- Each child should have been encouraged (as language users) to generate their own sentences to study and read from – this would have enabled a differentiated teaching and learning opportunity as each 'baseline' drafted sentence would therefore have been unique.
- Written representations of the children's oral language/contributions in the form of modelling/scribing print in action are essential components of the child's conceptual development as a reader.
- An integrated whole language approach including rich dialogue would have deepened the children's learning experience, particularly in a group situation (social mediation of learning: Vygotsky).
- There was no metacognitive approach to the learning situation from the teacher, for example the interrogatives 'Why', 'How', 'What', 'When', were not relayed to the children.
- Having each child's baseline at word level would have revealed questions such as, Step 1: Is the child aurally able to hear initial phonemes?; Step 2: Can the child isolate individual phonemes?; Step 3: Can the child hold the phonemes in their short-term memory?; Step 4: Can the child blend isolated phonemes into a whole word? And finally, can the child produce orally the target sound?

Case study 2   Sue's mathematics plenary session

Context: Whole class plenary – Differentiation (Year 2). The teacher is talking the whole class through a differentiated maths problem devised by one pair of the children (Joe and Daniel).

Teacher: I can remember what we did yesterday that was quite difficult – it was Joe's question about [takes it from the child and reads] the hen lays 65 eggs in 2 hours how many in 3 hours?

Joe: 65 doesn't have a half.

Teacher: That's right, now Daniel you worked out…

Daniel: You can't use 65 because it's either going to be 33 or 32 …

Teacher: Because 65 is an o… [motions to child to finish].

Daniel: Odd number.

Teacher: So we changed it, well you changed it to the hen lays 20 eggs in 2 hours – how many in 3 hours? How did you solve that problem? What did you have to do?

Joe: Well I knew that there were 20 eggs in 2 hours but then I put on 3 hours – I put a 0 on it to make it 30…

Teacher: Yes, but what did we have to solve – work out?

Daniel: I had to work out – he had to work out much the egg lays in each hour …

Teacher: For 1 hour, yes, so when you knew that the hen lays 20 eggs in 2 hours – so what did you do then?

Daniel: Erm … I halved it, from 2 you get 1.

Teacher: Half of 20, is that 1?

Daniel: No I mean 1 hour.

Teacher: Oh I beg your pardon – so how many in 1 hour?

Daniel: Because it's 20 I took off 10, so it's 3 x 10.

Teacher: Fantastic, that is brilliant and I think that is an excellent one to end on. Where would you put that question? [Teacher motions to three boxes labelled 'hard' 'easy', 'OK' –child puts it in the 'OK' box. The child next to him says 'I would put that in the hard box'.]

Teacher: Who agrees? Who would put that in the hard box? [A mixture of hands go up for each 'level of difficulty' box.] So it depends who you are doesn't it? So you have to decide for yourselves, that's what you have to do, if you feel that something is too easy you have to find a question that is more challenging for you.

Analysis

Sue's plenary session provides an authentic example of developing children's metacognitive skills through an integration of the recursive elements of their learning. The teacher recalls a previous day's learning to consolidate this aspect and validates their mathematical problem through a differentiated strategy. This collaborative approach provided rich assessment information on their understanding of the divisible aspects of two-digit numbers and their ability to re-work a problem using even numbers. This differentiated pedagogy in which the child was allowed enough time and space to explain the 'how' and 'what' of their calculations revealed the multiple number operations at work within each child. This internal exposition allowed the rest of the class to access higher order thinking and demonstrated the individual/collaborative complexity which can be nurtured and developed through self-regulated learning and a differentiated pedagogy.

Summary

What is differentiated instruction?

- It is starting where the pupils are rather than using a standardised approach.
- It is responsive teaching rather than one-size-fits-all teaching.
- It is about helping teachers to plan varied approaches to identify what pupils need to learn and how they will best be able to learn it.

Observation and Evidence Elicitation

In this chapter we explore the use of a critical lens for observation and evidence elicitation. Building on careful observation, the teacher is able to adjust the child's learning process.

Our understanding of formative assessment is as a dynamic process of evidence elicitation, analysis and action. Formative assessment makes demands on teachers to interrogate their practice and to evaluate their pedagogical content knowledge. Our experience has evidenced that teachers who use formative assessment strategies are constantly observing and responding through flexible adjustment in the planning of their strategies to match children's learning progress.

Observation may be based on instruments or it may be purely intuitive; it can be detailed or superficial, deliberate or accidental, quantitative or qualitative, long or short, rigorous or approximate, occasional or systematic but it must be planned for the information gained to support the learning process. The scope of what can be observed is as varied and complex as the learning and development processes and the environment in which those processes are carried out (Cardinet 1986). There is no reason why one should not assess what has been mastered and carry out 'micro-summative' assessment. If the teaching approach is to be readjusted it is often necessary to have an idea of the degree of mastery already achieved. It is possible to look at the learning processes, the working methods, the pupil's attitudes and his/her integration within a group – all of these are cognitive, emotional and relationship aspects of the teaching and learning situation.

What is most important in observation is not so much the instruments used, as the underlying theoretical framework on which the interpretation of the observation is based.

In the absolute, an ideal teaching approach would do without all formative assessment. In other words all the feedback necessary for learning would be incorporated in the teaching and learning situation, without it being necessary for a teacher to observe and intervene in order to bring about learning progress' (Perrenoud 1991, p. 84).

However, even in Perrenoud's ideal situation, it is difficult to see how the teacher could do without formative assessment when planning for teaching situations, organising the transition from one teaching situation to another and matching pupils to one rather than another of those teaching situations. There would be at least 'proactive' adjustment (Allal 1988).

The link between interpretation of the evidence from those observations and formative assessment is integral. If the teacher does not form an appropriate 'picture' of what is going on in the pupil's thinking, then there is minimal likelihood of the teacher's action having a decisive effect in adjusting the pupil's learning process. This fact is emphatically reinforced through Perrenoud's research finding that: 'the more accurate the information, the more personalised it is' (1991, p. 88). Groups of pupils, no matter how carefully selected, are heterogeneous. When supplied with the same tuition, these pupils do not progress at the same pace or in the same way. 'If one is bent on formative assessment, sooner or later one must face the fact that no one overall adjustment can meet their (learning) needs. The only appropriate answer is [to differentiate] differentiated teaching' (Perrenoud 1991, p. 89). Formative assessment is a compulsory component of a system for personalising learning and differentiating teaching. 'If formative assessment is carried out on a fairly regular basis, the result is pressure to differentiate' (Perrenoud 1991, p. 89).

In fact, the learning that has taken place cannot be observed because it has or has not been internalised – it is the effects or outcomes of the teaching and learning situation that are observable. The teacher is therefore left with visible clues which include involvement in the task and participation in collective activities.

[The teacher is not] in the same situation as an engineer monitoring several independent indicators, who has to take the appropriate decision for each of them. On the contrary, the teacher must, as events proceed, make a two-fold interpretation: on the one hand s/he must single out and understand what will help [him/her] to organise the activity and on the other, s/he must single out and understand what will help [the teacher] to foster learning. (Perrenoud 1991, p. 97)

Cardinet (1986) suggests concentrating observation on learning conditions (classroom environment; roles and regulation of teacher and learners;

styles of teaching, etc.) rather than on results, particularly in an interactive adjustment situation – while acknowledging the complexity of the relationship between teacher and pupils in teaching situations which range from the models of transmission to transaction with all the intervening stages of those models.

Observation of classroom sessions

The following strategies, materials and data organisation techniques are required for classroom observation:

- Researcher's field notes of classroom observations concerning the spatial, material and social organisation of each phase of the lesson (learning areas – set up by whom?; learner-centred or teacher-controlled)
- Selective recording of whole class and small group discussions occurring during the lesson (quality of talk/ideas; participation/roles; types of dialogues)
- Copies of the students' worksheets reflecting their problem-solving activities in small groups before and/or after the whole class discussions (quality of stages of completion; divergence/creativity of learning concepts/journeys)
- Audio recording of interviews with the teacher after each lesson, including the teacher's explanations about the activities, interpretations of critical events, comments on students' worksheets, plans for the following lesson (planning and set-up of integrated teaching, learning and assessment activities; learner-centredness).

A synopsis of each lesson should be constructed summarising the successive phases; the tasks and forms of social organisation, the material used and the duration. The transcripts of these discussions will form a major component of data for studying the emergence, the progressive elaboration and the taken-as-shared function of the changes in the regulation of teaching and learning practices (the perennials of 'who', 'why', 'what' which shape the teacher's future planning). Two other sources of data will play a complementary role: the transcripts of the interviews with the teachers allow inferences about their goals and explanations as well as their perceptions and explanations of events occurring during the whole class interactions. The evidence of the pupils' dialogues and discussion during their problem-solving activities in small groups (twos, threes) and notes as recorded on their work sheets, will provide information on the procedures tried out before and/or after the whole class discussions.

Key questions before, during and after a lesson

Teachers need to develop the skills of observation in practice and integrate their critical lens into their teaching and learning strategies. Key questions may take the form of:

Questions for observation:

- What was the lesson about – subject/learning focus?
- How much pupil involvement/engagement?
- What was being learned? How did the teacher know that learning took place?
- What teaching and learning styles were present?

Planning for observation (process? outcomes? behaviours?):

- What are learning behaviours? (Look for effective domain, cognition domain behaviours.)
- What is the conative domain? How is it evidenced? (Recognise that some pupils act differently when 'in an observed situation', for example they become more vocal or introverted.)

The guided group situation offers optimal observation opportunity for the teacher. The guided group situation makes the assessment information you gather formative by using it in 'real time' to change your teaching strategy as required. However, teachers need to internalise that a 'guided group' is a teaching session which enables good observation, not a stand-alone observation session.

Group composition and group work

Group work requires the teacher to decide how best to manage and observe what is taking place as pupils work and learn. Group work is part of the routine of many classrooms and pupils are often assessed through observation while they are working in groups. This can raise classroom management issues such as the organisation of pupils not in the target group; how best to observe and therefore assess what each pupil in the target group is doing.

Group work may be set up by the teacher for a number of reasons:

- A successful outcome depends on a collaborative approach.
- The objective is the promotion of collaboration itself.
- Group work allows more efficient use of resources including teacher time.

The effective management of group work and its assessment depends on the particular reason for the assessment as well as:

- Whether assessment should be through systematic observation or critical incident techniques
- The context of the task
- The format of the groups
- Teacher decisions about his/her part in the process, for example the extent of intervention, control.

Systematic observation

Assessing pupils by observing them can be planned for on a systematic basis.

Assessing pupils by observing them demands close teacher attention and concentration – hence the optimal opportunity is provided by the use of the guided group teaching strategy (see Chapter 2). This attention and concentration can be reduced by interruptions; the danger of ignoring these interruptions or sending away a pupil who has a task-related question, is that this signals to the class that assessment is not a part of day-to-day classroom activity. In planning for classroom assessment, teachers need to think about activities which require on-the-spot observation and those activities for which the products can be looked at later. Therefore, in planning activities, the teacher has to plan for the distribution of activity in the classroom/learning sequences. Issues to consider include:

- Deciding how much independent activity there should be compared to teacher participation or intervention, or group discussion
- Demonstrating to pupils that any assessments which take place in the course of normal classroom activities arise from the teacher's constructive interest in their progress and types of learning strategies being employed, all designed to support their learning progress and to encourage the pupils themselves to develop habits of self-evaluation (self-assessment).

Observation of process

Observation of process has to be planned for. Such observation for assessment has to be analytical, moving beyond a general impression to seeing what the pupil is actually doing – even thinking. 'Formative assessment is not a test but a process which produces not so much a scope but a qualitative insight into student understanding' (Popham 2008, p. 6). By being systematic in his/her approach, teacher competence and understandings of pupil conceptions and misconceptions will increase.

Points to consider when structuring the observation of process include:

- Thinking about the clarity of instructions preceding a task
- Deciding what is to be observed, keeping it simple; assessment should be limited to one aspect. For example, when a complicated activity is taking place, there will be many noteworthy features or actions that denote pupil learning decisions. One feature may tend to overshadow another – in assessment of a pupil's narrative, does poor spelling influence the teacher's assessment rather than the pupil's creative ideas?
- Deciding where to be: where should the teacher be located – again, this illustrates the use of a guided group strategy for optimum teacher assessment
- Deciding whom to observe: a guided group should consist of no more than 5–6 pupils to enable focused assessment by the teacher
- Deciding on frequency of observation: once may not be enough for accuracy of a decision on whether an aspect has been assimilated and internalised by the pupil; the aspect itself may need to be assessed in different contexts
- Deciding on what constitutes sufficient evidence: for standardisation of assessment decisions teachers should discuss examples of acceptable responses with their peers.

Collaborative work and copying

Some teachers still have issues over collaborative work and the boundaries of assessment judgements. Collaborative tasks are deliberately presented to groups of pupils so that the contributions of more than one pupil are necessary for an achieved outcome – social mediation of learning (Vygotsky). In making assessments in group situations, teachers can express concern over their difficulty in distinguishing between effective collaborative work and 'copying'. Copying can be defined as when one pupil working in a collaborative group uses the contribution of another pupil inappropriately. Identification of what has been contributed or achieved by each individual pupil can be clarified by brief discussions with a pupil about his/her contribution. This leads on to other questions:

- Is the observed quality of collaboration reflected in the quality of the outcomes?
- Are pupils contributing questions, suggestions and solutions which take the task forward?
- Are there contributions from all members of the group?

Assessing group work

To support assessments of the work of a group, the teacher needs to consider:

- How pupils share the tasks within the group
- The levels of involvement of individuals in the task
- What kind of participation results in the task being taken forward?
- What kind of dialogue takes place – is talk centred on the task?
- How much time is spent off the task?
- How will the teacher plan her/his approach to observation?

Observation of interaction

Teachers need to assess how well pupils are able to participate as speakers and listeners in group activities, including imaginative play.

Sharing and co-operation first develop in play situations. If an older pupil in a primary school does not appear to be able to participate as intended in group situations, it could be a temporary effect due to the particular task or an issue of relationships within the group. Repeated observation will enable the teacher to focus on causes and indicate how help may be offered. There needs to be within-school teacher–peer discussion on the observation of interaction. It is recognised how difficult it can be to identify exactly how the interaction supports and brings about learning. It may take time as well as training and advice for a teacher to develop full confidence in the observation of interaction.

Case study   An unrefined observational lens

Context: This is a reading session with a Year 1 (age 5–6) class. The teacher (Doris) is working with a group of five pupils. She has supplied all the pupils with the same pre-typed sentence and has written that sentence on the whiteboard: 'The snowman is fat'. This is Doris's interpretation of a literacy session. (The teacher does not refer to the pupils by name).

Teacher to Child 1:	That's it, good girl. Now when you go to do the next one, you've got to remember to put a space [motions to the whiteboard where the sentence is].
Teacher to Child 4:	You have not stuck that in the right place. Can you take it off as it needs to start the sentence. You need to find [to Child 3] the word 'snowman' [Points to the word

(Continued)

(Continued)

'snowman' on the whiteboard]. Goodness me, he is fat. He has got a very fat tummy.

Child 1:   Is this it? [Holds up the word 'snowman'.]

Teacher: That's it, it's just the same, it matches. (Motions now to Child 3.) Put it up here, further up next to this one [signalling that the child has placed her word incorrectly within the sentence]. You have got to leave a space ... the snowman is fat [Teacher re-reads the sentence from the board and emphasises the word 'is']. Do you think he is fat?

Child 3:   He's a fat umpa-lumpa.

Teacher: Is he? Have you been watching Charlie and the Chocolate Factory? [Child looks confused and continues gluing] Now [to Child 4] you are looking for 'is'. [Points to the word 'is' on the board. Child continues to look for it.]

Child 1:   I have found 'is'.

Teacher: Good girl, you are good at this.

Child 5:   Can I go now?

Teacher: No, you have only done one word. Now you need to find 'snowman'. Have a look carefully [places container near the child to find the missing word 'snowman'].

Child 5:   I need two now.

Teacher: No, just one, that's it [Child 5 shows the word snowman].

Child 5:   Two and one, shall I take this one off? [attempts to take the word 'the' off the sheet].

Teacher: No you need that one. [Turns and talks to Child 3.] Can you put that one there? [Points to the word 'the' to go at the beginning of the sentence because the child is attempting to glue the word upside down.]

Teacher: No, no, turn it round ... that's it. [Teacher reads, 'the snowman is fat'.]

The children are then asked to draw a picture under their sentences and they continue in silence.

Analysis of the lesson

Doris's guided group reading session with Reception children aged (4–5), the majority of whom have English as an Additional Language, demonstrates fixed and rigid roles that the teacher and the child occupy in Doris's understanding of a guided group methodology. The context was favourable as it had been snowing for a few days and the children had been enjoying the snow, making snow people, etc.

In the opening sequence the teacher reveals how controlled the session will be as she has generated everything herself: the sentence, the vocabulary, theme and complexity and content of language that all of the children will duplicate, i.e. 'The snowman is fat'. The child's role is reduced from the active participant/learner to compliant reproducer of the teacher's construct.

The teacher, Doris, reads the sentence aloud and a child picks up the word 'snowman'. The child asks, 'Is that it?' and the teacher responds. 'That's right'. This cognitive assessment opportunity is missed by Doris on several levels: How did the child work it out? What reading strategy was she using in order to discriminate between the other words? Was she using the shape and length of the word, or isolating individual phonemes? Or was this a word that she had internalised from her reading books or from the environment? Or did the child simply guess at the word? The teacher could have shared these meta-cognitive aspects with the whole group as a means of deepening their own problem-solving abilities and reading strategies. This didactic pedagogical model ignores the skills of active problem–solving which is deemed essential for emergent readers.

Within the guided group session cognitive differences in reading and comprehension inevitably emerge as two children confidently begin to match and place the appropriate words needed to complete their sentences – however one child glues down 'The' and states 'I'm finished'. This demonstration of misunderstanding sentence construction, i.e. a word as a single unit of meaning, is cognitively mismatched to the child's conceptual stage as a reader. This assessment opportunity is missed by the teacher; there is no attempt to scaffold the child's understanding because the teacher's construct of the children in front of her is one of a group to be treated as a homogenous unit with a 'one-size-fits-all' pedagogy in her pursuit of a coverage model. The dominance of a controlling pedagogy emerges throughout as the children are told where to put the chosen words, the correct orientation and are read out the sentence by the teacher without the opportunity for any independent demonstrations of understanding. The importance of stimulating the children's affective domains remains untapped and unvalued.

Key teaching, learning and assessment from the guided group:

(i)   Poor understanding of a guided group, as the teacher uses the group situation in a didactic way and ignores all of the affective and focused cognitive strategies to support both children's interest and learning.

(ii) Teacher domination of the process limits learning and engagement; the children have no involvement in the learning process, being reduced to 'suppliers' of outcomes.

(iii) There is minimal extension of vocabulary on a context rich theme: despite the children being interested and motivated by the theme of 'snowmen' (it had been snowing in the area for a number of days), the teacher did not use this affective opportunity to stimulate rich, creative learning.

(iv) No differentiation: one size fits all in the group.

(v)   No scaffolding of pupils' reading skills – children were effectively directed/told where to glue the words down on their pictures (no problem-solving strategies explored/attempted).

(vi) No use of assessment opportunities or techniques to gather information to help individual children despite the size of the guided group providing the optimal assessment structure.

A more formative teacher would have recognised the importance of a visual literacy through:

- Fusion of illustrations and writing and reading to assist children's communication and understanding (Boyle & Charles 2011).
- Strong dialogic relationship between word and image (Marsh & Millard 2003).
- The integration of a whole language approach to reading acquisition, valuing the children's talk to generate their own sentences about 'the snowman'.
- Emergent readers being enabled to make the connections between oral, aural and visual modes of communication and to see the relevance of applying and solving those complex problem-solving tasks.
- Using the guided group context (which the teacher thought she had set up) to develop collaborative learning.
- Modelling reading behaviours, e.g. CVC decoding and supporting the development of high frequency words.
- Referring to the children by name and not through gendered phrases such as 'good girl', 'good boy' without any task specificity.

Case study   A developing observational lens

Context: This lesson illustrates a guided group working in a science lesson to explore the senses, in this case through tasting. Karen's science lesson with her guided group of Year 1 children (aged 5–6) demonstrates many of the formative principles that should be visible in a guided teaching group. The size of the group and its composition, five children of similar ability, allow the teacher to create a learning ethos that embraces the children as individuals and provides a manageable teaching situation in which she can focus on matching specific concepts/skills to the developmental needs of the group.

Children can be heard shouting out what types of food they like and do not like. The teacher has prepared a selection of real food for the children to smell and taste (sour, salty, sweet and savoury). The teacher holds up a book about 'Tasting'.

Jamelia:	I love chocolate [all of the group are smiling and nodding].
Samera:	No, I don't like onions.
Teacher:	No onions?
Samera:	No I like onions now I remember.
Teacher:	Not everyone likes the same taste, do we all like the same things?
Amir:	I don't like medicine [Adel, sitting next to him agrees with him and pulls a funny face].
Teacher:	[Points to a page in the book and starts to read] And we can ask our friends and family what their favourite foods are and what their least favourite foods are, so maybe when you go home today and you have a chat with your mum you could say 'do you know we tried some food that was horrible [some children motion by sticking out their tongues] and your mum or your dad or your brother or sister might say, 'I love that' just like when I was trying the lemon and lime [points to the plate with the fruit on] and some people said 'uugh I don't like that', I thought it was lovely [all of the children respond by saying 'I liked it' and begin licking their lips and rubbing their tummies].
Teacher:	[Calms down their enthusiastic responses.] Right stick out your tongues [children do it as she reads from the book].

(Continued)

(Continued)

	Your tongue is covered in tiny tastebuds OK, different parts of your tongue taste different things. Who can remember what this part of the tongue tastes? [Points to the front of her own tongue.]
Jamelia:	Sweet and salty.
Teacher:	What about the sides? [Points to her own tongue again.]
Children:	Sour.
Teacher:	What about right at the back?
Children:	Bitter.
Teacher:	Excellent, right so now I'm going to give you all a magnifying glass so that you can look at your partner's tongue [hands them out and the children become engrossed in each others' tongues].
Teacher:	What happens if you don't like the smell of something?
Amir:	It can make you sick.
Teacher:	Yes and sometimes it can put you off trying something if you don't like the smell. [The children have been given some paper and pencils to start recording their 'taste observations'.] Right I want you to write down what you think you can smell and remember tasting from yesterday.
Amir:	Mine is salty [has a plate of crisps in front of him].
Samera:	Mine is sweet.
Teacher:	OK, anything else? You need to write it down for me.
Samera:	Yummy. [She has a plate of pretzels.]
Adel:	Slimy. [He has a plate of onions.]
Teacher:	OK, right.
Jamelia:	Lumpy. [She has a plate of lemons and limes.]
Teacher:	Now anything else? When you tasted it did you go 'mmm' or did it make you go 'uuk'?
Jamelia:	I like this. [Points to a plate of maple syrup.]
Teacher:	Why did you like this one?
Jamelia:	Because I have it at home.

Teacher:	So when you tasted it, it reminded you of home, what did you have with it?
Jamelia:	Bread.
Teacher:	Can you remember what Adel said he liked about it?
Jamelia:	[Shakes head.]
Teacher:	What did this maple syrup remind you of Adel?
Adel:	Ice-cream.
Teacher:	That's right, ice-cream, he said it was like ketchup for ice-cream. [Adel hands his paper to the teacher with his words written on.]
Teacher:	Now your chocolate didn't taste sweet did it? Normal chocolate does, but this one tasted different, why? [Adel looks confused – Amir appears to know why.]
Amir:	It tasted yuk?
Teacher:	Why was it so different?
Amir:	Because it had too much sugar and too much sour [screws up face].
Teacher:	Oh it wasn't sour, which part of our tongue did we say we could taste? [reminds children of where they are positioned on the tongue] So where could we taste it?
Amir:	In the front.
Adel:	It was sour.
Teacher:	It wasn't sour, what did we say it tasted like?
Samera:	Yummy.
Teacher:	Come on, which part of the tongue did we say that we could taste that chocolate? Because it wasn't yummy chocolate was it?
Samera:	Yes it was horrible chocolate wasn't it?
Amir:	It was bitter.
Teacher:	Yes it was bitter wasn't it? Where can you taste bitter?
Samera:	At the back.
Teacher:	Yes at the back, it was bitter. Now Adel, it didn't taste like normal chocolate did it?
Adel:	[Shakes head and begins to write another word.]

Analysis of the lesson

The teacher welcomes the children's involvement as she refers to 'the tongue' and talks about what happens to it when we are ill. This creates an opportunity for one child to talk about her own illness. The teacher signals positively and clearly that their contributions are welcomed. This values the consistent use of the affective domain relating to cognition and increases the likelihood of the child becoming involved in learning. This sharing of knowledge is demonstrated further as the teacher uses an illustrated information book on 'tasting food' and invites the children to talk about their favourite types of food. This guided group methodology provides assessment opportunities in which the children demonstrate both their affective and cognitive domain behaviours. (The children demonstrate that they value each others' comments as they ask questions that visibly demonstrate their enjoyment of this collaborative aspect.)

The teacher's pedagogical style does not dominate the teaching session. Karen does not set a 'fast' pace which the children must keep to, they take their cue from the teacher and take their time and enjoy investigating/observing each others' taste buds using a magnifying glass. She allows time for discussion and reflection and encourages cross-collaboration within the guided group. This maintains the children's level of interest and enthusiasm – again, the teacher demonstrates her understanding of linking the affective domain to the development of cognition.

An important element of a guided group philosophy is the development of transference of the skills being taught. This is demonstrated through the children being able to show/evidence their individual understanding without explicit help from the teacher. This group of children begin to illustrate their levels of written automaticity as they describe the taste and smells of different foods. This supplies an assessment opportunity which allows the teacher to observe the complexity of language use from individual children and the phonological word representations they use as information in their next steps in learning. (The teacher misses the opportunity to model and scribe written words to aid spelling development and sentence construction – using a flip chart as a resource in a guided group session will always provide language to model for children).

Key teaching, learning and assessment from the science guided group:

(i)   The teacher has planned for five children and this group size works well as she teaches and assesses.

(ii)   The teacher has created a positive collaborative learning ethos – matching teaching to developmental needs.

(iii) The teacher values pupils' oral contributions and the pupils demonstrably value their peers' contributions.

(iv)   The teacher's teaching style within the guided group allows her to collect optimal information on individual pupil learning.

 (v)   The teacher demonstrates the importance of allowing time and pace for discussion and reflection.

(vi)   The teacher perceptively demonstrates the learning benefits of integrating the affective and cognitive domains in her guided group.

Case study   A developed observational lens

Context: The pupils are assembled on the carpet as a whole class with the teacher reviewing the previous day's maths lesson on the '5 times table'. The complete unedited transcript has been used because it represents a 'developed observational lens', while still having 'flaws' in pedagogy, for example too much teacher talk and some gender issues, as in higher order questions being directed solely at boys. However, it remains a 'developed' model because this teacher really explores mathematical norms (e.g. exploration, process, interrogatives).

Teacher: We're just going to go over our 5 times table, we have done it in different ways – we've danced it, sung it and we've done all sorts to it. We are going to use our 5 times table in the next part of the lesson. Some of you need a little revision and I'll talk it through with you what we expect today. Just to remind you of the 5 times table we're going to start off with this little programme [whiteboard displays 5 times table as a touch screen graphic game]. I think we'll go in alphabetical order I think, so that we can take it in turns – alright? Who's first to go on this one [chorus of 'me me' from the children]. Let's go by the surnames in the register as you will know that better. Right come on **Matthew** [walks to the whiteboard in silence, touches the screen to place the correct missing number in the sequence and walks back to his place]. Come on **George** you are next [he looks at the screen and sees that '20' is the missing number in the sequence, presses '20' and smiles]. Well done, you are

(Continued)

(Continued)

all really good, come on **Ben** you are next [he presses '65' as the correct missing number in the sequence and dances back to his place]. Well done, big improvement. Right Louise [she touches the screen to place the correct missing number '55' and sits down]. Come on Olivia is that too hard? Or can you work it out? [She looks at the screen longer as the numbers have changed to three digits, e.g. '105',110, 115 – voices from the class shout 'It's too hard for me'.]

Teacher: Ssh children don't put her off ... (Olivia takes her time as she searches for the missing number). Olivia look at the pattern, 105, 110, 115, what are we in one...

Olivia: One hundreds.

Teacher: So there's a clue, now what must it end in? Look at the number there [teacher points to the top of the screen where the numbers are to choose from]. Where is there another 100? [Olivia points correctly to the missing number '120'?]

Teacher: Good girl Olivia, was that a guess? [She nods] Good that was the only '100' that would fit the pattern. Right who hasn't had a turn? OK – right I'm going to ask Daniel what is the pattern?

Daniel: 10 times table.

Teacher: Not the 10 times table is it? What is it? What have we been counting in? [Hands go up around the room.] Matthew?

Matthew: 5 times table.

Teacher: Yes, the 5 times table. Now in the 5 times table look at the last digit in each of those numbers [she points to the sequence on the whiteboard] and tell me the pattern. George what is the pattern in these numbers? [George studies the board with his fingers in his mouth.]

Teacher: Can you see a pattern? Come and show me the last digit in these numbers. [George stands next to whiteboard].

George: A number.

Teacher: Yes, a digit is a number. [George begins to sit down again.]

Teacher: How many digits in each of these numbers?

George: Two.

Teacher: Two, good, now tell me the pattern in the last digit. Look what they do. [Children with hands up all around the room, almost bursting with the desire to tell their answer].

Teacher: Look George at the pattern along that row [George looks confused]. Go on Daniel, tell me.

Daniel: 5s.

Teacher: Yes, but what else does it do, Ben?

Ben: 0.

Teacher: Yes, 5 and 0. So if it is in the 5 times table, the last digit must be what, Hannah?

Hannah: 0

Teacher: 0, or ...?

Hannah: 5.

Teacher: That's a good clue to when you are picking out the answers to the 5 times table, which one ends in a 5 or 0? That's right. Now Daniel, do you realise that when you picked 46, it ended in a 6 and it could not be in the 5 times table. [Daniel mutters it could be in the 6 times table. Teacher moves on.] I will tell you what we are going to do now. All look at me as I am going to tell you what we are moving on to next. This is what we are going to work on. Do you remember the lesson when we talked about Jack and his problems [Reference: Jack and the Beanstalk]. How it had grown 5 leaves every day so that helped us with our 5 times table because we were working in 5s and we were counting in 5s. Then you in pairs had to go away and write a problem. Now the pairs had to write their problem about the 5 times table, something in your problem had to be about the 5 times table. It had to be in two parts and if you felt you were clever enough you could throw in a red herring. Can anybody explain to me what that was about?

Joe: It's something that you don't have to worry about.

(Continued)

(Continued)

Teacher:	Yes, it's something that you don't have to worry about, like what? [More children with hands 'up', bursting with answers.]
Joe:	It is something that has nothing to do with the problem.
Teacher:	Yes, that is right. It is something that gives you extra information and it might worry you when you are trying to work out your problem but you don't have to. That's not the number you have to be worrying about so you put that to one side. That is very good. So there were your two rules: it had to have something to do with the 5 times table, some of you got carried away as you did excellent problems but you moved away from the 5 times table but I am not too worried about that because some of you made your problems even more difficult. Now today you are going to work on those problems but you are going to work with your partner. So, first of all, you are going to take a problem, try and solve it and if you have trouble solving it you must ask the person who wrote the problem to help you with it, because if they wrote the problem hopefully they will know how to solve it but you try and solve it for yourself first. But if you can't work with your partner try not to come to Mrs Hollywood or myself because I want you to work with your partner and to use them to help you. [Child interjects.]
Jane:	You could ask your team.
Teacher:	Well if you don't have a partner that is excellent – you ask the team they may be able to help you. So, that group that were working here [points to the table in front of her], you have got the straws, the leaves, all the apparatus to actually work out the problem. So, Melissa, for example, what else might you do to help you record your problem? You say the beanstalk has 5 leaves every day and after 6 days how many leaves does it have? [Child is silent.] How might you work that problem out? What kind of a sum is it?
Melissa:	It is an add sum.
Teacher:	It can be an add sum because what would you do each day? How would you write it on a piece of paper? Can you think, Melissa?

Melissa:	Do a sum.
Teacher:	Do a sum? How would you do it?
Melissa:	Like add [starts to nod head to represent each 5].
Teacher:	5 + 5 + 5 + 5 and you would do it for how many times?
Melissa:	8.
Teacher:	Well if it is on 6 days, for how many times would you have to add 5? [Child next to her mouths '6'.]
Melissa:	6.
Teacher:	Yes, 6, so it is an add sum but it is also … [Points to child sitting at the back of the class].
Matthew:	It is the 5 times table.
Teacher:	Yes, it is the 5 times table. We are saying it is 6 lots of 5. That is excellent, thank you Matthew. Now that is what the people on that table are doing. That is a little reminder and I will tell you who these people are. Now some children, you had a problem with the egg laying, the hen laying all of those eggs and you were working with eggs being laid in so many minutes, now you got quite complicated questions and I am wondering now if you are able to work them out because I am going to read some of those questions out. They were excellent but some of them are quite difficult [reads from a selection of the children's questions]. This one is quite difficult, this is James's, I think he might have to work this one out first and then perhaps he can help somebody else. James, do you want to read it out?
James:	No.
Teacher:	OK, in 5 minutes, the hen lays 60 eggs, how many in 6 minutes?
Seyhan:	How many?
Teacher:	In 5 minutes the hen lays 60 eggs, OK? [Silence in the room.]
Seyhan:	300.
Teacher:	Oh no, but I know what you are trying to do there, but listen to the rest of the question, in 5 minutes the hen

(Continued)

(Continued)

lays 60 eggs, how many in 6 minutes? What have you got to work out there, let's see [hands up all around the room]. Matthew, what has he got to work out?

Matthew: He has got to work out … he can double 24 … no, I mean [puts hands over face] … double 12, that makes 24.

Teacher: Think about the question and what you have to work out. The hen lays in 5 minutes 60 eggs, all right? So before you can move on to the next part of the question, can anybody else decide what he has got to know first? Can you Daniel?

Daniel: Did it lay 11 in one minute?

Teacher: Very very close, not 11, think again. I know what you are trying to do. What are you trying to do? Tell me what you are trying to do.

Daniel: I am trying to think of the number that the hen lays in one minute.

Teacher: Yes, so in fact what you are doing is a different kind of sum. You are trying to divide which is a very clever thing to do, how many 5s there are in 60. How many 5s are there in 60? [Looks around the rest of the class. No responses.] Because that is the opposite of what we have been doing with the 5 times table [Lots of hands go up]. No, how many 5s in 60, not 5 x 60.

Emily: 12.

Teacher: 12, so that tells you that you were close [now looks back at Matthew] because you were working on the 12s. I know what you were trying to do.

Matthew: So 4 x 12 … [is interrupted].

Teacher: I see, you were ahead of me and my thinking. You had already worked out how many the hen had laid in one minute, 12. Then you got to how many in 6 minutes, so that is another times table sum, which is what? So it is 6 lots of …

Emily: 6 lots of 6.

Teacher: 6 lots of 12 [looks at Daniel].

Daniel: 72.

Teacher [smiles]:	So that is a really difficult one. Let's see some we did yesterday. [Flicks through other questions and reads.] A hen lays 40 eggs in 5 minutes. The next day 20 eggs got smashed [smiles]. How many were there left? What kind of sum is that then?
Chorus of voices:	That's a take away.
Teacher:	It is a take away, that's right. So that was Ben's, a very good problem, I think a very good one, and you can solve that today [voices start to get louder around the room].
Teacher:	Shhh … listen … quiet … just a minute [teacher's voice is very low and quiet]. This is a good multiplying one … ooh, I gave you a clue. The hen lays 5 eggs in 5 minutes, how many in 10 minutes?
Daniel:	It is easy.
Teacher:	What did you do?
Daniel:	He lays one in one minute.
Teacher:	You did a dividing sum then you multiplied. Well done. Did anyone do it another way?
Peter:	I put in 2 in one minute.
Teacher:	Does he lay 2 eggs in one minute? He lays 5 eggs in 5 minutes so you have to do …
Peter:	Double it.
Teacher:	That is another good way, that is excellent, you are really thinking. So what we are going to do. You are going to solve as many of these problems as you can. Don't do the same one twice. We will come back and we will talk about it at the end of the lesson. We are going to do it for our plenary. We are going to put them into three separate sections (holds up questions), very challenging questions that you found very difficult, questions that you had to do a little bit of thinking about and it helped that you knew the 5 times table and then you are going to put some of them into the 'easy' section. You know that didn't really challenge me

(Continued)

(Continued)

and maybe some people who found the middle section a bit hard, they can then take an easy one all right? Then you can match the problem that you feel that you are ready to do. So, you are really saying what kind of a problem that you really want and hopefully you are going to go for the thing that you find challenging. What you find challenging, somebody else might not find challenging. So we will decide at the end what we have worked out with our problems. Now the other group that we talked about, I think it was with George's group, you were carefully making your problems but you were using the compost and you were actually putting your potfuls of soil, egg cups, and you were working it out and using the 5 times table and you did some really good problems [turns around in chair to find their written problems]. Can you remember one of yours because I cannot find them, OK Millie, go and have a look and you can read yours out [Millie hands the question to the teacher to read out].

Teacher: OK, we planted one pot with 5 egg cups of soil on day one, how many egg cups did it take to fill 6 pots. Now what did you have to do to work this out?

Millie: I got 6 pots and counted them in 5s [voice is very low].

Teacher: Did you and what was the answer?

Millie: 30.

Teacher: I think that was quite a hard question. Did you find that easy or did you need the apparatus to do it? Did it help to have all the soil there in the cups?

Millie: Yes.

Teacher: Because you could have done it without.

Millie: [Nods head].

Teacher: Do you think you could do it without?

Millie: [Nods].

Teacher: How would you have done it without the soil?

Millie: I would have got 6, 6 in my head, and then I would have counted in 5s.

Teacher:	And you could have also done it on your fingers. Right, maybe then that is the next stage for you. Maybe you won't need the egg cups, the more you get to know [Louise interjects.]
Louise:	Can she come and do the eggs with us?
Teacher:	Well I think she may have to do a little more. She may have to tell us when she is ready to do the egg ones, OK? More practice with the egg cups, then on to the leaves, and if you feel happy with that you might want to move on to the egg questions? After this we might hopefully move on to something else but these cards will always be available to you to do some problem solving with the dinosaurs [refers to previous classwork].
Louise:	If you finish any work, you can still do them.
Teacher:	Yes, absolutely Louise. Yes, Melissa?
Melissa:	How many do you do?
Teacher:	As many as you can get through in the lesson. So I will give you about 20 minutes to work on them so that you can look at the clock and then we are going to come back to discuss the problems. Does anybody not know what we are doing. [No response.] Can you remember which groups you are in? [Lots of chatter from the children as they disperse.]

Analysis of the lesson

These pupils are encouraged by their teacher to explore, investigate, negotiate and to research mathematical processes. The pace is their pace and time is allowed for immersion and reflection. A conducive learning environment and culture has been created and the pupils are confident in exploring learning issues. The teacher has captured the philosophy (Vygotsky) of the social mediation of learning, that pupils listen to and model language and thought processes from more capable peers. Although she retains the children in passive mode through a long introduction to the task, there is minimum disengagement on the pupils' part from the task discussion. This engagement is because she has clearly established a culture of 'pupil involvement' in the lesson and the pupils understand that the instruction phase is specifically linked to their forthcoming active phase.

Summary

- Successful learning outcomes depend on a collaborative approach.
- The objective of group work is the promotion of collaboration itself.
- Group work allows more efficient interaction and use of resources including teacher time.
- The effective management of group work and its assessment depends on whether assessment should be through systematic observation or critical incident techniques, as well as the context of the task and the format of the groups.
- Teacher decisions about his/her part in the process, for example the extent of intervention and control, are important.
- Assessing pupils by observing them demands close teacher attention and concentration – hence the optimal opportunity is provided by the use of the guided group teaching strategy (see Chapter 2).

5

Analysis and Feedback

In this chapter we focus on the role of analysis and feedback in formative assessment. We consider content and correct information, and the analysis of misconceptions, and provide detailed coverage of feedback.

What is the focus of analysis?

There is a tacit presumption of 'content' as 'correct information', selected in advance as lesson objectives. If there is a lack of discussion with pupils about the nature of disciplinary objectives (learning objectives), there is a traditional view that 'content' is the information that pupils should retain (i.e. as the right answer to a problem). So if the pupil gets the information 'right' (as the teacher has envisioned [planned] the problem) there is no genuine consideration of other ideas. Omitting the discussion over 'objectives' means that the teacher will pay little attention to the substance of the pupils' reasoning (so the response is either 'right' or 'wrong'). For this reason, the intention (e.g. the AfL mantra) of making learning goals explicit in lesson plans and as part of the instructions (Heritage 2011) engenders a simplistic view of content as a body of information. Therefore, standards are predominantly composed of target information or propositional knowledge (Coffey et al. 2011, p. 1118)

Analysis of misconceptions

There is a widely held view of misconceptions or preconceptions as inaccurate or incorrect conceptions which pupils hold that are contrary to the learning (instructional) objectives. Much of the research on misconceptions was written to challenge the idea that it is sufficient or even of primary importance to 'explain the correct concepts'. In particular, researchers have intended highlighting the rationality of pupils' prior conceptions. Strike and Posner (1992) argued that 'if conceptual change theory suggests anything about instruction it is that the handles to effective instruction are to be found in persistent attention to the argument and less in the attention to right answers' (p. 171).

Strike and Posner (1992) also argued that 'it is very likely wrong to assume that misconceptions are always there in developed or articulated form ... Misconceptions may be weakly formed, need not be symbolically represented, and may not even be formed prior to instruction' (p. 158). Researchers (Nobes et al. 2003; Taber 2000) have raised empirical and theoretical reasons to doubt the view of prior conceptions as obstacles to learning (some positivity/originality from the learner that it is valued and deemed 'correct' in terms of analysis).

What is feedback?

Feedback is a simple message. How can it assist the learning process? This can only happen when pupils take it into account, because it affects their cognition.

> Communication theory teaches us that the effectiveness of a message is measured at the level of the recipient; an intervention or a piece of information only helps a pupil learn better if their thought processes are modified. This is an abstract way of saying that no learning takes place without the learner. One can only stimulate, reinforce, re-orient, readjust or accelerate the pupil's mental processes in the hope of modifying the learning processes. (Perrenoud 1998, p. 86)

This approach can only be effective if a 'window is found into the cognitive system of the learner' (Perrenoud 1998, p. 86). There is no point sending him or her messages if these messages are treated as 'noise' or are regarded as redundant rather than as information to help in understanding, remembering, assimilating knowledge or developing skills. The problem is that many of the messages which teachers think are feedback messages do not achieve that aim for the child. This failure may be caused by a range of reasons and conditions: 'because their form, their tone, their content (verbal or non-verbal), the moment chosen, the point reached [by the pupil] in the work and the interactive situation in which they occur do not allow the pupils to understand them or do something with them' (Perrenoud 1998, p. 87).

Therefore, to enable feedback to be effective and to take place on the regular basis which is necessary for pupil learning to be affected, there is the requirement for the teacher to have 'a clear understanding of the way the pupils function and the manner in which they incorporate contributions external to their own thought processes. This understanding should be both general and particular (in so far as the pupils do not all function in the same way)' (Perrenoud 1998, p. 104).

Perrenoud's research (1998) outlines three major issues or difficulties. First, 'even the most advanced theoretical models, generated by research, are not yet adequate to take into account, in a precise manner, the mental processes of a pupil in a classroom situation and the exact use he or she makes of feedback' (p. 87). Secondly, teachers act, most of the time, on the basis of intuitive models, even more rudimentary than those of researchers, based on common sense rather than well-honed concepts or cognitive functions; thus the finer points and strategies advanced by Astolfi (1997) containing the errors of pupils are far from being recognised by teachers. And thirdly, even a teacher possessing all the theoretical tools would have considerable difficulty using them in an optimal way in a given situation, because of other priorities and uncertainties which cannot be dealt with in a given time (Perrenoud 1998, p. 87). Basically Perrenoud is stating that much of the feedback that is dispensed by teachers 'is like so many bottles thrown out to sea; no one can be sure that the messages they contain will one day find a receiver' (1998, p. 87).

The function of feedback

Feedback is a 'consequence of performance' (Hattie & Timperley 2007, p. 81). Consider instruction and feedback as a continuum. In some cases, there is a clear distinction between the provision of instruction and the supply of feedback. However, instruction and feedback can become combined to the extent that 'the process itself takes on the form of new instruction, rather than informing the student solely about correctness' (Kulhavey & Wagner 1993, p. 212). Butler and Winne (1995) claimed that 'feedback is information with which a learner can confirm, add to, overwrite, tune or restructure information in memory, whether that information is domain knowledge, metacognitive knowledge, beliefs about self and tasks or cognitive tactics and strategies' (p. 252).

Feedback has no effect in a vacuum; there must be a learning context to which feedback is addressed. Feedback is 'most powerful when it addresses faulty interpretations, not a total lack of understanding' (Hattie & Timperley 2007, p. 82), because 'the pupil has no way to relate the new information to what is already known' (Kulhavey & Wagner 1993, p. 220).

Effective feedback

Extrinsic rewards are typically negative in their effect because they 'undermine a pupil's taking responsibility for motivating or regulating themselves. Rather they are a controlling strategy that often leads to greater surveillance, evaluation and competition, all of which have been found to undermine enhanced engagement and regulation' (Deci et al. 1999, p. 659).

Effective feedback can be measured against three questions:

> Where am I going? (What are the goals?), How am I going? (What progress is being made towards the goal?); Where to next? (What activities need to be undertaken to make better progress?) These questions correspond to notions of feed up, feed back and feed forward. How effectively answers to these questions [support learning] is partly dependent on the level at which the feedback operates. These include the level of task performance, the level of process of understanding how to do the task, the metacognitive process level and the personal level. Feedback has differing effects across these levels. (Hattie & Timperley 2007, p. 86)

The more that the pupil is involved, the more effort that the pupil makes, the more likely it is that the feedback will be effective. Pupils will increase their effort when 'the effort leads to tackling more challenging tasks or appreciating higher quality experiences rather than just doing "more"' (Hattie & Timperley 2007, p. 86). They are more likely to increase effort when the intended goal is clear, when high commitment is secured for it and when belief in eventual success is ensured (Kluger & DeNisi 1996, p. 260). Pupils may also develop their own effective 'error detection' skills which lead to their own self-feedback aimed at reaching a goal. Such error detection can be very powerful provided that pupils

- **Step/Question 1: Where am I going?**

- Feed up

- What are the goals?

- **Step/Question 2: How am I doing?**

- Feed back

- What progress is being made towards the goals?

- **Step/Question 3: Where do I go next?**

- Feed forward

- What learning support is needed for me to make progress to achieve the goals?

Figure 5.1   The Three Step Model: Hattie & Timperley (2007)

have some understanding of the task about which to strategise and self-regulate (Hattie & Timperley 2007, p. 86). By inference, therefore, pupils can pursue better strategies to complete the task or be taught those strategies. Teachers can also assist by clarifying goals, enhancing commitment or increased effort to reach the goals through feedback. Vitally, goals can be made more accessible by narrowing the range of reasonable hypotheses available to the pupil. Teachers are therefore creating the conditions for a learning environment in which pupils develop self-regulation and error detection skills – part of the process of building pupil commitment through nurturing and modelling (Hattie et al. 1996).

Feedback is effective when it consists of information about progress and how to proceed. Pupils often ask for information about 'how am I doing?' Feedback specifically related to the task is more effective when it is simple rather than complex. Research indicates (Kulhavey et al. 1985) that pupils process additional feedback information at a surface level because they do not perceive it as being directly linked to the main issue (for the pupil) of identifying the correct response. However these results were mediated by the pupils' confidence in their responses. Those with high response confidence who had little trouble understanding or interacting with the task were more likely to make efficient use of the feedback, whatever its complexity. Similarly, when delivered in group situations, the feedback messages may be compounded by perceptions of relevance to self or to other group members. 'The effectiveness of feedback about the task in these situations depends very much on pupils' commitment and involvement in the task and on their notions about whether it relates to their performance' (Hattie & Timperley 2007, p. 92).

The effectiveness of marks or written comments has also been investigated. There is evidence that providing written comments is more effective than providing grades (Butler 1988; Crooks 1988). Butler's research demonstrated that feedback through comments alone led to learning gains whereas marks alone or comments accompanied by marks or giving praise, did not. Butler claimed that this proved the ineffectiveness of the whole culture and the system of giving marks, grades, merit awards, gold stars and competition rather than a focus on supported self-regulated personal improvement (Butler 1988).

Feedback about the self: This is often present in teacher–pupil interactions and often used instead of feedback about the task, feedback about the task process and feedback about self-regulation (Hattie & Timperley 2007). Personal feedback ('great effort' 'good boy') usually contains little task-related information and is rarely converted into more engagement, commitment to the learning goals, enhanced self-efficacy or understanding about the task. Feedback about the self can have 'impact on learning only if it leads to changes in pupils' effort, engagement or feelings of efficacy in relation to the learning or to the strategies they use when attempting to understand tasks' (Hattie & Timperley 2007, p. 96). The effects of the self-level of feedback are 'too diluted, too often uninformative about performing the task and too influenced by pupils' self-concepts to be effective' (Hattie & Timperley 2007, p. 96). Too often it deflects the pupil's attention from the task. There are also the situations when praise is delivered publicly by a teacher in the presence of a peer group that does not value or esteem school performance or achievement.

Timing of feedback: This will vary depending on the levels of feedback. Immediate feedback during task acquisition can result in faster rates of acquisition; immediate feedback during fluency building of conceptual understanding by the pupil can detract from the development of pupil automaticity. The effectiveness of delayed compared to immediate feedback varies correlative to the difficulty of the items. Research by Clariana et al. (2000) suggests that difficult task items are more likely to involve greater degrees of processing about the task and that delayed feedback provides the opportunity to do this. Conversely 'easy' items do not require this processing and delaying feedback is unnecessary.

The effects of positive and negative feedback: Kluger and DeNisi (1996) stated that both negative and positive feedback can have beneficial effects on pupil learning. However Hattie and Timperley found that 'negative feedback is more powerful at the "self" level while both negative and positive feedback can be effective at the task level. While there are differential effects relating to commitment, mastery or performance orientation and self-efficacy at the self-regulatory level' (Hattie & Timperley 2007, p. 98). At the self level, no praise is more effective than praise if accompanied by task-related feedback. There is evidence to suggest that negative feedback or disconfirmation can be more powerful than positive feedback or confirmation at the self level (Brockner; Brunuit 1979 et al. 2000; Hattie 1992). Individuals will go to extremes to confirm their self-perception by taking note of feedback information after experiencing negative affect, exhibiting less motivation on a subsequent task and attributing the feedback less to effort and more to ability. At the feedback on task level, corrective feedback is powerful for enhancing learning, especially new skills or tasks. Disconfirmation with corrective information can be effective but disconfirmation without this information is of little use because it provides no information on what to do or how to respond next time (Breakwell 1983). Feedback on task can be ignored by children if it is poorly presented or if their knowledge is insufficient to accommodate additional feedback information. Howie et al. (2000) reported that it was the poor presentation or lack of information value in the feedback, rather than children's faulty knowledge, which in the majority of cases explained the low power of much feedback information.

Feedback and the classroom: Effective feedback places demands on teachers if they are to use corrective information to support teaching and learning. 'First they need to undertake effective instruction ... feedback is what happens second [after teaching], and to make the feedback effective, teachers need to know how to make appropriate judgements about when, how and at what level to provide appropriate feedback' (Hattie & Timperley 2007, p. 100). The frequency of feedback in classrooms is universally low (Bond et al. 2000) and the frequency of feedback across teachers 'who did and did not pass certification as "accomplished" teachers ... was low across both groups' (Hattie & Timperley 2007, p. 100).

When feedback is given it is likely to be self-related or at best corrective task related and to be influenced by perceptions of pupils' needs. Teachers give 'poor' pupils more praise and the minimal self-regulated feedback is usually negative (Blote 1995). Teacher feedback to boys is more related to a lack of effort or poor behaviour and to girls feedback is more about ability attributions (Dweck et al. 1978). Feedback is not only differentially given but also differentially received. The environment and learning culture of the classroom is critical 'if disconfirmation and corrective feedback at any level is to be welcomed and used by the pupils and teachers. Errors and disconfirmations are most powerful in environments in which they are seen as leading to future learning, particularly relating to processing and regulation. Pupil engagement in learning will be constrained by the prevailing culture of the classroom because there is personal risk involved in responding publicly and being seen to fail. With inefficient learners it is better for a teacher to provide elaborations through instruction (modelling) than to provide a feedback on a poorly understood concept. If feedback is directed at the right level it can support pupils to understand, engage and develop effective strategies to process the information intended to be learned. To be effective, feedback needs to be clear, purposeful, meaningful and compatible with the pupils' prior knowledge and to provide logical connections. It needs to prompt active information processing on the part of the learners, have low task complexity, relate to specific and clear goals and provide minimal threat to the person at the 'self' level. The major discriminating factor in its use is whether it is clearly directed at the task, process and/or regulation and not at the self level. This highlights the importance of classrooms in which self and peer assessment and the culture of learning from misconceptions are valued and practised.

A critical conclusion is that teachers need to learn from feedback – just as much as the pupils learn from receiving that feedback. Too often assessments are used by teachers to provide summaries or snapshots of learning rather than to provide information that pupils can use to support their own learning. Assessment should always be feedback instruments that are integrated with and integral to teaching and learning – assessments are not 'add-ons' which 'round off' the process with a neat label or grade for the pupil. It is the feedback information and interpretations of children's learning locations, not the scores, levels and grades, that are important in the learning process. In too many cases, assessment is used synonymously with testing 'as the measure to judge whether change has occurred rather than as a mechanism to further enhance and consolidate learning by teachers and pupils' (Hattie & Timperley 2007, p. 104). However, when feedback is combined with effective teaching, it is very powerful in enhancing learning. Kluger and DeNisi (1996) noted that 'a feedback intervention provided for a familiar task, containing cues that support learning, attracting attention to feedback-standard discrepancies at the task level, and void of cues that direct attention to the self, is likely to yield impressive gains in students' performance' (p. 255). Feedback can only build on something; it is of little use when there is no initial learning or surface information: feedback happens second (Hattie & Timperley 2007, p. 104).

In their meta-analysis of 131 papers on performance feedback effects, Kluger and De Nisi (1996) found that, whereas feedback interventions improved performance on average, over one-third of feedback interventions weakened performance, 'a finding that cannot be explained by sampling error, feedback sign, or existing theories' (p. 254). However the possible social comparison component of performance feedback has been neglected. Monteil and Huguet (1999) proposed the following social comparison feedback theory:

(a) Cognitive productions can be regulated by social comparison experiences associated with the performance, competence or status feedback;

(b) Social comparison effects can depend on the individuals' degree of social visibility;

(c) The influence of social comparison and visibility is connected to the individual's academic or performance history;

(d) The interaction between current and past academic experiences can foster an attention-consuming situation;

(e) Since attentional resources are limited, attention thus partakes in the regulation of academic productions; and finally

(f) Through the modification of the attentional locus, social comparison feedback can thus influence cognitive performance. (Monteil & Huguet 2001, p. 368)

The underlying mechanism of this influence is therefore that of attenion referring to individuals' past history activated by the social conditions created by means of the involvement of an outside agent. The interaction between the individual's past experiences and the current situation supplies part of the contents and organisation of the long-term memory and can direct the allocation of attentional resources. Therefore the cognitive structures which record generic knowledge about the self also organise and direct the processing of information concerning the self. Likened to an autobiographical type of structure, the characteristics of the self would become involved in the use and direction of attentional resources (Monteil & Huguet 1999). Therefore a strong compatibility of past academic experiences with the current conditions of performance entails a cognitive context of self that requires few attentional resources. However, a poor compatibility between past academic experiences and the current conditions of performance induces a more costly cognitive context of self with respect to attentional resources. For children with positive academic self-knowledge, their usual expectations lead them to pay attention to the task, especially in high social visibility situations. For children with negative academic self-knowledge, their expectations, generally linked with failure, lead them to neglect the task, leaving their attention free to process other elements of their close environment. For students with a positive academic self-knowledge, negative feedback coupled with strong social visibility creates a cognitive context which interferes with attention. However, because it fosters conditions of protection with regard to the effects of a social comparison feedback, poor visibility allows these children to pay enough attention to the task to maintain expected performance. For children with a negative self-knowledge a positive (unfamiliar) social comparison feedback coupled with a strong social visibility leads to concentrated attention on the cognitive context of self-precluding an efficient processing of the focal task (Monteil & Huguet 2001, p. 369). Therefore, the variations observed in cognitive performances should not be considered as the direct product of a modification of the social context understood as an environmental factor. These variations are the product of the social context in relation to elements of the individual pupils' performance history.

Teachers need to have the ability to:

- Undertake close analysis of, for example, children's narrative writing to uncover the inhibitors to better writing.
- Match the individual needs of children to the next micro steps in teaching.
- Deploy a systematic approach to enriching writing which links writing to all aspects of language.

- Guide children at the correct pace to become autonomous self-regulated learners.
- Prepare personalised learning strategies that have precision and effectiveness.

The focus of this chapter is on how to assess to gain information in order to supply effective feedback to the pupil. Too much use is made of the word 'feedback' without linking it to an analysis of the learning information on which that feedback will be based. The intention of the case study in this chapter is to enable the teacher to better understand the learning progress which the child is making and through that understanding to plan the child's learning journey more accurately. Analysing pieces of work: where do we start?

Have you analysed a child's work before? What did you focus on? What were you looking for? What did you understand about what the child was doing in her response? Did you understand what the child could have been doing (alternative routes to learning)? How easy did you find it writing comments which identified what was going right/ wrong? Did you know enough to write clear next learning steps? How did the analysis help you understand where the child was in her learning journey? How did you help her 'move on' in her learning?

Rather than relying on allocating levels, sub-levels, grades or marks, the teacher is analysing the child's work and learning behaviours so that misconceptions are supported and the child's next specific learning steps are clarified. Through this analysis the teacher is able to write specific commentaries on what the child has learnt and where the child is going next. The thinking behind the formative commentaries is that there is an integral link between planning for teaching and learning, differentiation of the learning programme to match children's learning needs and the specific feedback to support and report children's progress through the commentaries (see examples below).

At four or five key points in the year (to be selected by the teacher without external interference) the teacher will carry out an analysis and write a detailed commentary on a piece of the child's assessed work. This commentary identifies the learning that the child has demonstrated in this specific piece of work and the further support or new learning which is required for the child's next step in the learning journey.

The teacher then has a progressive record across the year of the child's learning development, the learning issues and the scaffolding and support strategies which have been used in that period. This provides a full reportable record of each child's learning development for that year. The record is transferable to the next teacher and is an accurate document for reporting progress to parents, talking with the child and reporting

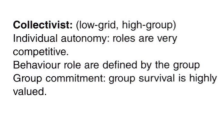

Collectivist: (low-grid, high-group)
Individual autonomy: roles are very competitive.
Behaviour role are defined by the group
Group commitment: group survival is highly valued.

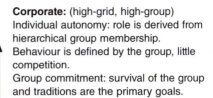

Corporate: (high-grid, high-group)
Individual autonomy: role is derived from hierarchical group membership.
Behaviour is defined by the group, little competition.
Group commitment: survival of the group and traditions are the primary goals.

Individual: (low-grid, low group)
Individual autonomy: roles are competitive and in constant flux.
Group commitment: few insider-outsider rules.
Minimum commitment to group goals or survival.

Bureaucratic: (high-grid, low-group)
Individual autonomy: roles defined through race, class, heritage, etc, no competition.
Group commitment: members believe in, but do not identify with the group hierarchy.
Minimum commitment to group goals or survival.

Figure 5.2   Grid–group typology classification (derived from Douglas 1992, Harris 1995, Rohrmann & Renn 2000)

externally to a range of accountability stakeholders. Each assessment piece reflects what has gone on in the classroom.

We decided to track three teachers from the same primary school using the grid group typology used extensively in risk perception and organisational culture research (e.g. Lupton 1999; Sjoberg et al. 2000; Spitzer 1975). In this theory of socio-cultural research 'Grid' refers to the extent to which the members of a group adhere to hierarchy and procedural rules and their level of individual autonomy. 'Group' refers to the extent members are committed to the social group and isolation from non-members' (Howard 2007, p. 2; Douglas 1992). The grid-group typology classifications are Collectivist (low-grid; high-group), Individual (low-grid; low-group), Corporate (high-grid; high-group) and Bureaucratic (high-grid; low-group) (see Figure 5.2).

In our earlier research we collected data from a comprehensive survey of practices of formative assessment in a nationally representative sample of primary schools in England (Boyle & Charles 2010). Analysis of these responses enabled us to develop a second typology to reference school levels of prioritisation of formative pedagogy as a practised philosophy for teaching and learning. Our research evidenced the following typology: differentiation; divergence; definition; depth and demythology.

Differentiation was defined as 'to the extent that pupils do not have the same abilities or the same needs nor the same way of working, an optimal situation for one pupil will not be optimal for another ... one can write a simple equation: diversity in people + appropriate treatment for each = diversity in approach' (Perrenoud 1998, pp. 93–4). It is important that teachers understand that differentiation of instruction is 'planned rather than just added on after observing difficulties' (Allal & Lopez 2005, p. 246). Teachers for pedagogical or philosophical, legacy or conceptual reasons clearly have problems with understanding differentiation. Differentiation has been evidenced as equating with setting and labelling children in static inflexible groups that remain constant throughout the time that a child remains in a year group (usually based on the sole evidence of test scores from the previous year). 'Differentiation implies the imposition of different curricula for different groups of pupils – or it means nothing' (Simon 1985, p. 6).

Divergence was not present in the pedagogy surveyed because

> in the face of pace, objectives, targets and tables that have become part of the dominant linguistic and conceptual discourse of education reform in England, we might wonder how confident good divergent teachers will be to stray from pre-set paths for better pastures. We might wonder what the absence of divergent thinking will mean, in the longer term, for children's motivation and interest in their learning experiences. (Dadds 2001, p. 53)

The following of a formulaic whole class lesson plan seems to be the sole pedagogical model, so there is no 'divergence'.

Definition is the third element in the typology and for us it represents the fact that 'formative assessment takes place day by day and allows the teacher and the student to adapt their respective actions to the teaching/learning situation in question. It is thus for them, a privileged occasion for conscious reflection on their experience' (Audibert 1980, p. 62). The understanding of formative assessment (or its synonym Assessment for Learning) and its practical operation is poor, and so there is no clarity of definition.

The fourth element of our typology is depth. In defining depth, 'teachers bring skills in devising and constructing tasks to elicit revealing and pertinent responses from children' (Sadler 1989, p. 80). Pedagogy is driven by 'coverage' and 'pace', which have precedence over depth and security in learning: 'Coverage and elicitation of facts rather than the creation and co-construction of inter-connected learning' (Myhill 2006, p. 34).

The final element of our typology is demythology, by which we mean 'the search for theoretical frameworks could lead to an increasingly abstract vision of formative assessment cut off from the realities of classroom practice. This is why it is essential to articulate theoretical work with the study of how assessment is actually practised in the classroom' (Allal & Lopez 2005, p. 251). The associated gimmicks camouflage what is the simple truth of formative teaching, that is, a child's learning needs should be at the centre of a teacher's planning, and therefore the concept of formative assessment needs demythologising (Boyle & Charles 2010).

Armed with these typologies we were allowed to embed ourselves in a school in the north-west of England for the cycle of a full school year. The school was situated in a low income, predominantly Bangladeshi community (95% school population). There was a high turnover of school staff and performance issues were raised in the latest Ofsted inspection.

Case Study

Visit 1: 29 September

The head teacher selected the Year 1 teaching group and the three teachers who taught that year group; we met with the teachers and talked through with them the process of the five assessments for the year. We made it clear to the teachers that we understood the pressures of summative accountability which the teachers were under and explained that we had used this formative methodology to report learning progress 'to provide information for learners, parents and teachers' (Green & Oates 2007, p. 7). We explained to the teachers that they would manage the assessment cycle; they would choose the genre from within their literacy framework; and they would design the assessment pieces. The teachers then met and planned the format for assessment one; they collaboratively produced a worksheet with six stimulus pictures positioned in a linear sequence under the story title 'Little Red Riding Hood'. We made a methodological decision to be present as observers when each of the assessments were being administered: 'The teacher adopts a fly on the wall technique to observe things as undisturbed by his/her presence as possible' (Woods 2006, p. 10). These observations included the verbal and non-verbal working methods of both teacher and children, completion behaviours of the children and the delivery style of the teacher.

We used three data collection instruments on our visits to the school: (1) an observation schedule for the five occasions when the three teachers administered assessments to the children; (2) a semi-structured interview schedule to be used for each teacher post the assessment administrations; and (3) a semi-structured interview schedule for the five post-assessment analysis interviews which were carried out with each of the teachers (to ascertain how the three teachers were using the assessment information in their teaching).

In observation schedule one problems arise when the checklist controls the focus of the observation or encourages the observer to become judgemental. 'Such specifications are to be regarded as intelligent, not necessarily correct' (Hopkins 1993, p. 100).

(Continued)

(Continued)

Figure 5.3 Little Red Riding Hood

The observation schedule checklist covered the following teacher behaviours:

(1) Emphasises learning goals, makes them explicit and expects children to be able to master the curriculum?
(2) Carefully organises and sequences curriculum experiences?
(3) Clearly explains and illustrates what children are to learn?
(4) Frequently asks direct and specific questions to monitor children's progress and check their understanding?
(5) Provides children with ample opportunity to practise, gives prompts and feedback to ensure success and correct mistakes, and allows children to practise a skill until it is over-learnt or automatic?
(6) Reviews regularly and holds children accountable for work?

Data collection instrument two was the semi-structured interview schedule used by us after each assessment. 'The assessment activity should arise from current classroom practice; the task should build on a pupil's previous experience and be clearly introduced. In these circumstances children can perform confidently and have less anxiety about assessment' (Christie & Boyle 1991, p. 9). At the conclusion of each assessment we tape-recorded a semi-structured interview with each teacher, 'interviews which have some pre-set questions but allow more scope for open-ended answers' (Woods, 2006, p. 13). This interview schedule was based on Boyle and Christie (1991).

(1) How did you design the assessments? (Task set up)
(2) How did you teach prior to the assessment? (Quality of instruction)
(3) How do you integrate the teaching and learning needs that have emerged from the children's responses to the assessment? What has emerged from the children's responses to the assessment? (Breadth of understanding)
(4) Is there anything from doing the assessment today that has changed your thinking? (Reflective teacher/modification)
(5) Would the children have noticed anything different in your behaviour from your normal teaching style? (Testing v. assessment styles)

The third instrument was designed to ascertain the depth of analysis and the integration of the information acquired through those analyses into the teaching and learning activities (based on Silverman 2000).

(1) How did you find doing the analysis? (Process)
(2) What did you find that the children were doing as writers from your analysis? (Learning behaviours; conceptual understanding)
(3) Were there any other aspects of their learning or was the analysis just at the word level? (Word, sentence, text – three interrelated strands)
(4) Is there anything about your teaching which will change because of your analysis of children's work? (Reflective practitioner)
(5) Are your models of assessment based on any literature? (Professional development; theory in training)
(6) What about individual needs? (Differentiation; guided group methodology)
(7) What is your understanding of assessment? (Testing v. assessment; integration)
(8) What teaching style do you use for the assessment? (Repertoire, e.g. whole class/individual/groups)

The three teachers involved in the research were: Teacher F: a newly qualified young female in her early twenties, who has signed up to follow a Masters programme. She was clearly the junior member of the key stage 1 team as this was her first teaching post. She was trained to teach 'sort of 3–9' age range (transcript 15 October). Teacher J: a young female, mid-twenties, who had worked at this school for five years. This school is her second teaching position since qualification. Teacher O: a middle-aged female, 'I was trained sort of 3–9, then I did infants for lots of years and then went up to the Juniors for five years' (transcript 15 October); experienced across the primary age range; last year she taught year 6, this year she is leading the key stage 1 team.

Observation comments on teachers' assessment administrations

(1) *Emphasises learning goals, makes them explicit and expects children to be able to master the curriculum?*

Teacher F did not emphasise what short-term learning goal she was looking for the child to achieve.

Teacher J emphasised surface features of text construction, e.g. full stops, capital letters; no modelling of skills.

Teacher O made decisions based on curriculum expectations which did not correspond to the children's current level of writing ability.

(2) *Carefully organises and sequences curriculum experiences?*

Teacher F did organise but did not sequence the curriculum experience.

Teacher J did emphasise the speaking and listening elements of literacy through the use of puppets to demonstrate the oral structures of character dialogue.

Teacher O asked no direct nor specific questions; she was operating at the procedural stage, i.e. as a supplier of excessive information which was surplus to the child's conceptual needs. ('instead of being founded on and around the needs and interests of children as they naturally develop and on their activity, writing is given to them from without' [Vygotsky 1978]

(3) *Clearly explains and illustrates what children are to learn?*

Teacher J did not explain nor fully illustrate (some use made of puppets) what children were to learn; there was no connection established between the child's experience and the story, evidenced by observation of the children's behaviours when left to think independently.

Teacher F did explain the story but did not illustrate what she wanted the children to learn, e.g. she did not attempt to model specifically how a story was constructed in written form.

Teacher O set up the curriculum experience but did not sequence or structure it.

(4) *Frequently asks direct and specific questions to monitor students' progress and check their understanding?*

Teacher F did not ask questions to check children's understanding, e.g. cueing children back to their taught experiences – what a letter looks like.

Teacher J was not anticipating nor asking questions about misunderstandings. The children were all struggling and found writing very difficult; 'what does it look like a "b"?', 'miss, where is "the" ?' as the child held up a single letter.

Teacher O did not model the relevance of the learning required to complete the assessment activity, e.g. 'miss, where is "w"?' Teacher not connecting with individual needs as she is operating at the level of abstraction while children still need support at concrete operational level.

(5) *Provides children with ample opportunity to practise, gives prompts and feedback to ensure success and correct mistakes, and allows children to practise a skill until it is over-learnt or automatic?*

Teacher F gave the children ample (if not too much) time; she did not provide prompts or cues but supplied direct answers to children's requests; she did not model correct words and therefore allowed errors to continue without remediation, e.g. child's construct of the word 'fw' (flower) was not addressed.

Teacher J allowed ample time but the children were not at the stage of making reasoned attempts at the problem-solving aspect of writing, e.g. the majority of the group were either at the initial phonemic word construction stage, role play writing or experimental writing phases. 'Miss, miss, it's too hard'.

Teacher O allowed time for the children to complete, but that completion was only achieved through massive teacher support at the level of the individual, e.g. no modelling for the child who wanted to write 'w' for 'woodcutter'.

(6) *Reviews regularly and holds children accountable for work?*

Teacher F praised children's efforts verbally and with external rewards, e.g. stickers.

Both teachers F and J did not demonstrate the next learning steps for each child and seemed unaware of the potential development within direct requests, e.g. 'What does a "b" look like?'

Teacher O did not discuss what the child had produced in terms of demonstrating achievement and did not review with the child in a strategic developmental manner, i.e. deconstructing what the child had done against the teacher's expectations for the child at that moment in her learning.

Post-assessment interview (based on Christie & Boyle 1991)

(1) *How did you design the assessments? (Task set up)*

Teacher F described her methodology for constructing the assessment as 'I got the pictures and just made lines'.

Teacher J: 'We all talked about how we would do it, sequencing pictures so it gives them a visual aid.'

Teacher O: 'The three of us sat together and decided we were going to do the same thing, the only thing we didn't all agree on and decided to go our own way with was whether we would have any keywords.' (No keywords were used.) 'I didn't want to hamper the children, I want them to think "oh that has to be in here".'

(2)   *How did you teach prior to the assessment? (Quality of instruction)*

Teacher F: 'We have been looking at Red Riding Hood for two weeks, so they should have a very good understanding and we did things like finger puppets ...'

Teacher J: 'We have been doing Little Red Riding Hood, we have already done Goldilocks and we had already wrote and so we all talked about how we would do it, sequencing pictures so it gives them a visual aid. We read them a different story and a larger book.'

Teacher O: 'If you want to find out something specific you would set something up to find that out so that you might want to find out how you count to 10 so you might set up something specific where that is my objective and who can and who can't do so then I can plan the next...'

(3)   *How do you integrate the teaching and learning needs that have emerged from the children's responses to the assessment? What has emerged from the children's responses to the assessment? (Breadth of understanding)*

Teacher F: 'I think looking at the pictures, there are too many pictures. I would give them one picture at a time so that they were more confident talking about it in a threesome.'

Teacher J: 'I think for Y1 I should have got some word cards for them to copy. I don't know whether it takes it away from them using their own knowledge.'

Teacher O: 'It is their phonic knowledge and the grapheme/phoneme, they can hear the sounds; the other issue is that two of the children don't know that a word is a unit so we are doing a lot in guided reading with me'.

(4)   *Is there anything from doing the assessment today that has changed your thinking? (Reflective teacher/modification)*

Teacher F: 'Definitely we are right at the start of the year but I have noticed that child Y was able to read hers back and then there was child Z who couldn't read what she had written so there is that diversity within their ability.'

Teacher J: 'Yes I think so, I need to be considering their abilities, you think they are all similar abilities.'

Teacher O: 'I would personally have just used a picture and just got them to do some writing.'

(5)   *Would the children have noticed anything different in your behaviour from your normal teaching style? (Testing v. assessment styles)*

Teacher F: 'In teaching I would have used the whiteboards more as they don't know their sounds yet.'
Teacher J: 'I think they would have noticed that I didn't guide them in the assessment situation whereas I would have guided them in the classroom teaching situation.'
Teacher O: 'In these Y1/Y2 classes, I think with the Y2 they have got that already but with the Y1 they start to queue up, yes I think it's about Y2 going off to do their "sats" and they think "that's going to be me next year. I am going to be working that hard".'

Post analysis interview (based on Silverman 2000, p. 88)

For each child's assessment each teacher wrote a commentary which focused on the child's demonstrated writing behaviours and identified the child's next learning steps.

Visit 2: 15 October

(1)   *How did you find doing the analysis? (Process)*

Teacher F: 'Well to be honest I actually analysed what they were doing while they were carrying out the task. Mine is based on how they had interpreted the actual task and then I just looked at their writing and then I looked at next steps for them as teacher.'
Teacher J: 'Fine it helped me with the Y1s. As they were doing it I was making notes on what I was asking them and what they could do and what help they needed and I felt it was easier with the Y1s doing that especially because they are new this year.'
Teacher O: 'No different to what I normally do.'

(2)   *What did you find out about how the children were doing as writers from your analysis? (Learning behaviours; conceptual understanding)*

Teacher F: 'Even though this assessment is all new, as a teacher I have done a piece of writing to find where the children are at and done it at different stages of the year to see how they have progressed and I would have obviously looked at the writing and been analysing as a teacher as to what they can do and where they need to go from here.'
Teacher J: 'Year 1 there was more of a difference than what I thought originally, some of them were getting the initial, medial and final sounds, child H was just getting initial sounds and so that's more of her needs now and something that we are in the process of sorting

out our phonics groups and how we sort them into ability groups, so obviously we need to get that going.'

Teacher O: 'It is their phonic knowledge, the grapheme/ phoneme, they can hear the sounds, they are not even at the stage of hearing the initial sounds, actually hearing initial, medial and final sounds but they don't know what these sounds look like so they have had a lot of work done in Reception in listening to sounds so they have never really been pointed to the letters so we are working through the 'jolly phonics' programme which is set up so that they can start CVC pretty fast, we have started that already. The other issue is that two of the children don't know that a word is a unit so we are doing a lot in guided reading, with me, 'show me your pointing finger', starting to see the unit of meaning, cutting up words when they are reading, so those are the two main teaching points.

(3) *Were there any other aspects of their learning or was the analysis just at the word level? (Word, sentence, text – three interrelated strands)*

Teacher F: 'They are all at different levels. Some have mark-making, some have got some sounds, but although these three particular children have got some letter recognition, for me with the Y1s I knew that letter recognition was going to be a focus with the Y1s anyway'.

Teacher J: 'When they were with the puppets they were describing the story. The Y1s were saying more of the speech of the story language to re-tell the story (long pause) so what I have done we have got these books for them, the continuation books and I have put their writing assessments in there and stuck the analysis in there for each child and we have also been collecting other pieces of work. It might be teacher-led or independent. We have done that for all the children. As you can see from this work it's them choosing to go and write.'

Teacher O: 'So whenever we do a story we re-tell it so they know what happens at the beginning, middle and end, but it was just a focus for them – what's happening in that picture? He's going to see grandma. So, what are you going to write? Getting them to say the sentence again, I was getting them to match something to the picture.

(4) *Is there anything about your teaching which will change because of your analysis of the children's work? (Reflective practitioner)*

Teacher F: [Pause] 'Well I am going to have more focus on letter recognition and sounds just to push them forward and also with the formation of sentences so to have the structure within the sentence so maybe not with them to be writing for themselves but for them to be putting words into order to form a sentence and to form a sentence and to see if they can spot because we have done that and I suppose it has been in light of this to have the structure of the sentence like what comes at the beginning? What do we need to remember? Get them to read through what they are writing to help them make sense of what they are seeing and to help them as they are writing, do you know what I mean?'

Teacher J: 'Yes, anyway we need to set up the phonics group, teach the 'jolly phonics', to write the sounds because a lot of them they are actually good at sounding out but they can't identify the letter and that is what's stopping them from writing more.'

Teacher O: 'Yes, yes, these are early days and it was an initial assessment so you do your assessments and the next week you have moved them around again so you think that they have got different needs to that group, as a result of that I know what different children need.'

(5)   *Are your models of assessment based on any literature? (Professional development; theory in Initial Teacher Training (ITT)*

Teacher F: 'I think as I said to you assessment for me is going to be a huge target for me this year because I have got very little experience using it.'

Teacher J: 'No, no, there has not been anything that I have read.'

Teacher O: 'No [firmly], it is based on what I know.'

(6)   *What about individual needs, how do you feel about that? (Differentiation; guided group methodology)*

Teacher F: 'Maybe I should have done a "top", a middle and a bottom because I think I would have been able to see a difference in the development across the three abilities but here because they are about the same level I think I am going to see them all moving on the same.'

Teacher J: 'Well I am not used to sitting with individual children, homing in on how they are thinking, questioning them, so that is, you know, a different way of assessing them that is very informative and may be...'

Teacher O: 'This an assessment, OK but now that I have made my judgement on it and decided what the ... was going to be, they may not be with me the next time you come so I might just have child A and B with me because they are on different stages whereas child B and child C they may come another time because they have slightly different needs.'

(7)   *What is your understanding of assessment? (Testing v. assessment; integration)*

Teacher F: 'Assessment for me is going to be a huge target this year because I have got very little experience using it.'

Teacher J: 'But I wouldn't do these assessment pieces every day, they are just one-offs for the benefit of this, whereas I am teaching and scaffolding all other times, the days that I am working with them. If I am not there (i.e. when the assessment is done unsupported) what can you do without me? Without the teacher that is truly what you can do, sometimes the children can become reliant on the teacher being there, you know, 'what do I do now?' and the teacher tells them, which is fine, but I also think the children need to know that they don't always need that teacher and when she is not around they can still do it.'

Teacher O: 'I knew I was going to be doing this with Y1 so I was assessing their developmental writing and they did not need to have any keywords so teacher F's class is different to mine so we decided that we all would have the same format but we would do the assessments in the way that we wanted to do them.'

(8) *What teaching style do you use for the assessment? (Repertoire, e.g. whole class individual/groups?)*

Teacher F: 'Maybe I could have helped them and that way I would have had a more true reflection of what they can write because they were forgetting what they had done, like child Y, she was really using her fingers, she was pointing at all her words as she was reading it back.'

Teacher J: 'Because it was an assessment I would have seen that as showing them the way too much. In the weeks before, I was modelling and writing a different story. At the beginning of the story you'd be looking at finger spaces, capital letters and full stops. Yes, I see this [the assessment] as if we want to see what they can do they need to do it individually with no help so you get a true picture of what they can do.'

Teacher O: 'Yes, it wouldn't necessarily be an assessment session it would just be general practice. I might now and again set something up specific to see if they are using what we have put into practice, so because we have been doing some phonics recently I might check to see if they are using...[voice trails off].'

Visit 3: 17 November

Observation comments on teachers' assessments

(1) *Emphasises learning goals, makes them explicit and expects children to be able to master the curriculum?*

Teacher J: Wanted the children to master the curriculum, focus was on process goals; learning goals not expressed; projection of learning not explicitly made.

Teacher F: Made learning goals explicit and enabled the children to succeed.

Teacher O: Did not emphasise learning goals, did not identify individual learning goals; emphasised minimum requirements of completing the task.

(2)   *Carefully organises and sequences curriculum experiences?*

Teacher J: Meticulously set out resources for each child; modelled a completed task content, child was expected to replicate.
Teacher F: Organised experiences carefully and enabled individual competences to be demonstrated.
Teacher O: Teacher generated resources; developmental steps were not appropriate and with omissions throughout.

(3)   *Clearly explains and illustrates what children are to learn?*

Teacher J: Over-explained and provided a total example of what the children were to do and to complete.
Teacher F: Through the resources the children each had a clear illustration to support them in their writing; she monitored her explanations through a metacognitive approach, e.g. 'I like how you have gone back to re-read your sentence to make sure you have not missed any words out'.
Teacher O: Explained what the children were to *do* and to complete; no mention of individual 'learning' and process

(4)   *Frequently asks direct and specific questions to monitor students' progress and check their understanding?*

Teacher J: No direct or specific questions which addressed the children's learning; focused on presentational features rather than learning.
Teacher F: Intermittently asked pointed questions to individuals specifically in relation to their work and what they had done: 'Have you finished that sentence?' 'How do we know?'
Teacher O: Made statements rather than asking specific questions, e.g. repeated use of 'How many words? Count them with me.' Eg 'I like parrots'.

(5)   *Provides children with ample opportunity to practise, gives prompts and feedback to ensure success and correct mistakes, and allows students to practise a skill until it is over-learnt or automatic?*

Teacher J: Theme had been taught and practised over previous two weeks; no feedback during the session.
Teacher F: Individualised support towards learning goal; discussed miscues with children, e.g. child omitted word 'man' in a sentence, teacher encouraged child to locate the omitted word in another sentence. Climate of success: one of the three children in the sample is now demonstrating automaticity.

Teacher O: Children interested in 'pets' theme and teacher indicated that a lot of oral work had taken place; teacher supplied solutions rather than encouraging children to enquire about their own interests and thoughts on the theme.

(6) *Reviews regularly and holds children accountable for work*

Teacher J: No review, teacher over-scaffolded support so that children were not accountable for their own work.

Teacher F: Reviewed regularly at key learning points, e.g. at completion of child's sentence, teacher got child to read sentence and this supported the child's development of the next sentence in the sequence; teacher did not tell children their next steps in sequence of learning, e.g. use of correct vowels.

Teacher O: No evidence of review or accountability.

Post-assessment interview

(1) *How did you design the assessments? (Task set up)*

Teacher J: 'Last time I looked at it as if it was an assessment without any help from me because I have never done it before. So this time I did it more as a lesson and how I would teach.'

Teacher F: 'Well I listened to what you said last time about having the words, so the words wouldn't mean anything because they are still struggling to read and I thought that the pictures which are kind of sequenced and that it's made for a purpose so that they can look at the pictures to help them.' [Assessment had pictures of 'food' nouns that would aid the children in their writing. Assessment sheet was of high quality for the more independent learner.]

Teacher O: 'In terms of what they actually do?' [Assessment was designed around the children's interest in animals and pets.] 'So I thought I would take it in that direction so it was a mixture of what they had been learning in their information books and what we had been doing in class.'

(2) *How did you teach prior to the assessment? (Quality of instruction)*

Teacher J: 'We have done lots of work on instructions and we have used a lot of the sequencing words and doing instructions.'

Teacher F: 'We have been looking at non-fiction texts all last week and half the week before and looking at features of non-fiction and how they give information. That kind of language as well so we have just been building up, this isn't something that I have done whereas it was before' [i.e. in the first assessment I observed]. 'I think for the first time there are all these expectations of what you wanted to see and now this is about me and my teaching and so I shouldn't having to be planning something completely different so this is what I wanted to do.'

Teacher O: 'So for the last two weeks we have been looking at closed sentences using words like … and then the last two weeks we have been looking at key words.'

(3)   *How do you integrate the teaching and learning needs that have emerged from the children's responses to the assessment? What has emerged from the children's responses to the assessment? (Breadth of understanding)*

Teacher J: 'We look at what they are interested in and use that as a kind of thing to run with so they have been interested in food so what they like to learn about food so we made cakes and then we thought we'd find out about flour … so we have looked at what they want to learn and put that in the context of writing.'

Teacher F: 'I think they need to practise saying the sentences out loud so it's a step back from the writing. Like child A is able to read out her sentences and questions like 'Does that still make sense?' 'What words are missing?'

Teacher O: 'With those three children? Child Z is not as far on as I thought she was because child D has moved on from doing initial sounds and maybe final sounds and now he is spelling whole words, whereas child Z is not.'

(4)   *From doing the assessment today is there anything that has changed in your thinking? (Modification/reflective teacher)*

Teacher J: 'I think they sat for a long while and maybe I chose too many pictures and … I should have chosen three pictures with those boys.'

Teacher F: 'I think they need to practise saying the sentences out loud so that it is a step back from the writing. Like child A is able to read out her sentences and questions, like 'Does that still make sense?' 'What words are missing? and we need the practice of putting sentences back in order so that they are not always writing, and I felt that this worked really well [points to alphabet chart] for them to be able to identify the letters to connect with the sounds.

Teacher O: 'With those three in particular? Child O, the girl in the middle, she has just come back from Pakistan last week, she is very quiet anyway, I think I am going to change her group because she needs more attention. It's not because she can't do it, she needs a kind of relationship, she doesn't like to be in a big group. Child Z is not so far on as I thought she was because child D has moved on from doing initial sounds and maybe final sounds and now he is spelling whole words, and child Z is not. In fact she just wrote a string of initial sounds and she was not reading back what she had written and so she has not moved to where child D is at. She is very erm, erm…on the special needs because of her behaviour.

(5)   *Would the children have noticed anything different in your behaviour from your normal teaching style? (Testing v. assessment styles)*

Teacher J: 'No, they would not have noticed anything different because I do model writing. Maybe I had more word cards for them to use, e.g. flour, sugar, it's just getting all those things ready.'
Teacher F: 'I think I am more vocal, the stuff I was doing on the carpet I am doing more of because of the reading, and what I need to be doing all the time as part of the lesson, so before I didn't think I needed to keep doing it. It has given the children that reinforcement all the time because it is lots of repetition that's what they need. Again through the reading it has made me go back and simplify things for myself and for the level that the children are at, things I was doing but not doing enough.'
Teacher O: 'No, not at all.'

Visit 4: 15 December

(1)   *How did you find doing the analysis?*

Teacher F: 'I thought it went really, really well. The fact that they had the pictures to go along with the words helped them to read so lots of children were looking at the initial letter [to help them] to read. I thought the fact that they had the words helped them to be more fluid in their writing. The reading helped [me] a lot but common-sense things you overlook. You think you are doing certain things but you are not, I realised I was not saying enough of "Keep saying the sentence out loud", "Does it sound right so you do not miss any words out". [Refers back to first piece of reading that was distributed to all three teachers (Iverson & Depree, 1994). In the first assessment piece that the children did when they were looking for initial sounds by giving them the alphabet mats [suggested in the literature] they were able to find the letter to match their sounds, using the mat with less intervention from me, which gave them more confidence in their own ability.'
Teacher O: 'It was interesting, they came out very different from what I expected, after grouping them initially and thinking they were all at similar levels but now they have all got completely different needs so I don't think I can work them as a group.'
Teacher J: 'Well it seems so long ago now … it went well, they enjoyed doing it and [the girl] worked very enthusiastically and the

two boys worked well, they chose to carry on working and finish it in the afternoon, as well as that writing going on, we also have the children making cakes with the different ingredients.

(2) *What did you find out about how the children were doing as writers from your analysis?*

Teacher O: 'Yes, they have all got such specific needs, child D is fine, he has got the concentration, he has got a lot of skills, remembers key words, he has got good phonic knowledge, so whoever he would work with he would be a good role model. Child T, she was on the special needs and I dropped her down a level, she has got such concentration issues but she is young and I am not expecting any more, I think I am expecting too much so, see my class is a completely different nature to the other two classes, I have the really young children, she [child T] finds it really hard to concentrate for anything longer than 5 to 10 minutes and that [session] was too long for her to sit at the table. No, child C, she can't make her needs known, she needs to be in a one-to-one situation. I wouldn't work those three together again, they really have got completely different needs.

Teacher J: 'Really well, they have got so much willingness to do it and I have just started doing one to one reading with them and we also do guided reading groups that are ability based and those three children are in the same group and we have got books at their level which they can't read but they can look at the pictures and they are really enjoying it and they say "when is it our turn, when can we do our reading?" And we have also started our phonics groups and they are going well.

(3) *Were there any other aspects of their learning (that you were focusing on) or was the analysis just at the word level?*

Teacher O: 'No, it's not based just on writing it's on the children and where they are at personally, their personal development, especially children this young, you know, child T needs these short bursts because of her concentration, child U needs a friend, she needs that security of having a friend around her.

Teacher J: The guided reading sessions are helping, there are lots of things contributing, also it is the speaking and listening.

(4) *Is there anything about your teaching which will change because of your analysis of the children's work?*

Teacher F: 'I think it has made me realise the importance of just talking. Initially I would have given this activity out and I would have said "Now remember your full stops and capital letters and say your sentence out loud", but now that is not enough. For example, child A just got on with it and I think she will become a good role model for the other children. It will be helping the other children because they won't keep turning to me, they will use each other to develop their thinking and more independence because lots of children now are coming up to me especially these three children because they are very keen writers and they are constantly writing in the classroom and they will ask me, "How do you spell this ..." and I say "How are you going to find that out for yourself?" and get them into the habit. They are also looking at other children's work which is important for them. Children probably learn more from other children. The fact that I have tried it out with these three children, they then became the role models for the other children but are still role models between themselves and they are all at different stages even though they are the top children, it is the starting point for lots of different things. I think role modelling and getting the children to learn amongst themselves is my next step. I overlook a lot of things and to give more importance to physical resources rather than just talking, for me that would be my next step forward, to push on the conversation, questioning, questions which develop their thinking more.'

Teacher O: 'I think initial groupings, I don't think groupings actually work in my class, I like it as and when they want to do something, generally with the Y2 I might take a lower group, the Y1 will just come over when they want to, they don't work in ability groups, having said that I wouldn't have grouped them initially based on their phonic knowledge.'

Teacher J: 'I would say that a writing task [is done] every week and I am more conscious of doing it with the Y1 and I am also doing it one to one which takes time to get through but I don't think I need to do it for the whole year. Yes it is making me more focused on the Y1 so it is more manageable rather than do it in a group of six; I think they get more out of the three grouping and that is their ability level right now, but further down the line I might have two or three children.'

(5)   *Are your models of assessment based on any literature?*

Teacher F: 'Because I have not managed to find something like that I don't feel that any [previous] reading has really impacted on my teaching but having read those small pieces that were easy to digest it was so common-sense in small doses I can use it in different ways in my teaching and extend what I do.'

(6)   *What about individual needs? How do you feel about that?*

Teacher F: 'I think these two children, child H and child Z, lots of oral forming of the sentences, working in pairs, using child Y (more

advanced as an independent writer) in there to be that role model, she is more independent than those two, she gets a little bit tired because we don't expect the Y1s to do that much writing so that when they do, again she does get tired but her ability can push the other two children on further in a different way than what I can do. I still think everything seems a little bit too formal. Child Y got on with it but I sat in between child H and child Z, so I think child Y should sit in between those two and I think they would have benefited more from talking to each other and given them more confidence. They don't realise how much they can do, especially child H when I say to her "Have you done all that by yourself?" and the look on her face was lovely … sharing their work and recognition from their peers so a lot of it is all to do with their confidence.'
Teacher O: 'Well what I have done is that I have identified that I need to do more modelling of writing, definitely spend more time using the board so that they are seeing it over and over again and what I am also doing is going in with them to the different areas to see if they are drawing and for me to write alongside them so they see me write.'
Teacher J: [No response]

(7)   *What is your understanding of assessment?*

Teacher F: 'It comes back to my personal idea of what I thought assessment was about, an understanding of that it is about having lots of scaffolding in place and what [effect] that has on the children in terms of moving them forward, their confidence, and in terms of me getting a true picture of what the child can do, and I think this is the key and I think when you leave a child to work independently you think that is a true reflection, for example, using those word mats as prompts you get a completely different picture of what the child can do, it is not just about leaving the child on their own, it is not necessarily going to give me a true picture. I don't think exams help them. I think the assessment for learning is helping teachers now that they know that their teacher assessment is going to count and it has made me realise that this is as valuable [points to child's work which she has analysed].'
Teacher O: 'It is what we do every day, you constantly make some sort of judgement, some sort of assessment, every step of your day is linked to the children, whether it is a form of a test, it is like getting babies off the bottle trying to get people away from tests and getting people to make judgements not just about where we are but it is something you just have to do. This is something I have been doing [shows self-made checklist], I have identified the reluctant writers and what I think they need so I am going to try and do some, build up word banks with them, so for example this is a boy [outside the sample] who has speech problems so every day I will tick off what we have tried. I mean my

TA would say, "We have done this…" and they are very specific and I could probably do this for everyone in the classroom.'

Teacher J: 'Originally assessment was, you know we talked about the continuation books and I saw that as being an assessment, whereas now when I am working one to one as well, I can see them progressing and I can see where their next steps are and see that writing focus as an assessment as well as being a writing task.'

(8)   *What teaching style do you use for the assessment?*

Teacher F: 'Yes it has changed, it is the whole scaffolding process, just thought assessment was giving the children a completely different piece with no help, but that is not moving them on because you are knocking the confidence of the children. So they know their sounds but they have not got the letters and the key words are not flowing and if you are not giving them the opportunity to practise before they are ready to write it down then it is not helping them and it is all of that kind of thing. It is to give children support that is appropriate to individual children to help them to provide a piece of work that is their ability at that time.'

Visit 5: 12 January

Observation schedule (Teacher F absent on this occasion)

(1)   *Emphasises learning goals, makes them explicit and expects children to be able to master the curriculum?*

Teacher J: Emphasised general goals but not individual goals, e.g. generic use of capital letters, full stops, finger spaces. Used an initial framing sentence of 'I remember when…' to start each child's response.

Teacher O: No emphasis on individual learning goals, emphasised use of full stops (surface features) and the use of two target words 'went' and 'the'.

(2)   *Carefully organises and sequences curriculum experiences*

Teacher J: Used a common planned sheet which sequenced the content/responses; did not use stimulus pictures on the assessment sheet but used the Jill Murphy storybook, *Peace at Last*, to orally structure the story for the children, she then reinforced the oral structure by writing up the children's related experiences.

Teacher O: Supplied [5] stimulus pictures directly from the Jill Murphy story and ruled lines to provide a structure for the child; she rehearsed sentences and content as a class and then with the group being assessed.

(3) *Clearly explains and illustrates what children are to learn?*

Teacher J: Clearly explained and illustrated her expectations for learning and completion of the task she had set.
Teacher O: Very clearly reinforced what was required and supplied the actual words of the response.

(4) *Frequently asks direct and specific questions to monitor children's progress and check their understanding?*

Teacher J: Teacher asked questions to monitor children's progress and ascertain understanding. Asked each child to read back their completed sentences for syntactical accuracy but missed significant teaching points, e.g. failed to pick up on errors such as inappropriate tenses and significant overgeneralisations in some spellings of words, or turn these into teaching points.
Teacher O: Questions from the teacher emerged only when children stopped or could not complete the required answer. This was largely down to the artificiality of the task which (i) did not involve or interest them and (ii) had been over-rehearsed to restrict it to a 'copying' of four/five words. The children were regurgitating what 'teacher' had already supplied and there was no sense of exploring new knowledge.

(5) *Provides children ample opportunity to practise, gives prompts and feedback to ensure success and correct mistakes, and allows children to practise a skill until it is over-learnt or automatic?*

Teacher J: Supplied many extended opportunities, e.g. restructuring the group composition in the class, i.e. working more on a one to one basis with children, also extending that thinking to small guided reading sessions, i.e. integration of phonic work, linking it to writing time/tasks. Signs of a developing automaticity are emerging from the children and this is evidenced by the decrease in demand for 'help', 'what do I do?' from the children. Some evidence that learning is being internalised by the children, e.g. in the quality of the sentences constructed by the children.
Teacher O: Prompts extended too much into 'detailing' the exact nature of each individual's response, i.e. all five picture/ sentences were reduced to the same model, there was no deviation from her original script; feedback did not support movement or progression in learning; feedback was supplied but was limited to phonemic representation, e.g. a sound of an initial letter, 'f' for fridge. There was a focus on sight vocabulary in having two key words, and one of these was included in her script for each sentence.

(6) *Reviews regularly and holds children accountable for (own) work?*

> Teacher J: Was reviewing positively to indicate progress for the child, e.g. 'Now look what you have done, you couldn't do that last time on your own'.
> Teacher O: No evidence of reviewing or of checking with the children on their accountability, e.g. as a child completed the sentences he/she was simply released to play in the classroom.

Post-assessment interview

(1) *How did you design the assessments?*

> Teacher O: 'I wanted something very simple and one in which we could use the pictures [from the story] so we would have the picture cues where they would have a very simple sentence and with two key words on which we would focus [went, the].
> Teacher J: 'I didn't want it to be too long for them so I put the lines down for them to write in and the boxes for them to draw their pictures and giving them the beginnings of three sentences, e.g. "I remember when…", "I felt…" and "In the end…".'

(2) *How did you teach prior to the assessment?*

> Teacher O: 'This morning? This week? … We have pictures for every part of the story so all of the Y1 got up and the Y2 had to sequence the pictures, to put in order what had happened then we went round the Y1 children and said the sentences, for example "Snore, snore went Mrs Bear" and we said the sentences all the way around. Then after we play we picked out a couple and wrote the sentences and we did a bit of work using the magnetic letters.'(sic)
> Teacher J: 'We introduced the book [the Jill Murphy storybook] and read the book. We talked about the different things to keep the bear awake and we talked about their own experiences and what kept them awake. They came up with things like nightmares, baby crying, shouting, television on, work going on outside and then when we came back after play I took one of the children's ideas and wrote a sentence together. Mainly me thinking up the sentence but using the child's previous ideas and getting them to count the words and then getting them to come up and write the word 'I' and getting them to sound out the words, the simple words that they could hear, especially the Y1 and then get the lower Y1 to come up and put the full stops in and to focus on the finger spaces. I was really impressed at how the children have started to read back their writing.'

(3) *How do you integrate the teaching and learning needs that have emerged from the children's responses to the assessment? What has emerged from the children's responses to the assessment?*

Teacher J: 'I think reading back the sentences was very useful and I am going to focus on that more. There are still some letters that the children do not know and that is something we are still doing, our phonics groups. Counting, remembering the sentence, more carpet work in which I say a three-worded sentence and the children have to write it down, count it, and now let's try a sentence with four words in it.'

Teacher O: 'Really I still like to personalise it, they have all got individual needs. Child R is definitely at a par if not further than child C. He has really picked up things very quickly, he seems to be a good match for child T and I also wanted to assess at which stage he was. So the boys who came a bit later have all got such specific needs. They need more words so they are looking at initial sounds, they are not understanding a word as a unit. Child H is very very clever.'

(4) *From doing the assessment today is there anything that has changed your thinking?*

Teacher J: 'I wanted to do this type of writing because it is different. We have done imaginative stories, recounts and I wanted them to write their own but I think maybe what I could do next is not necessarily have them at the tables writing. Maybe we could go outside, specially the boys as child U is slouching in his chair and maybe he needs to be a bit more active, maybe using a clipboard and getting them to write from that rather than a table. I could do more paired work as well with the Y2; they do like to read to the Y2 and we do that a lot with the reading, even when the Y1 have these very basic books, the Y2 still listen so I think if we do it as paired writing and do that a lot more with the Y2 children.'

Teacher O: 'The little boy who came second really, at the beginning of the year he was just mark-making. He would come and write very happily but it would be just marks but he is making words now. No bother with the cubes even though he didn't get "tick tock" but put "went" at the top. He is not necessarily getting the order and when he read it back, he actually went up here and said "tick tock" went the clock and read the words in whatever random order he read them. He is recognising words as units and he is actually pointing to the words so that has gone from letter strings.

(5)   *Would the children have noticed anything different in your behaviour from your normal teaching style?*

Teacher J: 'No. I don't think so, no. I support them...'

Q: 'Would you say that the way that you work now has become a very natural part of your everyday teaching?'

Teacher J: 'Yes, yes, yes. I don't think they would notice anything different, maybe if I went into one of the areas and started writing they would think that was a bit different and they would think "Miss does not usually do that...".'

Teacher O: 'No. That's the same as we always do.'

Q: 'What would you call that session?'

Teacher O: 'I would call it a guided writing session, you know we are being guided in our writing basically and it is the sort of thing they do further up the school, it is not free writing it is guided.'

Case study 2

The work of four children is used to exemplify our approach and the type of analysis undertaken to support the young writers. To enable us to analyse we used an instructional framework of questions (Depree & Iverson 1994) such as: Did the child enjoy listening to a range of stories read by the teacher? How did the child demonstrate this engagement? While observing the child writing his/her assessment, did he/she appear to be enjoying the task? What are the child's psycho-motor skills? Do these include levels of co-ordination, dexterity, strength, speed, fine and gross motor skills? Were the children at the single phoneme, consonant framework, multiple phonemes, whole word construction stage? Were the children able to retain, internalise and transfer the whole or parts of a story? (Boyle & Charles 2011).

Data and discussion

The class had been working on 'traditional stories' as part of a five-week theme. 'Goldilocks' was one of the traditional stories which the children had experienced as part of their Literacy programme. The first piece which the guided group wrote is based on that story. Their second piece of writing, written five weeks later, was a story about an imaginary journey which was stimulated by classroom work on the topic of 'journeys'.

Child One: Xenab at the start demonstrated a lack of confidence and did not appear to view herself as capable of producing written text like her peers. Research by Perrenoud identifies that:

Difficulties in schooling can be explained in the differences between pupils, often described as failings or shortcomings in pupils who do not reach the norm: socio-cultural handicap, linguistic poverty, poor family background and lack of motivation and support; so many expressions which stigmatise pupils in difficulty. (Perrenound 1998, p. 93).

It was apparent that Xenab's affective domain (intrinsic motivation, self-esteem) needed support, and from the provision of that support it was hoped that her confidence in herself as a writer would develop. Teaching strategies utilised to address this included involving Xenab in the (metacognitive) process of analysing her own writing with support. We ensured that she had consistency of conditions within the guided group with whom she talked and wrote collaboratively during teaching sessions. Young learners learn to write from correctly contextualised modelling (Berninger et al. 2006) and within this collaborative process miscues were discussed and resolved (Boyle & Charles 2011).

Child Two: Hana's reluctance to orally retell her version of the story to the rest of the group was indicative of her overall shyness. However, through the means of a guided group strategy she listened to the other children retell their stories which provided her with prompts and important sequential events. Hana required oral support with repetition of

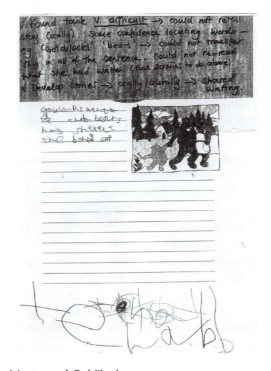

Figure 5.4 Xenab's story of Goldilocks

each phrase/sentence she chose to write. She was able to use her growing sight vocabulary to read and then write the beginning of her story from the prompt 'bubble' ('one' 'day' 'went' 'bears'). Hana's story using Applebee's (1978) construct of story suggests that it has elements of a 'focused and unfocused chain'.

> When a child is able to create a story with a main character at the centre who then goes through events that are linked ... based on Vygotsky's concept theory (1962) the organisation is not conceptual but "a pseudo concept ... before true concepts emerge children make use of pseudo-concepts which are superficially similar but which remain perceptually rather than conceptually based". (Applebee 1978, p. 62)

Hana understands the structure of a story but has not learned to focus and give the story direction; there is some cohesion to the events of her story and little content as it abruptly trails off in its conclusion (Simmons & Gebhardt 2009).

Research on the merits of guided group teaching and learning (Hayes 2008; Tomlinson 2001) and on how the value of reading aloud to children affects vocabulary development (Robbins & Ehri 1994; Whitehurst & Lonigan 1998), acquisition of literary syntax and vocabulary (Purcell-Gates et al. 1995), and story text (Duke & Kays 1998). However, researchers have found a negative relationship between the amount of time teachers spend on reading aloud in kindergarten and children's decoding skills (Meyer et al. 1994). These studies suggest that merely reading books aloud is not sufficient for accelerating children's oral vocabulary development and listening comprehension. Instead, the way books are shared with children matters (McGee & Schickedanz 2007, p. 742).

Child Three: Burhan retold his version of the story to the group and his enthusiasm and enjoyment spilled over into his narrative characterisations (voice, actions, phrases) in which the teaching roles became de-regulated (Perrenoud 1998) and the guided group in Vygotskyan (1978) terms 'had a greater opportunity to understand, internalize and therefore lay down the foundations for the development of dialogical skills that support text production' (Rijlaarsdam et al. 2008, p. 60). Burhan did not require any oral support for his written account of his story or any additional support for his spellings. Using Applebee's (1978) construct of story, Burhan's written piece suggests elements of a 'focused chain' alongside some aspects of 'narrative'.

> Narratives expand on the focused chain by including additional features. The centre of the story is developed while a new idea or circumstance develops out of a previous idea. This propels the story forward, often ending with a climax, in narrative everything is held together by the core which relies on abstract or concrete bonds (Simmons & Gebhardt 2009, p. 3)

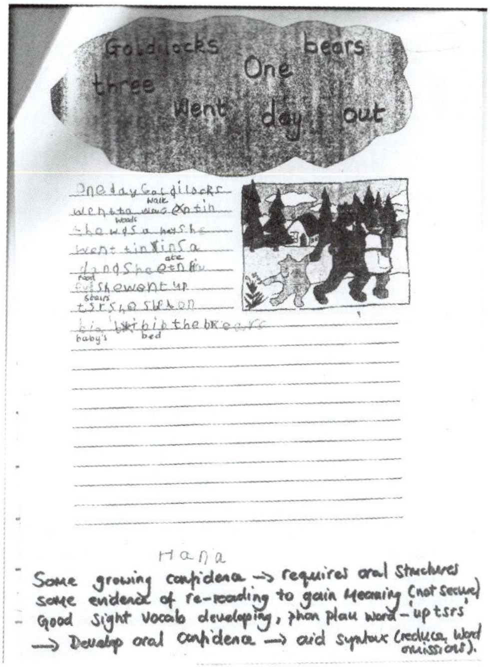

Figure 5.5 Hana's story of Goldilocks

In a 'true narrative', the incidents are linked both by 'centring and chaining and are more fully controlled' (Applebee 1978, p. 69). Burhan understands the structure of a story but is limited in syntactical, grammatical and text cohesion features which result in a loss of flow to his story. However, his creative imagination and awareness of audience are developing, note how he concludes his story: 'The house disappeared' (Figure 5.5). The importance of Burhan's ending is significant in this context, as he is the only member of the group to write one. In an attempt to understand Hana and Xenab's omission of a story ending, see Berninger et al. (2006) who draw attention to an understanding that 'language is not a unitary construct ... and that Language by Ear, Language by Mouth, Language by Eye and Language by Hand are each complex functional systems that draw on common as well as unique processes to achieve different goals' (p. 62). This suggests that Hana and Xenab were constrained by transcription processes and the demand on working memory to complete conclusions to their stories (Bourke & Adams 2010; Hayes & Flower 1986).

Child Four: Sultan's oral retelling of the story featured elements that he found interesting and important as events in the story. His written account demonstrates that he does not always write for meaning as he confuses the word 'bear' for 'day' in his opening sentence. He writes

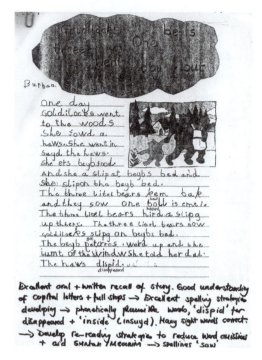

Figure 5.6   Burhan's story of Goldilocks

predominantly in the correct tense and occasionally confuses his use of prepositions. Stein and Albro (1997 in Senechal & Young 2008) suggest that children who produce well structured stories must organise the events that occurred in a sequential meaningful way (p. 30). Sultan's story with its predominant constraints on Language by Hand (Berninger et al. 2006) is clearly following a sequential series of events through 'focused and unfocused chains' (Applebee 1978).

The second piece of narrative writing continued within the guided group format. Because we felt that Applebee's framework was limiting our analysis in this instance we decided to use Hudson and Shapiro's (1991) narrative framework. We felt that the latter was more structurally comprehensive and provided more elements to the stories which enabled richer analysis. The children were asked to write an imaginary journey stemming from the original Big Book entitled: 'Biff's aeroplane'. The children collectively composed their version of Biff's journey:

> One cold day Biff wanted to take her aeroplane to the park. Biff wished that her aeroplane was magic so she pretended if she pulled the string it would go to new places. Biff got smaller and the aeroplane got bigger. She got inside and went to London to play in the zoo with the animals. Biff got tired and got bigger and went home.

As the teacher scribed their ideas they were encouraged to keep re-reading the text to maintain cohesion and the overall flow of the story.

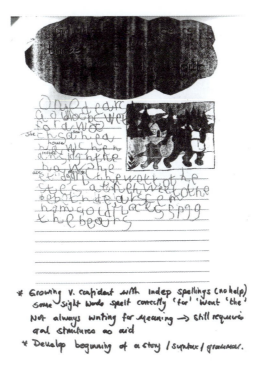

Figure 5.7 Sultan's story of Goldilocks

Burhan chose to narrate his idea of 'pulling the string to get smaller to fit into the plane' and Xenab decided to include 'London' as a location when asked by the teacher, 'Where will Biff travel to when she is in the plane?'. The question 'What will she do when she is there?' enabled Sultan to respond: 'Play in the zoo with all of the animals'. Hana chose not to orally contribute to the group's composing process. Burhan concluded the story with 'Biff got tired and got bigger and went home'. Fisher and Williams (2000) remind us that story writing for children 'provides them with the most complex of intellectual challenges' (p. 70). All the richness of the dialogue used by the group hasn't been captured in the brief version of the story above.

Guided group story writing is one of the processes in the social construction of learning. Vygotsky (1978) stated that 'learning is socially constructed during interaction with others and the relationship between literacy and social interaction is complex and significant to [children's] learning' (p. 243). Although the stories generated by the four children share similar content knowledge, closer analysis reveals differences in structural, micro-linguistic and contextual knowledge (Hudson & Shapiro 1991, p. 89). Three of the stories contain a formal beginning (Xenab) 'One day', (Burhan) 'One snowy day', (Hana) ' One sunny day', while Sultan has no formal beginning. Interestingly, Xenab's opening is the only one to attempt 'an orientation to introduce

Figure 5.8   Xenab's story of an imaginary journey

setting and characters' (Hudson & Shapiro 1991, p. 100): 'Biff was play-ing in the park'. The other three stories introduce a character with no setting: (Sultan) 'Biff pulled the string of the aeroplane'; (Burhan) ' Biff has an aeroplane'; (Hana) 'Biff pulled the string of the aeroplane'. All four of the stories assume audience awareness and do not give any back-ground information as to the central character's actions, motivations and intentions. Hindi and Hildyard (1983, in Hudson & Shapiro 1991) and Kemper (1984, in Hudson & Shapiro 1991) suggest that the 'inclu-sion of internal goals, motivations and reactions making more sophisti-cated story productions is absent from children's fictional stories before the age of around 8 years' (in Hudson & Shapiro 1991, p. 101).

In initiating 'events-goal directed actions'(Hudson & Schapiro 1991), three of the stories include references to this aspect of narrative construc-tion as Burhan, Sultan and Hana wrote: 'Biff pulled the string of the aero-plane'. Xenab omits this structural element and wrote: 'Biff went to London'. Interestingly all four of the children locate the central character in place and time (Sultan uses no time reference). The inclusion of cumula-tive events to add coherence features in Hana and Sultan's stories: (Hana) 'It flew higher and higher. Biff got smaller and smaller'; (Sultan) 'It went faster and faster Biff got smaller and smaller'. In contrast, Burhan uses the theme of 'shrinking' (which he initiated during the group composition) to conclude his story and moves away from a traditional/conventional

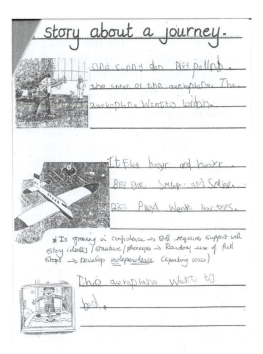

Figure 5.9   Hana's story of an imaginary journey

ending. Xenab does not include any reference to 'shrinking' which may suggest, as Hudson and Shapiro (1991) propose: 'For young children, the fit between the structure of knowledge and memory and the structure of the narrative genre is critical in determining narrative coherence ... and the amount of "translation involved between knowing and telling"' (p. 126).

All four children give minimal narrative detail in their stories, and the structural coherence specifically with regard to (Hudson & Shapiro 1991, p. 100) 'a problem or obstacle to achieving the intended goal and a resolution of the problem'. Their central character, Biff, travels on a journey (achieving the intended goal) in all of the stories. However, Sultan and Hana begin to develop how this goal was achieved: (Sultan) 'The aeroplane went to London. It went faster and faster. Biff gets smaller and smaller'; (Hana) 'It flew higher and higher. Biff got smaller and smaller'. In contrast, Xenab provides no detail of how this goal was achieved: 'Biff went to London'; similarly, Burhan: 'Biff went to England. It was snowy'. There are varying degrees of implied reader awareness across the four stories that generate quite different questions to different children: 'Why did Biff get smaller' (Sultan and Hana); 'How did Biff get to London?' (Burhan and Xenab). Is this more about memory, cognitive load, physical constraints on transcription, narrative awareness, motivation or lexical limitations in an analytical attempt to explain the differences across the four stories?

The fusion of illustrations and the children's writing is seen as a 'visual literacy integral to the composing process' (Boyle & Charles 2011, p. 12). Curtis and Bailey (2001) agree that 'pictures provide something to talk about ... and can be used to reinforce literal, critical and creative thinking' (p. 11). All four of the children appear to conclude their stories; Burhan's ending 'she got bigger and the aeroplane got smaller' suggests a movement into another episode and the reader is left with an air of expectancy and mystery. Similarly, Sultan's ending: 'Biff saw an aeroplane on the bed' suggests that he has not given his narrative a 'formal ending device' (Hudson & Shapiro 1991, p. 100). In contrast, Hana and Xenab's endings are more definitive in their descriptions: (Xenab) 'She went home'; (Hana) 'The aeroplane went to bed'. Pradl (1979) observes that children reach the end of their 'inventiveness span' fairly quickly and will abruptly finish stories with 'tag endings' (p. 23). Each of the children provides a different ending to the same illustration. Smith (1975, in Protheroe 2010, p. 33) suggests that 'many children find pictures difficult to interpret' and Pressley (1977, in Protheroe 2010, p. 33) argues that 'children need training before they can interpret representations of three- dimensional space in two dimensions' (in Protheroe 2010, p. 33).

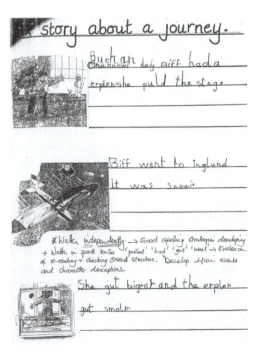

Figure 5.10 Burhan's story of an imaginary journey

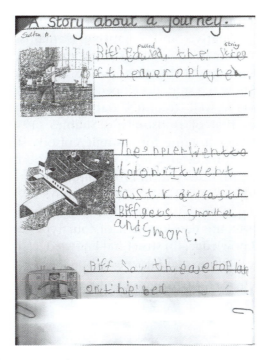

Figure 5.11   Sultan's story of an imaginary journey

A more conceptual analysis, as proposed by Protheroe (2010), suggests that 'understanding is not simply a matter of taking a literal interpretation of the meanings in a text ... meaning requires an interaction of information from the text with background knowledge ... and the inferences that they make' (p. 36). In short, all four of the children do not go beyond the illustrations except when each narrative reaches a 'high point' when Biff travels to London. For the writer, the developmental necessity of 'knowledge-based inferences can provide missing information, resolve discrepancies and predict unmentioned facts or events' (Mason & Just 2011, p. 314).

Findings

The study involved a relatively small number of teaching sessions and only reports on the first two stories, so cannot and does not claim to be conclusive. However, it does demonstrate that, on a small scale, close analysis guided by acknowledged research frameworks can be effective in supporting teaching pedagogy (Salvetti 2001, p. 79).

We addressed the issue of 'one size fits all' in teaching writing to emerging writers through utilising sound research methodologies in the field and a classroom structure of a guided group to address the children's affective, conative and cognitive domains simultaneously. Applebee's (1978) framework enabled us to analyse the young writers' stories against a conceptual structure. His six stages provided an initial understanding of how the story developed for the children from a simple 'heaping' of events to well structured narratives. The second analytical tool we used was that of Hudson and Shapiro (1991) based on the characteristics of the structure for a single episode story: (a) a formal beginning; (b) initiating events; (c) a problem or obstacle to achieving the intended goal; (d) a resolution of the problem; (e) a formal ending device (p. 100). In addition, Hudson and Shapiro's (1991) partial framework for studying narrative production was also incorporated with specific reference to the development of four types of knowledge and skill: (a) content knowledge, (b) structural knowledge, (c) micro-linguistic knowledge, and (d) contextual knowledge (p. 89).

Conclusions

Through using these analytical frameworks we obtained specific information about each child's progress and were able to scaffold support based on those individual learning needs. Because of this information and the affective domain environment of the guided group, we suggest that improvement in the children's stories was facilitated between story 1 and story 2 through this nurturing pedagogy (Goouch 2008). For example, Xenab still requires support with scribing to lessen her cognitive load and enable her to focus on her other needs, narrative structure, spelling and cohesion while she develops as an independent writer. This collaborative process within the guided group can be described as the establishment of 'a socio-cognitive apprenticeship in which teachers and students collaborate, inform, question, think aloud, self-correct, challenge and construct meaning together' (Englert et al. 2001, p. 211). In short, this should become a core pedagogical strategy for Xenab to develop as a story writer. Similarly, Sultan still requires strategies to support cohesion and narrative development, but his dominant need is motor development, and transcription, mapping by hand (Berninger et al. 2006). In contrast, Burhan is already demonstrating that he has been exposed to a wide range of narratives and his need is for knowledge-based inferences and evaluative-based inferences (Mason & Just 2011). He does not necessarily need illustrations to structure his story telling. Finally, Hana requires a paired collaborative approach (Boyle & Charles 2011; Topping 2001) to facilitate the oral aspect of story rehearsal, reducing the pressure on her for a written output.

Co-construction: The Active Involvement of Children in Shaping Learning

In this chapter we look at the pedagogic transactions between teacher and student. Not all children want to participate in their own learning; in this chapter we consider how the teacher can help to shift the student's attitude to active involvement in their own learning.

Generalisation is inevitable when an observer describes the profile of any class. There are always some children in the class who are willing to work harder in order to be noticed, to win praise, to outperform or outscore their peers, or for a range of other reasons, including to learn more. These students therefore fit well with formative assessment, because to work well formative assessment requires the student's co-operation at both the information-gathering stage and the adjustment stage. However, some children dislike the notion of demonstrating or evidencing how they think, how they organise themselves, how they construct a line of text or develop an argument and hypothesise. These pupils display active or passive resistance to the teacher's curiosity about their cognitive processes. A number of pupils do not aspire to learn as much as possible and are content to 'get by', just getting through the school day. The teaching contract in those cases is a fragile compromise: the teacher has to take care not to be unduly demanding, for that would elicit open revolt or defence strategies that are more difficult to control, such as cheating, absenteeism, displays of indifference and boredom (Chevallard 1986). Formative assessment inevitably presupposes a shift in this 'equilibrium point' towards a more serious and open attitude from the child towards learning based on the premise that he/she will benefit from the increased application and effort in the medium term.

Co-construction

Co-construction (or, its synonym, the active involvement of children in sharing learning) is a key aspect of formative teaching, learning and assessment. The 'changing of the regulation' (Perrenoud 1991, 1998) between teacher and pupil is key to rich, deep learning – and that is the aspiration and purpose of formative assessment. In England the Department for Children, Schools and Families (DCSF 2007) introduced a guidance paper *Improving Writing with a Focus on Guided Writing*. However, the main thrust of the guidance was identified as a means to focus on improving measured performance standards in writing as 'improving standards of writing at the end of key stage 2 is a national priority' (DCSF 2007, p. 5). The guidance does, however, define and promote the use of guided writing as a supportive structure for developing writing for each individual, that is 'the teacher is able to observe and respond to the needs of individuals within the group' (p. 6). However, if the development of the child as an autonomous writer (Boyle & Charles 2009; Zimmerman 2000) requires the child to be involved in the construction of their own learning, the guidance falls short in that it is didactic, highly structured and teacher-centred, e.g. the 'teacher provides opening' (DCSF 2007, p. 22), 'the teacher constructs an imaginary situation' (p. 18), 'the teacher introduces the lesson objectives' (p. 32). The child is clearly seen in a fixed subordinate role evidenced by the guidance's instructions on setting up writing opportunities (p. 18), and the pedagogical model being suggested echoes Alexander's (2004) 'closed recitation script'. The DCSF's guidance fails to recognise the complexity and level of demand required for one to emerge as a proficient writer; it does not acknowledge the 'individualisation of the learning trajectory' (Perrenoud 1998, p. 98). The guidance rather follows the model of linear stepped progression to becoming a writer which was critiqued by Flower (1989) in her analogy of the 'writer as switchboard operator, juggling a number of different demands ...' (in Yarrow & Topping 2001, p. 263).

Case study 1

Context: Whole class maths lesson, children sitting in a large circle facing a medium-sized container filled with coloured straw and the numbers 1–20 buried inside for the children to 'locate' them.

Teacher:	Let's find a number [all of the children rush to the container to pick out a number]. No, no, when it's your turn, you must go back to the circle and wait your turn. Eden pick out a number. [Eden takes his time to rustle through the straw, he picks out a number card, looks at it, then puts it back. The teacher does not notice as she is reminding the children to sit correctly. Eden picks out the number 2.] What's that number Eden?
Eden:	20.
Teacher:	Not 20, turn it around it's number t..t..t
Eden:	2.
Teacher:	Ismail go and choose a number.
Ismail:	3.
Teacher:	Bilal come and choose a number. [He turns around number 12 with a smile on his face but with no answer.]
Teacher:	Let's see if your friends can help you. [Hands go up around the circle with a chorus of whispers '12'.]
Teacher:	Amar come and choose a number, Mrs Hodge [classroom assistant] would you like to choose a child? [Two children stand up and pick out a number each. Amar is still standing holding her number '15' unsure of what it is.] What number has Sophie got? [Children shout out '9', teacher calls out four more children at the same time to pick out a number.]
Teacher:	Quick, get one out. [Mohammed holds up 14.] What comes before 13?
Mohammed:	15.
Teacher:	No, that's after, what is 14 and 1 less? You have to go backward. [Child's eyes look up into the air.] Oh I can see that you are working it out.
Mohammed:	18.
Teacher:	No. Who can help him out? [Children shout out '13'.] Good girl, good boy. [In the meantime, Amar did not receive any help with her number and quietly sat down unnoticed.]

(Continued)

(Continued)

Teacher:	Who has got number 1? [Child stands up.] Stand up who has got 1 and 1 more? [Child stands up], 2 and 1 more? [Children shout '3' and child stands up. The teacher continues with this number patterning until the children begin to predict what the next number will be before the teacher asks the question with '1 more', etc.]
Chorus of voices:	18.. 18.
Teacher:	No, no I don't want to hear 18, what is 17 and 1 more? [Some children shout '18'.] Now what is 18 and
Chorus of voices:	19.
Teacher:	No I don't want to hear that, what is 18 and 1 more? [Some children say the right number. Teacher continues until all the children are standing up with their numbers, they then count forwards and struggle a little counting backwards, the teacher then concludes the session by asking the children to place their numbers back in the tray.]

Analysis

Developing processes of co-construction

The first step is that children have to explain their problem-solving procedures to the rest of the class. Closely associated with this process is the idea that once one or more procedures had been presented, children should make additional proposals that differ from those already proposed. This second step demonstrates emerging comprehension of what constitutes a 'different procedure' (Lopez & Allal, 2007, p. 259). Qualitative classroom observation data were collected in two third grade classrooms (Gasim's and Miriam's) over a full school year. Although these two steps were the same in the microcultures of Miriam and Gasim's classrooms, other norms differed and therefore affected the way in which the first two steps (norms) functioned. One major difference concerned the norm of how students should take account of other children's proposals during whole class discussions. In Miriam's classroom, children were expected to reformulate (in their own words) the explanation given by another child or to pursue an explanation started by another pupil. In Gasim's class, children were expected to express an opinion about the relevance and the effectiveness of their peers' proposals and explanations. This difference in the norms regarding peer interaction was closely associated with different (sociomathematical) norms regarding the forms of problem solving that were considered acceptable or preferable. In Miriam's class, emphasis was put on trying out different equally acceptable procedures, whereas in Gasim's class priority was given to the progressive adoption of the procedures judged to be more effective for problem solving.

In Miriam's classroom, children were expected to present their explanations of problem-solving procedures in a very detailed, step-by-step way, from the starting point until the final answer. The children's explanations were often guided by teacher scaffolding based on a series of precise questions. When new procedures were explained, they were nearly always written up and remained available as a shared reference for subsequent work during the session. The norm that students should re-explain or pursue the explanation given by another child was a way of verifying that the children understood each other's proposals and therefore helped to build up a pool of meaningful procedures. However, the children were not involved in the assessment and validation of each others' proposals; this role was reserved for the teacher. Miriam's assessments of the children's proposals often included reformulations that introduced conventional (mathematical) terminology. However, she guided the discussion towards the validation of a variety of different solution procedures, all considered equally relevant and legitimate even though some of them were more distant from conventional mathematical solutions than others. The main sociomathematical norm regarding problem solving was that children should find several ways of solving a problem, try out different procedures and look for new methods so as to better understand underlying mathematical concepts. Throughout the year pupils continued to use a range of more or less sophisticated procedures that were all accepted as part of the 'taken-as-shared' practice in this classroom (Lopez & Allal 2007, pp. 252–65).

In Gasim's class, the children were expected to explain the general direction of their procedures without giving a detailed step-by-step account of each intermediate result. Gasim's style of questioning was more open-ended than Miriam's. Some elements were written up on the whiteboard but complete procedures leading to solutions were not recorded – as Miriam had done. Although Gasim encouraged the pupils to present and explain different procedures that were relevant for finding a solution to a problem, he gradually introduced a more restrictive sociomathematical norm. By questions leading pupils to compare their procedures and by direct statements, the norm was established that some procedures are more effective than others and that it is preferable to identify these procedures and use them. However, rather than validating the children's proposals himself, as Miriam did, Gasim tended to orchestrate peer exchanges during which several students expressed opinions about the relevance and effectiveness of other students' procedures and explanations. This led children to differentiate between mathematical procedures that are 'relevant' (going in a direction that can ultimately lead to a correct solution) and those that are 'relevant and effective' (leading rapidly without major risk of error to a correct solution). In contrast to the microculture of Miriam's class, the children in Gasim's class participated to a larger extent in the validation of acceptable practices, but because of the predominance of the norm of effectiveness, this led to a greater degree of standardisation of problem solving than in Miriam's class (Lopez & Allal 2007, pp. 252–65).

Our classroom research (Boyle & Charles 2010) has left us with unanswered questions: Why is it that only a small percentage of teachers have a strong and balanced pedagogical base for their practice? Is this caused by a misunderstanding of the definition of pedagogy? According to Alexander (2008):

> Pedagogy is the observable act of teaching together with its attendant discourse of educational theories, values, evidence and justification. It is what one needs to know and the skills one needs to command in order to make and justify the many different kinds of decisions of which teaching is constituted. (p. 29)

This rich pedagogy as outlined by Alexander is based on differentiated treatment of children (Perrenoud 1998). The following example of an enriched pedagogical experience was recorded in a mathematics lesson with a Year 2 class, and formed part of our research sample (Boyle & Charles 2010).

Case study 2

Two children, Matthew and Fatima, are working on the concept of 'doubling' within the learning objective of 'formulating word problems' in the context of Jack and the Beanstalk. The following dialogue took place when the children asked their teacher's advice on developing their word problem:

Teacher: Why don't you write a more difficult question?

Fatima: The tree grew 45 leaves on day 1.

Teacher: What about those words we used about 'doubling'?

Fatima: Is it 90, because he did the same with 1,000 metres [points to Matthew].

Teacher:	Well maybe Matthew can help you to think of a question using 'doubling'. Go and talk about it first. Don't try and write it until you have talked a good question through [The teacher continues working with her group as the two children go off to re-draft their question.]
Fatima:	Right, on day 1...
Matthew:	It grew 65 leaves and the next day it doubled.
Fatima:	65 doubled ... oh, that's a hard one [Fatima scratches her head].
Matthew:	And then the next day it doubled and the next day it doubled.
Fatima:	Oh no, not four doubles please.
Matthew:	No three doubles.
Fatima:	So 65 doubled, OK, 120 doubled equals 240.
Matthew:	No, 65 add 65 add 65.
Fatima:	65 and 65 would be 40, then another 65 would be 140 [Fatima looks very confused and unsure and Matthew shrugs his shoulders]. Oh, it would be 305, maybe not. [Fatima holds head in hand in total confusion].
Matthew:	You're not getting this.
Fatima:	I don't know the answer [with a smile on her face]. You think of it.
Matthew:	I don't know the answer to my question.
Fatima:	You have to know the answer. If you don't know then you shouldn't tell it.
Matthew:	But you are working it out.
Fatima [pauses]:	It should be 240 shouldn't it? Maybe. I need another leaf [reaches over to get more paper].
Matthew:	Let's go back to the teacher.
Fatima:	He's done 3 x 65 and I am thinking that it is 240.
Teacher:	Well I heard you working that out by doubling 60.
Fatima:	65 add 65.
Teacher:	No just double the 60 first of all.
Fatima:	120.

(Continued)

(Continued)

Teacher:	Then double 5.
Fatima:	130.
Teacher:	Ok then you have 130 and you have got to add one more 65. Would it help if you write it down before you forget, so you have 130 and another 65 to add to that.
Fatima:	I know what it is. It is 195.

Analysis

There are two contextual points which need underlining about the children's dialogue. First, the children are exploring the concept of doubling two digit numbers and as a consequence have also demonstrated their misconceptions of trebling two-digit numbers. Secondly, the teacher had set up this active learning situation as a way of confirming and exploring the children's understanding of those concepts. We suggest that because of the co-constructed nature of the activity (Schunk & Zimmerman 2007) the teacher learned far more about the children's processes of mental calculation than from supplying a worksheet on doubling. The children were given opportunities to access the 'elaborated code' of knowledge construction through being empowered to de-regulate the learning situation (Perrenoud 1991, 1998) and through being enabled to explore learning parameters which are traditionally imposed.

The teacher reviews with the pupils what has been done on the number operations theme previously. She does this in depth, indicating that she has reflected on the previous learning and values the experience enough to want to further it. She has therefore set up the context for the children to co-construct with her the next phase of the learning on this theme. This contrasts with the approach of the didactic teacher who delivers the next task to the children so that they can compliantly respond.

The teacher explores one child's mental calculations in her written problem. She frames her questions with the cognitive interrogators 'how', 'what' and 'why'. These encourage the child to verbalise and explain how she calculated her problem. The teacher observes the child's non-verbal cues, for example the teacher interprets the child's repeated nodding of her head as acting out the language of repeated addition. The teacher extends the sequential element in the calculation by asking: 'how else can we write this?' to which a boy responds '5 x 6'. The teacher is making explicit the internal mathematical thinking – she is exposing the whole class to collaborative problem solving using her formative assessment skills.

Conclusion

Our teaching philosophy is based on an understanding that learning flourishes through co-construction and self-regulation (Boyle & Charles 2010, 2011; Schunk & Zimmerman 1997, 2007) and that an optimum teaching environment requires a balance of affective, cognitive and conative domains. These conditions would enable every child to have access to a more equitable pedagogy (Allal & Ducrey 2000). The child should be at the centre of the teaching and learning process and it is the child's needs which should dictate the teacher's planning for learning, not the reverse (Alexander 2005). Myhill (2006) suggests that the dominant pedagogical model over the last 15 years has been 'the coverage and elicitation of facts rather than the creation and co-construction of inter-connected learning' (p. 34).

The chapter uses a practical case study of a teacher engaged in co-construction encouraging the involvement of pupils in shaping learning. The teacher and children co-construct the next phase of ongoing activity, with the teacher using cognitive interrogators to encourage children to reveal their thinking in problem situations. In this way a collaborative exploration of a learning situation is created and the teacher demonstrates a formative pedagogy by clearly locating the pupils at the centre of the activity and the learning.

Reflective Practice

In this chapter we deal with reflective planning. Effective assessment enables teachers to refine their micro-observations and to reflect and revise their planning according to learning needs.

What is reflection? Theories and definitions

The Office for Standards in Education (Ofsted) states that 'the most distinctive [feature] of very good teachers is that their practice is the result of careful reflection...they themselves learn lessons each time they teach, evaluating what they do and using these self-critical evaluations to adjust what they do next time' (Ofsted 2004, para. 19). In his definition of the 'reflective teacher' Andrew Pollard described reflective teaching as 'applied in a cyclical or spiralling process, in which teachers monitor, evaluate and revise their own practice continuously' (Pollard et al. 2008, p. 17).

Donald Schön (1983) developed the notions of 'reflections in action' and 'reflection on action'. These concepts can be translated simply as 'reflecting while doing the task' and 'reflecting after doing the task'. According to Schön's model of the 'actor' in his work, *The Reflective Practitioner* (1983), 'the everyday conduct of practitioners stems from a know-how that is mobilised on a situational basis and that is acquired through an accumulation of experiences; this knowledge is 'hidden' in their courses of action, meaning that this knowledge is implicit in the actions that they take and in their understanding of the situation confronting them' (Morrissette 2011, p. 251). A further development of Schön's work is the distinction between technical rationality and tacit knowledge. This distinction could be described as the 'theory-practice' gap. Schön contrasted 'scientific professional work such as laboratory research with 'caring' professional work such as education. He called the former 'high hard ground' and saw it as supported by "quantitative and objective evidence"' (Pollard et al. 2008, p. 21). Like Dewey, Schön believed that reflection began in working practice, particularly those areas of practice where professionals are confronted with unique and confusing situations – 'the swampy lowlands of practice' (Fook et al. 2006). These complex 'lowlands', according to Schön, tend to become 'confusing messes of intuitive action'. Such messes tend to be highly relevant in practical terms, 'they are not easily amenable to rigorous analysis because they draw on a type of knowledge-in-action, knowledge that is inherent in professional action. It is spontaneous, intuitive, tacit and intangible but it "works" in practice' (Pollard et al. 2008 p. 22). Teachers may well have acquired the theoretical knowledge of their subject or of the practice of teaching and learning, but while this might explain their classroom practice as it should be, it might not explain that practice as it actually is. From these real-life experiences teachers can develop tacit knowledge – a synthesis of theory and practice which they have developed for themselves – but our research challenges Schön's assumption. While empathising with the 'swampy lowlands', our research (Boyle & Charles 2010, 2012) has evidenced the 'theory-practice gap' that is present in the large majority of teachers' pedagogical understanding and practice. Without a strong philosophy, teachers have evidenced that they are prone to following verbatim the demands of short-term policy imperatives, for example the 'one size fits all' Strategies, for example, Assessing Pupil Progress (APP). How can we expect teachers to reflect when they have a large theoretical gap underpinning their practice – what is the basis for their reflections in that case?

Pollard alerts us to three issues. First, 'Reflective teaching requires attitudes of open-mindedness, responsibility and whole-heartedness' (Pollard et al. 2008, p. 19). Open-mindedness, for Dewey, is 'an active desire to listen to more sides than one, to give heed to facts from whatever source they come, to give full attention to alternative possibilities, to recognise the possibility of error even in the beliefs that are dearest to us' (Dewey 1933, p. 29). For Pollard, open-mindedness is 'an essential attribute for rigorous reflection because any sort of enquiry that is consciously based on partial evidence, only weakens itself. We use the concept in the sense of being willing to reflect upon ourselves and to challenge our own assumptions, prejudices and ideologies' (Pollard et al 2008, p. 20). The second issue is called 'intellectual responsibility': 'to consider the consequences of a projected step, it means to be willing to adopt these consequences when they follow reasonably ... intellectual responsibility secures integrity.' (Dewey 1933, p. 30). The third issue is 'wholeheartedness': as Dewey stated, 'there is no greater enemy of effective thinking than divided interest ... a genuine enthusiasm is an attitude that operates as an intellectual force. When a person is absorbed, the subject carries him [her] on' (p. 30).

Giddens (1987) conceived of the competence of actors as being closely bound up with the reflexive monitoring of conduct in the day-to-day continuity of social life, illustrated in Schön's (1983) reflective practitioner, who carries on 'reflective conversations'. Giddens distinguished between 'discursive consciousness' and 'practical consciousness'. 'Discursive consciousness' refers to everything that actors are able to give verbal expression to concerning the context and intentions surrounding their actions or the actions of other actors; it is dependent on the prevailing interpretative schemes, namely the modes of representation and classification that actors draw from their sociocultural references, viewed as conditions of their own action. 'Practical consciousness' refers to everything that social actors know tacitly – that is, everything they can accomplish in social interactions but that they are also unable to directly express discursively, such as routines (Morrissette 2011, p. 252).

This model of the teacher as 'actor' makes it possible to focus on the formative assessment practices of teachers from the perspective of their know-how and the reflectivity with which they conduct their day-to-day practice.

Case study

In this case, the researcher does not adopt the position of an expert who has come to train practitioners but that of a facilitator working to explicate practical knowledge.

Five female primary teachers (grades 4–6) from a school in the Quebec city area of Canada volunteered to draw on their experiences for the purpose of articulating their ways of enacting formative assessment; the researcher's role involved fostering the process of explicating and sharing practices and facilitating the debates that emerged. Three types of reflective activities were carried out on an alternating basis over a period of five months. Video-recording was conducted in their classes (three times) and the teachers were invited to view these tapes for themselves; where relevant they were asked to identify formative assessment episodes. Following this, three individual interviews were conducted on the basis of a feedback protocol referred to as 'shared reflection' (Tochon 1996), which involves the researcher and practitioner in the collaborative co-construction of professional knowledge regarding a subject of mutual concern. During these interviews the participants presented the previously identified episodes and explicated the reasons underlying their actions. Both these activities (video recording and interviews) laid the groundwork for five group interviews conducted on an alternating basis. Within this framework the teachers offered an account of their formative assessment episodes, commented on the practice narratives presented by their peers and negotiated the meanings of these practices from the anchoring in experience that individual interviews helped to make manifest. One of the aims of the group interviews was to add further depth to these teachers' reflections (Morrissette 2011, p. 254).

The 12 main themes which emerged during the course of the group interviews were grouped together under two main categories for ways of 'doing' formative assessment: 'ways of defining the situation of students towards learning' and 'ways of supporting students' learning'. In detail these two categories comprised:

- *Ways of defining the situation of students towards learning:* decoding students' non-verbal signs; using an erasable pad; correcting homework; employing formalised procedures; taking notice of the learning approaches used by students; sharing experiences and information with other educators.
- *Ways of supporting student learning: prompting reflection:* re-organising teaching-learning contexts; appropriate sharing out of ownership of learning between teacher and students; modulating individual/group ownership of learning; providing support during end-of-grading-period of evaluation (Morrissette 2011, p. 255).

For each of these 12 general practices, a set of specific practices was identified. For example, 'prompting reflection among students' was associated with six different specific practices: continually posing questions to students in order to stimulate and guide their reflection; allowing students' lines of reasoning to reach conclusion ('dead ends') in relation to a given problem; destabilising students in order to 'shake up' their usual way of doing things and to trigger personal engagement; using the portfolio to prompt students to assess their areas of progress; embedding feedback in an 'after-the-fact' logic; employing a letter-based code of feedback.

Analysis

The shared zone: conventions of a professional culture

Shared ways of doing things are those that were the subject of marks of mutual recognition whenever they were explicated among the group of teachers. Drawing on the work of Becker (1982) these shared practices are regarded as 'conventions' of the teachers' culture, as practices of their professional group that enable them to support their students' learning through formative assessment. Four types of conventions emerged in the research:

1. Reifications, such as certain categories of students
2. An identity-centred claim that linked formative assessment to the meaning that teachers ascribed to their occupation
3. Cultural interpretive schemes
4. 'a black box' (Morrissette 2011, p. 257).

The mobilisation of cultural interpretive schemes: the interpretation of students' non-verbal signs

One of the identified conventions concerns the mobilisation of cultural interpretative schemes that stem from the gradual integration of concepts, theories and procedures that have historically and socially proved their worth in a given professional culture (Giddens 1987). Certain ways that teachers have of 'defining the situation of pupils towards learning' appear to involve the interpretation of pupils' non-verbal signs, as appearing from situationally-based monitoring. The teachers stated that they took cues from the gestures of the children as part of an 'informal process of formative assessment' (Bell & Cowie 2001). This way of 'defining the situation' while engaged in a classroom activity appears to be based on tacit consensus about non-verbal signs of difficulty, for example a distraught look, a frown, that the teachers stated that they could confidently decode. The teachers all alluded to the importance of the interpretation of these non-verbal signs in the assessment process. The teachers appeared to ascribe meanings to these signs on the basis of a prior analysis of the tasks planned with the objective of proposing the tasks to their students. This advance preparation, which shaped their monitoring, would appear to be filtered by the knowledge they possess of their work tools, textbooks and ways of designing tasks. It would also appear to be filtered by the information that they deemed to be relevant concerning the family history and school record of pupils and which prompted them to focus on some pupils more than others. In summary, the teachers appeared to capably 'take their bearings' when interpreting pupils' non-verbal signs because of the perspective afforded by the common knowledge associated with their professional culture. (Morrissette 2011, p. 257).

A black box in the form of the notion of progress

An analysis that proceeds through the search for what was not explicated by the teachers provides an indication of another convention relating to shared ways of doing formative assessment. This convention can be viewed as a 'black box', that is, as representing a theoretical notion that actors use without necessarily understanding all the complexities inherent in it. When explicating their ways of doing things, the teachers made frequent use of the notion of 'progress', a core issue of formative assessment, a core issue of teaching and learning per se. They spoke of this notion as though its meaning was shared consistently and they did not have to make its meaning clear to themselves. One of their preferred ways of 'defining the situation of pupils' consisted of 'taking stock of the approaches employed by pupils' on the basis of all the written evidences that they left as part of their work or that appeared from verbal interactions that had been specifically organised for this purpose. In the teachers' views, these specific practices enabled them to adopt perspectives concerning individual 'progress' or the 'progress' of their group as a whole. That is also what they argued in relation to certain ways of 'supporting pupil learning' such as the teaching of knowledge or strategies, that is specific practices that they believed would enable their students to 'progress'. Therefore, what did the teachers actually mean by 'aiding pupils to progress'? Progress towards what?

The ways in which the teachers spoke about the different subjects of knowledge indicate what they meant by 'progress'. Where mathematics and writing were concerned the children's progress appeared to correspond either to the gradual appropriation and eventual mastery of certain notions in context or to the accumulation of knowledge. In relation to other disciplines such as history, geography, religious studies, the idea of progress was understood as a kind of gradual de-centering of oneself and an opening of oneself up to the world. (Morrissette 2011, p. 258)

Admitted ways of doing things manifested in terms of formative interventions focused on pedagogical differentiation. They also manifested in terms of 'theories in use' (Giddens 1987) or pedagogical principles relating to formative assessment.

The erasable pad routine

One of the teachers who took part in the research employed on an everyday basis what she conceived of as a formative routine when teaching her students a new concept. For this purpose she used erasable (write and wipe) pads on which the children could write down words or sentences with a dry marker and then wipe these after use. In concrete terms, while teaching a concept she regularly asked the children questions; at her request the children all raised their pads in the air so that she could get a view of the general understanding of the concept. For the teacher, this practice enabled her to make decisions on the next step in the target objective, or on how to follow up in the next lesson, or how to make adjustments on an ongoing basis. Following this quick 'pulse taking exercise' she sometimes provided additional explanations whenever the majority of the group appeared to be confronted with a problem of comprehension, offered other examples for clarification or to continue with exercises for the pupils to put into practice what they had learnt. The 'pulse-taking' exercise also served to inform her of those students who needed more personalised support – she was then able to conduct a support 'clinic' with this smaller group. In this process she began by diagnosing – in greater detail than was possible from the erasable pad – what those children had not understood, then to develop and to conduct interventions. This teacher explained that this teaching and learning routine constituted an everyday formative assessment, based on the information obtained from the children's responses to her teaching. (Morrissette, 2011, p. 259). While seeing the possibilities of this strategy with small group interaction, we are concerned about the limitations of attempting to conduct the strategy with a whole class. Our research bears witness to the use of the 'erasable pad' routine as an endemic whole class teaching strategy with nil refinement.

Learner-centred planning

This chapter is based around a case study of the work of one the authors in a classroom/school situation. This philosophy of the 'pupil at the centre' of planning for teaching and learning was behind the conceptualisation of the Revised Framework (DfES 2006) and has always been part of our philosophy as it is a formative philosophy. 'Teachers must respond to the children' was the summary of the Revised Framework supplied to the profession in Bloom's *Times Educational Supplement* piece (2006) as an alternative to teachers ploughing through the 1,600-page version on the DfES's Standards website. The intention of the revised framework was to challenge the established primary teaching weekly planning pattern of setting 'one-size-fits-all' objectives and then ticking them off 'done', covering them regardless of the learning needs of the children. Nigel Bufton, mathematics programme director for the primary national strategies, was reported as stating:

> 'teachers tend to take objectives and race through them rather than focusing on what progress has been made and addressing things children don't understand. Our new cycle is plan, teach, assess, plan, teach, assess. Teachers should be thinking what kind of approach will help children best' (Bloom 2006).

Charles's practice at the time of the research (her thinking was stimulated by Western Australia's First Steps Developmental Continuum, 1994) was already focused on removing the blocked-in five-day week planning model. This rigid planning system made flexible responses to daily demonstrations of individuals and their learning needs impossible – in most schools this was at best picked up at the end of each week at year group planning meetings or at worst no retrospective pick-up of pupil misconceptions occurred at all (Boyle & Charles 2007, p. 26). This model did not encourage the development of the teacher as 'reflective practitioner' (Pollard & Tann, 1995), evaluating one day's teaching and re-strategising for the next day against individual learning needs.

Charles as the researcher decided (in her then role of key stage 1 co-ordinator) that a change in strategy with her colleagues would be attempted. This would be based on an understanding of formative teaching and learning principles (Perrenoud 1998), focused on individual learning needs (Shepard 2000) and demonstrated through a more specific child-centred planning model.

To lead and model her colleagues (seven key stage 1 teachers, of whom three taught Y1 and four taught Y2) through this change in strategy required many sessions of detailed discussion, observations and modelling sessions – even at the level of explaining that she was not asking for *less* planning but more *specific* and *focused* daily planning. The original five-day planning model of the strategies (DfEE 1998C) was conceptually dismantled and the key stage 1 teachers' operational planning was reduced from writing a full five-day week in rigid detail in advance (as per that original model) to the first three days (for initial ease of transition). Then successive days were planned post-reflection on each day's teaching. The notion of suddenly becoming 'reflective practitioners' and then re-conceptualisers, revisers and implementers of differentiated planning based on individual learning needs proved daunting to the group. Their resultant initial attempts at reformulating planning reflected their levels of confidence, experience and curriculum knowledge. Over time the teachers reduced their fixed planning from three days to one.

A major aspect of our research involves observing and reflecting on teaching and learning and having conversations with teachers about their teaching, their philosophy and conceptualisations in planning for teaching, and how they see their role and their children's role in the teaching and learning process.

However, we observed more and more rigidity evidenced through very tightly planned lessons controlled totally by the teacher, which we saw (from the minimal engagement by the pupils) as constraining rather than challenging (Boyle & Charles 2007).

'This is a recitation script of closed teacher questions, brief recall answers and minimal feedback' (Alexander 2005, p. 21). Is this lack of flexibility because teachers feel forced to 'get through' or 'to cover' (two phrases which we heard regularly as defensive statements) certain amounts of work? Do these teachers have a 'menu' which they have planned to cover during the five planned days; a 'menu' which remains uninterrupted and unchanged even after reflection on what has been taught and learned? Who is setting the timetable for this pressurised 'dash' through the primary curriculum?

The majority of lessons which we observed are planned as 'tasks' with no deviation. (Boyle & Charles 2007) This rigidity may be derived from a misunderstanding of the flexibility which is available within the framework. The revised Literacy and Numeracy frameworks (October 2006) provided new opportunities and challenges for the teaching profession. The intention is that greater emphasis be placed upon the needs of the children

	Class: Year Group(s): Term: Week Beg: Teacher:		Guided Group Tasks (reading or writing)	Guided Group Tasks (reading or writing)	Independent Group Tasks			Plenary
	Whole class – shared reading and writing	Whole class – phonics, spelling, vocabulary and grammar						
Mon	Read What People Do. Discuss children's own experiences of different types of jobs.	Look at words ending in "ing" in the text.	Group D. Children to write about what they would like to be when they grow up.	Group A. Children to choose one job from the text and describe it in detail.	Group B. Resource Sheet 77. Children to fill in missing "ing" words.	Group C. Resource Sheet 78. Children to match names of jobs and descriptions with pictures.	Group E. Handwriting/ phonic revision work.	Review children's work. Ask children from Group A to show their work.
Tues	Discuss with the children the people in a school and the jobs they do.	Children to match the names and descriptions of jobs from the text.	Group E. Children to write about what they would like to be when they grow up.	Group B. Children to choose one job from the text and describe it in detail.	Group C. Resource Sheet 77. Children to fill in missing "ing" words.	Group D. Resource Sheet 78. Children to match names of jobs and descriptions with pictures.	Group A. Handwriting/ phonic revision work.	Review children's work. Ask children from Group C to show their work.
Wed	Discuss job adverts from newspapers. With children design an advert for a gardener.	Children to sort vocabulary from text into categories, "names of jobs", "objects involved in the work" and "things done by the workers".	Group A. Children to write about what they would like to be when they grow up.	Group C. Children to choose one job from the text and describe it in detail.	Group D. Resource Sheet 77. Children to fill in missing "ing" words.	Group E. Resource Sheet 78. Children to match names of jobs and descriptions with pictures.	Group B. Handwriting/ phonic revision work.	Review children's work. Ask children from Group E to show their work.
Thur	Ask children to describe what they think a typical day as a teacher might involve.	Ask children to suggest sentences to describe the pictures on pages 10 and 11.	Group B. Children to write about what they would like to be when they grow up.	Group D. Children to choose one job from the text and describe it in detail.	Group E. Resource Sheet 77. Children to fill in missing "ing" words.	Group A. Resource Sheet 78. Children to match names of jobs and descriptions with pictures.	Group C. Handwriting/ phonic revision work.	Review children's work. Re-read descriptions of pictures from Sentence work.
Fri	Ask children to talk about jobs they would like to do when they leave school.	Ask children to read and solve riddles about jobs. Ask children to make up riddles of their own.	Group C. Children to write about what they would like to be when they grow up.	Group E. Children to choose one job from the text and describe it in detail.	Group A. Resource Sheet 77. Children to fill in missing "ing" words.	Group B. Resource Sheet 78. Children to match names of jobs and descriptions with pictures.	Group D. Handwriting/ phonic revision work.	Review children's work. Ask children from Group C to read out their work.

Weekly Plan | Term 3 Unit 2

Figure 7.1 Rigid planning

rather than the coverage of objectives. 'Teachers should be thinking what kind of approach will help children best: children's progress should dictate lesson planning' (Bloom 2006, p. 8). Or it may simply be a failure to conceptualise teaching and learning with the child at the centre of the learning and a deep-rooted feeling that the teacher loses 'control' of the process of teaching and learning if there are modifications to the traditional role.

Our classroom observations indicated that what is clearly missing in this planning model is any origination of learning content which is based on individual children's learning needs. It would seem that both teachers and policy makers who originate strategies/frameworks are missing the point that children become de-motivated when they do not see the relevance for their learning menu – the 'what' that is being planned to learn and 'delivered' to them – because they have no role in negotiating aspects of that planning (Vygotsky 1978).

Sharing the objective

Even where processes appear to be in place that give the impression of the learner being 'involved in sharing the learning objective' (Arg 2003) this is an illusion, with a single objective selected and planted by the teacher. We see no sign of the 'intrinsic need' being aroused in the learners through their understanding of the meaningfulness and relevance of what they are doing (Vygotsky 1978, pp. 117–18).

Responding to such notions challenges the current model and ortho-
doxy of teacher-control of planning for learning:

> 'While it may be possible to determine what activity settings and models
> on interaction are likely to be conducive to effective learning and, on that
> basis, to propose the goals for class or group activities, the teacher always
> has to be responsive to the learner's goals as these emerge in the course of
> activity and by collaborating with them in the achievement of their indi-
> vidual goals to enable them to extend their mastery and their potential for
> further development. From the teacher's perspective then one is always
> aiming at a moving target. (Wells 1999, Chapter 10 p. 319)

The more generally rigid style of planning and delivery of structured
non-divergent content is not picking up on learners' individual learning
needs (See Figure 7.1). There is no evidence of the teacher's understandings of the differentiation required in planning to match those needs to
the teaching and learning anticipated:

> 'To the extent that pupils do not have the same abilities nor the same
> needs or the same ways of working, an optimal situation for one pupil will
> not be optimal for another ... one can write a simple equation: diversity in
> people + appropriate treatment for each = diversity in approach'.
> (Perrenoud 1998, pp. 93–4)

Allal adds a note of caution to teachers which our own observations can
confirm as being necessary: 'Differentiation of instruction has to be
planned for rather than being just added on after observing difficulties'
(Allal & Lopez 2005, p. 246). We have observed little evidence to indicate that the teacher is a reflective practitioner, constantly reflecting,
amending, revising and refocusing planning to meet the revealed needs
of the children (Boyle & Charles 2010). Worse there is no indication of
teachers' understanding of a triadic system linking teacher-learner-
knowledge being addressed (Bain 1988). This is seen as the teacher's
task and that domain is guarded even more jealously in the current
controlling climate.

Formative teaching and assessment

Why go for a formative, more flexible model? If formative assessment is
used as a framework for teaching, teachers change the way they interact
with learners and how they set up learning situations which guide children to becoming 'learning learners' (OECD 2005). So formative teaching
and its natural partner formative assessment should fit well within the
current standards drive to improve outcomes of teaching and learning in
schools. If teachers understand better how to loosen their regulation

(Perrenound 1991), in other words change from a didactic role to enable learners to have an active involvement in both the planning and the actions of learning, motivation to learn will be less reliant on the teachers' imagination or stimulus. It will become intrinsic to the learner because the learner has been the instigator and the innovator in co-construction with the teacher of that learning.

If teachers enable dialogue and negotiation between themselves and learners and between and across learners, this will 'constitute a framework of social mediation that fosters the learners' increasing capacity to carry out more autonomous self-assessment and self-regulated learning' (Allal & Lopez 2005, p. 252).

With respect to the teacher facilitating learner involvement see Audibert's maxim that formative assessment takes 'place day by day and allows the teacher and the learner to adapt their respective actions to the teaching/learning situation in question. It is thus a [privileged] occasion for conscious reflection on their experience' (Audibert 1980, p. 62). The reflection on the experience is the key to this process: planning is NOT a fixed schema, the reflective practitioner uses the evidence from the current lesson to change planning for the learner.

Individual targets are not imposed but negotiated with the learner; feedback comments are clear and specific to the learning intention – not to be confused with grades, levels and marks. This is the concept of 'regulation of learning' (Cardinet 1986). This is further defined by Allal as 'interactive regulation contributes to the progression of student learning

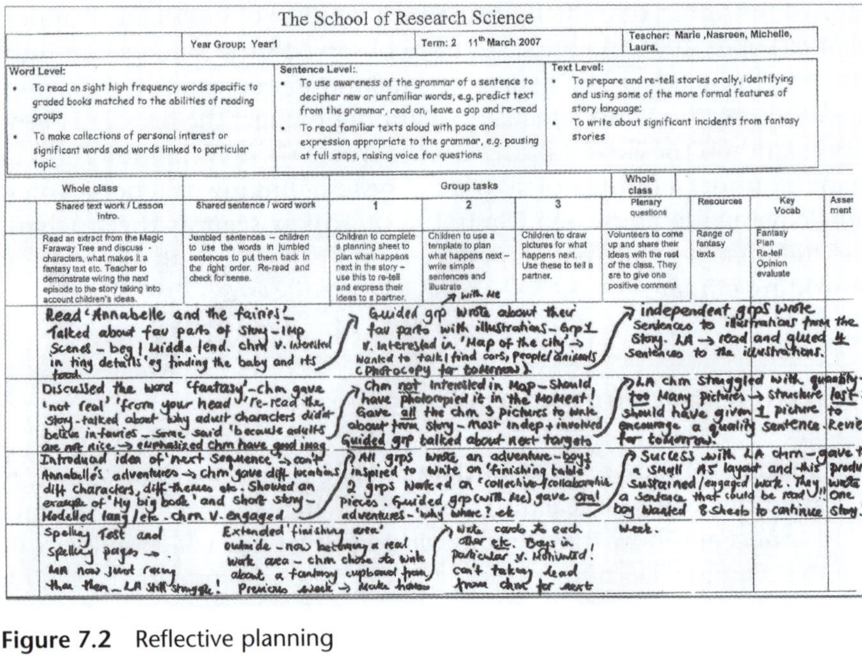

The School of Research Science

	Year Group: Year1	Term: 2 11th March 2007	Teacher: Marie ,Nasreen, Michelle, Laura.

Word Level:	Sentence Level:.	Text Level:
• To read on sight high frequency words specific to graded books matched to the abilities of reading groups • To make collections of personal interest or significant words and words linked to particular topic	• To use awareness of the grammar of a sentence to decipher new or unfamiliar words, e.g. predict text from the grammar, read on, leave a gap and re-read • To read familiar texts aloud with pace and expression appropriate to the grammar, e.g. pausing at full stops, raising voice for questions	• To prepare and re-tell stories orally, identifying and using some of the more formal features of story language: • To write about significant incidents from fantasy stories

Whole class		Group tasks			Whole class			
Shared text work / Lesson intro.	Shared sentence / word work	1	2	3	Plenary questions	Resources	Key Vocab	Asse ment
Read an extract from the Magic Faraway Tree and discuss - characters, what makes it a fantasy text etc. Teacher to demonstrate wiring the next episode to the story taking into account children's ideas.	Jumbled sentences – children to use the words in jumbled sentences to put them back in the right order. Re-read and check for sense.	Children to complete a planning sheet to plan what happens next in the story – use this to re-tell and express their ideas to a partner.	Children to use a template to plan what happens next – write simple sentences and illustrate (with Me)	Children to draw pictures for what happens next. Use these to tell a partner.	Volunteers to come up and share their ideas with the rest of the class. They are to give one positive comment	Range of fantasy texts	Fantasy Plan Re-tell Opinion evaluate	

Read 'Annabelle and the fairies' – Talked about fav parts of story – imp scenes – beg / middle / end. chn v. interested in tiny details 'eg finding the baby and its food. → Guided grp wrote about their fav parts with illustrations – Grp 1 v. interested in 'Map of the city' → wanted to talk / find cars, people / animals (Photocopy for tomorrow). → independent grps wrote sentences to illustrations from the story. LA → read and glued 4 sentences to the illustrations.

Discussed the word 'fantasy' – chn gave 'not real' 'from your head' / re-read the story – talked about why adult characters didn't believe in fairies – some said 'because adults are not nice → emphasized chn have good imag. → Chn not interested in Map – should have photocopied it in the moment! Gave all the chn 3 pictures to write about from story – most indep + involved. Guided grp talked about next targets → LA chn struggled with quantity – too many pictures → structure lost: should have given 1 picture to encourage a quality sentence. Review for tomorrow.

Introduced idea of 'next sequence' → con't Annabelle's adventures → chn gave diff locations / diff characters, diff themes etc. Showed an example of 'My big book' and short story – Modelled lang / etc. chn v. engaged → All grps wrote an adventure – boys inspired to write on 'finishing table' 2 grps worked on 'collective / collaborative pieces. Guided grp (with Me) gave oral adventures – 'why' where? etc → Success with LA chn – gave them a small A5 layout and this produced sustained / engaged work. They wrote a sentence that could be read!! One boy wanted 8 sheets to continue story!!

Spelling Test and spelling pages →. MA now just racing than them – LA still struggle! Extended 'finishing area' outside – now becoming a real work area – chn chose to write about a fantasy cupboard from previous week → Make [illegible] → Write cards to each other etc. Boys in particular v. motivated! can't taking lead from chn for next week.

Figure 7.2 Reflective planning

by providing feedback and guidance that stimulate student involvement at each step of instruction' (1988).

Figure 7.1 illustrates the rigid inflexible version of the Framework planning which focuses on coverage of content. Figure 7.2 exemplifies a typical week planning based on conscious reflection – reflective planning. At the end of each day the teacher adapts and refocuses his/her planning for the next day's learning. A glance at Wednesday in Figure 7.2 indicates the teacher's awareness of the learners' misconceptions and on the following day (Thursday) he/she re-strategises of the focus of learning to address those conceptual issues – matching teaching to individual support needs. Equally, Friday demonstrates that the teacher and learners are co-constructing the next steps in the Fantasy theme.

Conclusion

This chapter has demonstrated a model of planning which as a pedagogical tool has focused on flexibility based on individual learning needs. The straitjacket of five day planning has been gradually reduced and the learner's needs gradually introduced so that there is opportunity for the reflective teacher to plan to support, scaffold and reinforce on a targeted daily basis.

Self-regulated Learner:
Learner Autonomy

In this chapter we look at self-regulated learning and the emergence of the learner. We explore self-regulation in relation to formative assessment, consider various definitions of self-regulation, and how students can become autonomous learners.

The specific focus for this chapter is self-regulated learning (SRL). This concept is much quoted but also much misunderstood. As a theme for researchers and educators who want to understand how pupils become independent in their educational journey, it is a priority of pedagogical exploration. At a simplistic level, it is clear that pupils who rarely complete their projects or assignments, forget to do homework and are generally uninterested in their work, display little self-related learning. In contrast, those pupils who demonstrate attentiveness and involvement in their work, take notes, follow up their assignment research out of school time and manage their own time well, are demonstrating that they are in charge of their own learning.

Self-regulation involves interplay between pupil commitment, control and confidence. It addresses the way in which pupils monitor, direct and regulate actions towards the learning goal. It implies autonomy, self-control, self-direction and self-discipline.

Along with the difficulty of formulating and transmitting effective and relevant feedback at the right time (see Chapter 5), can be added a confusion among teachers of the levels of regulation. Among the regulations orchestrated by the teacher it is important to distinguish the regulation of ongoing activities from the regulation of learning processes. The regulation of the activities of pupils is easier to validate since the teacher can immediately observe the results of his/her contribution. The question is to see whether this regulation of activity guarantees the regulation of the learning process itself (Allal 1993; Perrenoud 1998).

> The question is first and foremost a conceptual one: ought we to consider any influence on the learning process as regulation, or should the concept be confined to modulation or an adjustment of these processes? To avoid identifying all actions of the teacher with permanent regulation we need to address the issue of the regulation of activities of pupils to: refer to activities specifically conceived with the intention of stimulating particular learning processes among pupils; confine regulation to the visual navigation through these activities or, in other words, to the initiatives taken to thoroughly engage pupils to help them to understand the purpose of the activity and to find their own place in relation to it in order to prevent them from abandoning it at an early stage'. (Perrenoud, 1998, p. 88)

In reality the regulation of learning activities does not always have as its main objective the regulation of the learning process. In the majority of classroom experiences, what is important is that the pupils become involved in the tasks set, finish in the required time and succeed. The teacher consequently has a strong normative influence on the work of the children, for reasons which are not always positive to their learning processes. There is a case to be made (Perrenoud, Allal) that this control of learning activities hinders the regulation of learning. This is especially so when the teacher (focused on the quantity of outcomes required) steers his/her course without enabling the children to hesitate, make mistakes, enter into dialogue – in fact, regulates against all the requirements of pupil learning. In active and constructivist teaching, the teacher is less concerned with the product and more centred on the child's learning process or journey to learner autonomy.

Where the aim is to regulate learning, the regulation of activities can only have an indirect effect on mental processes.

> It is difficult to ascertain at which point in time and under which conditions the regulation of the activity induces effects on the learning process. Thus teachers will say of some pupils: they are active, they seem interested, they ask questions, they enter into dialogue, they seem to be learning but the next day, there is nothing left. (Perrenoud 1998, p. 89)

One element of regulation can be delegated to the didactic apparatus itself, to interaction between children, to technologies, to various forms of metacognition (Perrenoud 1991, 1993). In a class which uses formative assessment and methodically analyses the results and methods or in a class which is working on metacognitive skills (Allal & Saada-Robert 1992), the child becomes an important source of auto-regulation, controlling and even dispersing external feedback. This is why the regulation potential in a learning situation is never an analysable abstraction consisting of the skills and the availability of the actors present.

The nature of regulation and the role of formative assessment depend on the definition, broad or narrow, which we choose to use; this in turn pre-supposes a particular understanding of teaching-learning. Teachers who want to be associated with formative assessment employ a range of concepts and practices. Some limit themselves to information based on feedback, others opt for a total integration of teaching and formative assessment. It is difficult in the extreme to compare classes in which the status of regulation and formative evaluation are so different. These differences indicate our basic conception of education:

> In classes which favour active methods, teacher and pupils determine the learning situation; formative assessment becomes an integral aspect of managing learning.

In 'traditional' classes, teaching is taking a class or giving a lesson; assessment is a specific event (oral questions or a written test or assignment) while teaching is mainly in the form of teacher presentation and task distribution which does not allow for regulation. Take as an example the French TGV railway speed of 300km per hour as equating to the number of exchanges that pass between teacher and pupils during the course of a lesson, with over half of these emanating from the teacher. 'At such a pace it is hardly surprising that each pupil has only limited access to regulation' (Perrenoud 1998, p. 91). Traditional teaching inevitably reduces regulation to its simplest expression and confines formative assessment to tests which are quite distinct from lessons, even if those tests are sequenced post-lesson. 'The ensuing retroactive regulation is often restricted to re-working notions which have not been understood by a significant proportion of pupils' (Perrenoud 1998, p. 91). Therefore, formative assessment is restricted to a brief surface micro-summative evaluation followed by remediation.

The regulatory influence of formative assessment is weak if it is limited to a subsequent evaluation which, at the end of a phase, unit or even lesson of teaching, highlights gaps in knowledge, errors and only a shallow understanding, at best, of the concept that has been taught, leading to remediation at a future point by the teacher. 'We find ourselves dealing with retroactive regulation which Allal (1988) distinguishes from proactive regulation and interactive regulation, which operates during the teaching and learning activity through an exchange with the pupil (face to face or in a group)' (Perrenoud 1998, p. 91). Retroactive regulation only takes place at the end of a phase of learning and relates to levels of understanding which take precedence over learning processes and impedes the identification of the cognitive difficulties encountered by the pupils during the learning activity.

If one has a more demanding conception of formative assessment, going beyond the temporary acquisition of knowledge to interactive regulation of learning, there is little evidence of this in didactic, transmission model classrooms.

Mottier Lopez & Allal's research (2007) on the regulation of teaching and learning in the classroom is based on a model that concerns the relationships between regulations linked to contextual factors and processes of learner self-regulation. Three levels of context factors are considered: (i) the structure of the learning environment characterised by the affordances that support and constrain the learner's activity (Reed 1996); (ii) the teacher's interventions and interactions with the students; (iii) the interactions among students. The relationship between those factors and the processes of self-regulation is considered to be a dialectical one in the sense that contextual sources of regulation can foster or hinder student self-regulation and, conversely, student competencies in self-regulation can foster or hinder the exploitation of contextual resources (Lopez & Allal 2007, pp. 252–265).

In terms of the micro-culture of the classroom the researcher (on behalf of the teacher) seeks to understand the ways in which teachers and students in their actions together constitute environments for one another. Observations document the cultural and social organisation of the events that are observed, on the assumption that the organisation of 'meaning-in-action' (Erickson 1986, p. 12) is at once the learning environment and the content to be learned.

A definition of self-regulated learning should emphasise autonomy and control on the part of the individual who is monitoring, directing and regulating his/her actions towards his/her goals such as information acquisition, expanding expertise and self-improvement (Paris & Paris 2001, p. 89). For the child to become an autonomous learner, s/he should be involved in and sharing in the construction of their own learning. This philosophy is known as self-regulated learning. For Zimmerman (2000) 'self-regulation refers to self-generated thoughts, feelings and actions that are planned and cyclically adapted to the attainment of personal goals' (p. 14). Perry, Hutchinson and Thauberger (2007) state that the 'children develop the process of self-regulation through instrumental support from teachers and peers through the forms of modelling and scaffolding attitudes and actions' (p. 29). These three definitions, while not totally congruent, all include the central location of the pupil, 'knowing about knowing', and, more specifically, allow the pupil to systematically monitor his/her own learning. Research also indicates that 'authentic tasks encourage self-regulation because they give [students] a genuine purpose for participating in an activity' (Guthrie & Wigfield 2000, p. 406). However, Ruttle (2004) has identified some concerns regarding the dangers of 'metacognition theorising'. Specifically because it does not 'seem to help very much those children who cannot recognise the effects of, and cannot evaluate, their own performance in the light of these taught elements of metacognition' (p. 73). Similarly, Paris and Paris (2001) signal the problematic elements of self-regulated learning in that it becomes the transmission model in which 'students who comply with teachers and use instructed strategies are regulated by others, and not self' (p. 96). The importance of Perrenoud's work (1998) is evident here, in demonstrating that the roles of teacher and student have to be 'deregulated' from the traditional 'transmission and passive reception' model; in short, fluidity of roles should dominate the classroom environment.

The tension among the theorists on this issue is evidenced by Perry et al. (2007) who state that not all learners will be effective as self-regulated learners: 'some students have difficulty gauging their learning strengths and weaknesses and how these interact with the demands of particular tasks' (p. 28). Consequently they may have difficulty regulating strategic behaviour and 'rely on extrinsic, surface indicators (e.g. grades, teacher praise) and social comparisons (e.g. ranking) for feedback to their success as learners' (Pintrich & Schunk 2002, in Perry et al. 2007, p. 28). This reliance on extrinsic indicators, that is labelling children as level 2c or 3a of the current Standards agenda and the predominance of a testing culture, is producing children who cannot self-regulate and teachers who are still located in the traditional model of whole class didacticism. Research by Randi and Corno (2000) suggests that 'students have few opportunities in school to regulate their learning' (Randi & Corno 1997). The work of Alverez and Adelman (1986) (in Graham et al. 2005, p. 236) and Graham and Harris (1989) evidences that primary grade children are not able to accurately assess their own capabilities, which raises the issue of whether self-efficacy is a viable construct for such young children. Furthermore, Graham et al.(2005) indicate that additional research is needed to investigate why struggling writers overestimate their capabilities; similarly Ruttle (2004) questions:

> How contingent is the metacognition given by me, the teacher, to inexperienced writers? Allied to this it is now recognised that skilled writing for what it is, is a tremendously complex problem-solving act ... could my preconceived learning objectives, however well intentioned and metacognitively 'pure', get in the way of actually working with how some individual children think about their own writing? (p. 75).

Interestingly Ruttle concludes that 'the writing of the lower-achieving children has not improved to nearly the same extent' by keeping the majority moving at pace and ignoring individual learning needs (p. 71). Ruttle is cautioning teachers against both the rigidity of the pre-planned package version of teaching and the dangers of ignoring individual learning needs to keep the 'majority' moving at pace through the terms' objectives. Children do not simply arrive at this self-regulated position overnight. Meyer and Turner (2002) recognise the child's achievement of self-regulation as a learner by describing the process as 'assuming responsibility, this becomes contingent not only on the classroom climate and growing competence but also on the opportunities afforded to *demonstrate* that competence' (p. 23, original emphasis).

Self-regulated learning is at the core of formative assessment and *through the involvement of the learner* is an evidenced outcome that formative assessment is taking place. In 2008, Hayes reported on findings from classroom observations of 400 primary school pupils that they 'have limited choice in or control over the activities they engage in and although teachers are recorded as proposing active participation the findings did not show children actively participating in their learning' (p. 434) with 'children mainly observed worked silently' (p. 433).

Researchers (Alexander 2005, 2008; Dunphy 2008; Edwards 2001; Patrick et al. 2003; Wyse et al. 2007; Boyle & Charles 2010) have chronicled the sterility of the pedagogy that has emanated in England from 14 years of central government-imposed Strategies designed to improve test scores under a minimum competency model and a restricted definition of the term 'Standards'. 'Pedagogy is so palpably the missing ingredient ... and it is so obviously vital to [children's] progress and to learning outcomes that we have no alternative but to find ways of remedying the deficiency' (Alexander 2008, p. 22). So teachers and their trainers have to re-think the basis of pedagogy: synonymous with this process is an understanding that a child as an autonomous learner should be involved in sharing the construction of his/her own learning, that is self-regulated learning. For Schunk and Zimmerman (1997) 'self-regulation refers to self-generated thoughts, feelings and actions that are planned and cyclically adapted to the attainment of personal [learning] goals' (p. 14). For Perry et al. (2007) pupils 'develop the process of self-regulation through instrumental support from teachers and peers through the forms of modelling and scaffolding attitudes and actions' (p. 29); note the focus across both definitions on allowing the pupils to systematically monitor their own learning. The importance of Perrenoud's thinking is evident as he states that 'the roles of teacher and pupil have to be deregulated from the traditional transmission and passive reception model' (1998); so as a minimum requirement for teaching, teacher training should stress avoidance of the 'recitation script' style of pedagogy so criticised by Alexander (2005). The current summative metric model and didactic pedagogical style are producing children who cannot self-regulate (because they are not offered the experience of working that way) and teachers who are still located in the traditional model of whole class teaching and didacticism. Ruttle (2004) warns the didacts to reflect whether their 'preconceived learning objectives, however well-intentioned and metacognitively "pure" get in the way of actually working with how some children think about their own writing' (p. 75). Ruttle is cautioning teachers (and the teacher-trainers) against both the rigidity of the pre-planned package version of teaching and the dangers of ignoring individual learning needs to keep the majority moving at pace through the weekly objectives.

In England the influence of the government's National Strategies (introduced in 1997) which listed learning outcomes by lesson, by week, by term and by year encouraged teachers to believe that there was a requirement for strong pacing. The Office for Standards in Education (Ofsted), the government's school monitoring force, exacerbated this situation through its 'concern to sharpen pace in teaching which led to the pursuit of pace at all costs, regardless of the fact that pace without attention to [children's] understanding leaves all but the fastest learners stranded' (Alexander 2008, p. 18).

In practical terms, one step which would demonstrate a critical movement from the 'one size fits all' didacticism (Alexander 2008, p.18) is that of the teacher engaging in systemic guided group methodologies. The guided group is a pedagogical strategy which enables the teacher to focus on small size (4–6 pupils maximum) differentiated groups of pupils. The teacher still makes managerial decisions about the differentiated learning objectives and teaches and interacts with the whole class, but the notable difference is that the teacher then teaches the targeted group. She has specific aims and objectives for a 20–30 minutes maximum session of focused, uninterrupted teaching, having planned high-level, challenging, self-supporting activities from the lesson's theme for the rest of the class to engage with. This formative teaching and learning approach optimises the teacher's insights and understanding of the pupils' location and learning needs, for example the levels of language that a child has, such as complex/non-complex sentence structure, use and breadth of vocabulary, etc. It enables each pupil to have the necessary time and space to explore and internalise rather than being rushed through a 'coverage' model. The teacher, through the structure and formality of the guided group approach, can support each pupil's affective domain which consequently develops both conation and cognition (Allal & Ducrey 2000). Conation is in the 'work domain' of learning. Pupils will engage or disengage their will to learn based on whether the topic or subject matter has some personal or 'real life' meaning for them. 'Conation can be thought of as an "internal engine" that drives the external tasks and desires. The drive shaft links "what I want to know" to "how I feel about the task" and subsequently "how I will respond to the task"' (Huitt & Cain 2005, p. 2).

The trainee teacher will not understand self-regulated learning without tutoring and support, both theoretical and empirical. Meyer and Turner (2002) recognise the pupil's achievement of self-regulation as a learner by describing the process as 'assuming responsibility, this becomes contingent not only on the classroom climate and growing competence but also on the opportunities afforded to demonstrate that competence' (p. 23). Social collaboration and scaffolding are essential prerequisites for the classroom conditions to support the development of the self-regulated learner. Paris and Paris (2001) detail studies of the social and motivational conditions that support pupils' use of effective strategies. Teachers have used pair-share activities, reciprocal teaching and collaborative learning to enable children to coach each other to monitor and improve their own learning. Therefore, learning strategies have become important cognitive tools for teachers to model, explain and cultivate in their children (p. 91).

During the past 30 years the nature of classroom instruction has fluctuated – often influenced by government policies. Early training studies emphasised didactic methods, while the last 10 years have seen some movement towards reflective and scaffolded instruction, with that movement restricted by the tension caused by 'teaching to the test' for accountability purposes. Research in the 1980s situated strategy research in the classroom in four distinct ways: first, metacognition was added to the research on strategies so that training included explanations about how strategies operate and why they are useful rather than just a simple direction to use them. In retrospect it seems very short-sighted that researchers would not routinely explain how, why and when strategies are effective. However it was 'normal practice' that pupils were told what to do rather than being provided with explanatory rationales for their actions. Time and research have proved that fuller disclosure and the involvement of the child (co-construction; self-regulation) in the learning process at all points has led to better, deeper, richer learning (Paris et al. 1986; Pressley et al. 1992). Second, motivation and emotion were added to cognitive dimensions of learning. Consequently, training pupils to use strategies for learning involved making the strategies fun and functional – an inextricable weave of fun and information (Paris & Paris 2001). Third, discrete strategies were situated in specific disciplines, beginning with reading in the 1970s and extending to mathematics, science, etc. as researchers recognised that each discipline offered different frameworks for organising knowledge (Alexander 1995). Fourth, strategy research became embedded in classrooms as researchers needed an authentic environment to test whether children could be taught to use effective learning strategies in their regular curriculum. The result was a realisation that instruction is not telling children what to do or which strategies are to be applied. Cognitive instruction involves students in reflective discourses about thinking, with multiple opportunities to talk about the task and how to solve it. Explanations, guided inquiry, scaffolded support, reciprocal teaching and collaborative learning allow pupils to coach each other to monitor and improve their learning. Therefore, learning strategies have become important cognitive tools for teachers to model, explain and foster in their pupils throughout the curriculum. Formative assessment aims to help teachers attend to what their pupils are thinking during the course of instruction – only then can the instruction be tailored to scaffold and support the learning of those pupils. The heart of the matter of formative assessment should be seen as the attention to what and how pupils are thinking and participating. By not delving into the specific substance of pupil thinking, the literature – and subsequently practice – misses and may undermine its fundamental objective (Coffey et al. 2011, p. 1112).

Taking the development of writing competence as an example, in that writing is more complex than a discrete linear staged process and with the added variable of ESL (i.e. for some children English is their second language), it becomes even more complex (Flower et al. 1986). Flower's metaphor of writers as switchboard operators, juggling a number of different demands on their attention and various constraints on their behaviour, captures a learning model which, although pedagogically sound, has been made redundant. This failure to engage with such a rich and relevant teaching and learning model has been caused by a generation of teachers who feel no need to have this level of complexity in their pedagogy as they follow the outcomes-oriented demands imposed by the English government's National Strategies. Like a distant voice from history, Piazza (2003) recommends referring to content features which are divided into four critical components: the writer, the process, the text and the context. Examples of the writer factor include background, interests, self-efficacy, learning style, knowledge base in writing and developmental level. Piazza is demonstrating the relationship between the affective and cognitive domains essential for the development of automaticity in the writer. However, it is important to understand the contextual contrast between Piazza's findings and the current Standards agenda for Literacy in England. Teachers here are being told 'many schools are finding difficulty in raising standards in writing' (DCSF 2007, p. 55) and that 'improving standards of writing at the end of Key Stage 2 [age of 11] is a national priority' (DCSF 2007, p. 5).

For pupils to become strategic and have an understanding and awareness of their own learning requirements, optimal conditions require that these pupils are trained as self-regulated learners (Graham et al. 2005; Perry et al. 2007; Schunk & Zimmerman 2007; Schunk & Zimmerman 1997). The Vygotskyian style is at the heart of these interactions as learners become autonomous and actively construct knowledge (Vanderburg 2006, p.375). 'This recognises the importance … of the interactions of … teacher-student discourse in the classroom' (Vygotsky 1962p). However, children do not independently arrive at this position and this demands that teachers change from a didactic to a more child-centred pedagogy that leads to the recognition of a child's zone of proximal development (Vygotsky 1962). In support of this Perry et al. (2007)

observed writing activities in five grade 2 and 3 classrooms and character-ised them as 'high' or 'low' in opportunities for pupils to engage with self-regulated learning. In 'high' self-regulated learning classrooms students engaged in complex, meaningful writing activities, [they] made choices and had opportunities to control challenge in completing tasks. They received support from their teachers and peers that was instrumental to their self-regulated learning. (in Perry et al. 2007, p. 30)

Researchers (Alexander 2005, 2008; Boyle & Charles 2011; Dunphy 2008; Shepard 2005; Wyse 2007) have chronicled the sterility of the pedagogy that has emanated from 10 years of Strategy-led teaching, despite attempts (e.g. Revised Framework 2006), to encourage teach-ers to focus on children's individual learning needs and to plan accordingly. At present we have a model of writing which fulfils the targets of the Strategy, that is the pupil is enabled to achieve the outcomes as prescribed, such as 'using paragraphs' or 'writing for different audi-ences,' but is not developing automaticity as a writer. For this to be achievable teachers have to re-think the basis of their pedagogy: 'Pedagogy is so palpably the missing ingredient ... and is obviously vital to [children's] progress and to learning outcomes, that we have no alternative but to find ways of remedying the deficiency' (Alexander 2008, p. 22). Central to this model is a realisation that the pupil as an autonomous learner, should be involved in and share the construction of their own learning. This philosophy is known as self-regulated learning. For Zimmerman (2000) 'self-regulation refers to self-generated thoughts, feelings and actions that are planned and cyclically adapted to the attainment of personal goals' (p. 14). While Paris and Paris (2001) 'emphasise autonomy and control by individuals who monitor, direct and regulate actions towards goals of informa-tion acquisition, expanding expertise and self-improvement' (p. 89). Perry et al. (2007) state that the 'children develop the process of self-regulation through instrumental support from teachers and peers through the forms of modelling and scaffolding attitudes and actions' (p. 29). These three definitions, while not totally congruent, all include location of the pupil, 'knowing about knowing' and more specifically, allow the pupil to systematically monitor their own learning. Research also indicates that 'authentic tasks encourage self-regulation because they give [students] a genuine purpose for partici-pating in an activity' (Guthrie & Wigfield, 2000, p. 406). However Ruttle (2004) has identified some concerns regarding the dangers of 'meta-cognition theorising'. Specifically because it does not 'seem to help very much those pupils who cannot recognise the effects of, and can-not evaluate, their own performance in the light of these taught elements of metacognition' (p. 73). Similarly, Paris and Paris (2001) signal the problematic elements of self-regulated learning in that it becomes the transmission model in which 'students who comply with teachers and use instructed strategies are regulated by others, and not self' (p. 96). The importance of Perrenoud (1998) is evident here, in that the roles of teacher and student have to be 'deregulated' from the traditional 'transmission and passive reception' model; in short, fluidity of roles should dominate the classroom environment.

Principles of self-regulated learning to apply in classrooms

Paris and Winograd (1999) described 12 principles that teachers can use to design activities in classrooms that promote children's learner autonomy and understanding of self-regulation of learning. They provide a useful practical summary of the research into self-regulated learning and could make the application of self-regulated learning in classrooms more accessible.

The 12 principles are organised by four major features of research on self-regulated learning as follows:

1. Self-appraisal leads to a deeper understanding of learning.

    (a) Analysing personal styles and strategies of learning and comparing them with the strategies of others increases personal awareness of different ways of learning.
    (b) Evaluating what you know and what you do not know as well as discerning your personal depth of understanding about key points, promotes efficient effort allocation.
    (c) Periodic self-assessment of learning processes and outcomes is a useful habit to develop because it promotes monitoring of progress, stimulates repair strategies and promotes feelings of self-efficacy.

2. Self-management of thinking, effort and affect promotes flexible approaches to problem solving that are adaptive, persistent, self-controlled, strategic and goal-oriented.

    (a) Setting appropriate goals that are attainable yet challenging is most effective when these goals are chosen by the individual and when they embody a mastery orientation rather than a performance goal.
    (b) Managing time and resources through effective planning and monitoring is essential to setting priorities, overcoming frustration, and persisting to task completion.
    (c) Reviewing one's own learning, revising the approach or even starting anew, may indicate self-monitoring and a personal commitment to high standards of performance.

3. Self-regulation can be taught in diverse ways.

  (a) Self-regulation can be taught with explicit instruction, directed reflection, metacognitive discussions and participation in practices with experts.
  (b) Self-regulation can be promoted indirectly by modelling and by activities that entail reflective analyses of learning.
  (c) Self-regulation can be promoted by assessing, charting and discussing evidence of personal growth.

4. Self-regulation is woven into the narrative experiences and the identity strivings of each individual.

  (a) How individuals choose to appraise and monitor their own behaviour is usually consistent with their preferred or desired identity.
  (b) Gaining an autobiographical perspective on education and learning provides a narrative framework that deepens personal awareness of self-regulation.
  (c) Participation in a reflective community enhances the frequency and depth of examination of one's self-regulation habits.

What does it mean for children to be self-regulated?

Self-regulated children display motivated actions, that is goal-directed and controlled behaviours that they apply to specific situations. 'Self-regulated learning is the fusion of skill and will' (McCombs & Marzano 1990 in Paris & Paris 2002, p. 98). It is informed by metacognition from oneself and one's peers and is fuelled by affect and desire (Paris & Paris 2001, p. 98). What motivates and energises children? Are they motivated to display their competence, to impress others, to get good grades, to win the respect of teachers and parents or to avoid shame and embarrassment? All these factors might contribute but we need to examine how individuals become motivated to be self-regulated.

How children exhibit self-regulated learning is as much of an issue as why they display it. Historically self-regulated learning has been regarded as a set of positive learning strategies that good students apply judiciously. However, such a characterisation emphasises the acquisition of instrumental tactics and the approach of positive goals such as studying texts, revising and redrafting and monitoring one's problem solving. There is an alternative; for example if a pupil has failed high-stake multiple choice tests on several occasions s/he might feel pessimistic, a failure or angry when presented with another such test. To avoid another threat to self-esteem or another confirmation of low ability the pupil is absent ill, produces a half-hearted effort or cheats. These actions are deliberate and goal-oriented although not in a positive manner but are also self-regulated learning. Self-regulated learning can involve avoidance of behaviours as well as approach. A less aspiring student can be self-regulated in avoiding hard work or study and fabricating an evasion or excuse. Self-handicapping techniques are clearly the outcomes of motivated actions designed to minimise threats to self-esteem (Covington 2000; Paris & Paris 2001, p. 98). Self-regulated actions may be directed to the attainment or avoidance of goals that are held in either high or low regard by teachers.

How do pupils become self-regulated, autonomous learners?

Paris and Paris believe that every child constructs his/her own theory of self-regulated learning (2001, p. 98). Each discrete theory can be naïve and ill-informed or elaborate and appropriate. Students' theories of self-regulated learning change as they strive to achieve specific goals in different contexts – just as their theories of mind, school and self change (Paris & Cunningham 1996). Research indicates that pupils' understanding of self-regulated learning is enhanced in three ways: indirectly, through experience; directly, through instruction; and elicited; through practice.

First, self-regulated learning can be induced from authentic or repeated experiences in school. For example, children can realise that checking their work has benefits, it does not require much additional time and leads to greater accuracy, and therefore, better marks. For many students self-regulated learning may emerge as tacit knowledge about what is expected by the teacher and what is therefore useful reciprocal behaviour by the child. Second, teachers may provide explicit instruction about self-regulated learning. Self-regulated learning is directly taught, for example when a teacher describes the need to analyse each term in a story problem in mathematics, place each term in the proper location, perform the calculation and check the answer (Greeno & Goldman 1998). Self-regulated teaching instruction could emphasise detailed strategy instruction or it might involve increasing children's awareness about appropriate motivational goals and standards. Explicit instruction that is designed to avoid distractions and persevere in the face of difficulty is an example of volitional control that promotes self-regulated learning (Corno 1993). Third, self-regulated learning can be acquired through engagement in practices that require self-regulation, that is, in situations in which self-regulation is welded to the nature of the task. For example, collaborative learning projects often require each child to contribute one part of the overall project. If a child's contribution is inadequate, the need for further work and the direction of improvement may become apparent in the process of working on the project. It could also be pointed out explicitly by peers but the self-regulation aspect may be required as part of the activity. This is the intent of creating 'communities of learners', which is consistent with learning through participation and practice (Lave 1991; Rogoff et al. 1995). Rarely would self-regulated learning be acquired neatly in one of these three categories: indirect induction, direct instruction, elicited actions. 'All three probably operate together in classrooms as pupils create their own theories about learning in school and their own abilities as they work with teachers, parents, and peers' (Paris & Paris 2001, p. 99).

Summary

Self-regulated learning is a model which realises that the child is an autonomous learner and should be involved in sharing the construction of his/her own learning.

- For Zimmerman self-regulation 'refers to self-generated thoughts, feelings and actions that are planned and cyclically adapted to the attainment of personal goals' (Zimmerman 2000, p. 14).
- Paris and Paris emphasise 'autonomy and control by the individual who monitors, directs, and regulates actions towards goals of information, acquisition, expanding expertise, and self-improvement' (Paris & Paris 2001, p. 89).
- Perry et al. state that 'children develop the process of self-regulation through instrumental support from teachers and peers through the forms of modelling and scaffolding attitudes and actions' (2007, p. 29).
- These three definitions, while not totally congruent, all allow the pupil to systematically monitor his/her own learning.

Dialogue and Dialogic Teaching

> In this chapter we explore the concepts of dialogue and dialogic teaching as tools to support the learner.

Within formative teaching, learning and assessment there has to be an understanding that teacher questioning can change the discourse patterns of the classroom, broadening the understanding and practices of 'dialogue' beyond the typical initiation, response and evaluation model to a more free-flowing exchange of ideas (Minstrell & Van Zee 2003). This understanding of the primacy of dialogue in changing the regulation between teacher and pupil and consequently the pattern of learning is crucial in securing effective learning through formative methodologies. Alexander notes the external effect on the learner of experiencing a dialogue-rich classroom: 'The dialogue in dialogic teaching is not just between teacher and child or child and child, as the official "speaking and listening" formulation has it; it is also between the individual and society. It is about cultural and civic interaction, not just classroom interaction' (2010, p. 105). The potential effect upon lifelong learning and citizenship for the putative child is life-changing: 'What ultimately counts is the extent to which instruction requires students to think, not first report someone else's thinking' (Nystrand et al. 1997, p. 72).

Pedagogy of poverty and invisible pedagogies

Dialogue produces rich information about the substance of pupil thinking and therefore provides clues about pupil learning. In question and answer sessions, teachers measure pupil contributions against what is regarded as the 'correct answer' – there has to be a focus on the disciplinary substance of the ideas for their own value. Do teachers focus enough on the evidence required to support or refute the students' contributions?

Following Bernstein's research into elaborated and restricted codes of language (1973), he consistently rejected the interpretation of his work examining the relationships between social class, family and reproduction of meaning systems as stating that working-class language and culture were deficient (Danzig 1995), but stated that they 'are functionally related to the social division of labour, where context dependent language is necessary in the context of production' (Bernstein 1996, p. 147). For Bernstein, the fact that: 'schools require an elaborated code for success means that working-class children are disadvantaged by the dominant code of schooling, not that their language is deficient. Difference became deficit in the context of macro-power relations' (Powell 2001, p. 73). There is a danger, in Bernstein's terms of 'privileging texts' and also the possibility of the 'cultural transmission of contemporary, social principles, through invisible pedagogies' (Goouch 2008, p. 99).

The Bullock report (DES 1975) stated that 'many young children do not have the opportunity to develop at home the more complex forms of language which school education demands of them' (Ch. 5, 5.4–5.10) and this reinforces the crucial role of the teacher in supporting and structuring children's language development equitably. Tizard et al. (1983) did find that 'the most frequently mentioned aim of nursery education' listed by teachers was 'enriching language'. However, the researchers went on to state that, 'there was also a significant social class difference in the teachers' talk, with more complex uses being addressed to middle-class children than to working-class children' (Tizard et al. 1983, p. 537). A clear distinction of 'invisible pedagogy' is given by Hartley (1993) in his attempt to understand connections between constructs of childhood, society and pedagogy. He defines 'invisible pedagogy' as the way in which: 'control will be achieved implicitly: that is, the child may rearrange and personalise the context which has been pre-defined by the teachers; the child will have the apparent discretion as to what, when, with whom and how he/she acts within the pre-set arrangement' (Hartley 1993, p. 26). In England the machinery of the metric starts at 3 years of age. The Early Years Foundation Stage (EYFS) with its 147 assessment scales for 3–5 year-olds (DCSF 2007), introduces the young child to a school culture which is dominated by the 'pedagogy of poverty' (e.g. assessment through testing, asking 'right answer' only questions, 'patrolling teacher', 'lecture transmission style', etc; Boyle & Charles 2008; Hodges 2001) within this paradigm of the 'testocracy' (Guinier & Torres 2003). Bradbury (2011) adds that 'the practices associated with assessing children using the Early Years Foundation

Stage Profile work to produce educational inequality among children as young as four and five' (p. 660). Through his consideration of the workings of the types of educational practice, Bernstein 'contributed to a greater understanding of how schools reproduce what they are ideologically committed to eradicating: social-class advantages in schooling and society' (Bernstein 1996, p. 29). In the testocracy, the metric is laid down and teaching and learning become a process conforming to the testing metric. Its limitations and the humanistic and social implications are not even considered as flaws in the system.

The face of teaching and learning in classrooms is changing dramatically as it now includes other para-professionals working in schools. In 2010 almost half of the school workforce (45%) were support staff, a number of developments have contributed to the growth in the range and quantity since 1997. These include the delegation of funding for SEN, the introduction of the national literacy and numeracy strategies, and in 2003 the introduction of 'The National Agreement: Raising Standards and tackling workload', which set out to raise pupils' standards and tackle teacher workload via new and expanded roles (DISS 2003–08). These support staff, also known as Teacher Assistants (TAs), generally provide support for 'low-achieving' groups and children with Special Educational Needs (SEN) (Blatchford et al. 2009). This growing workforce has major implications in terms of developing and supporting dialogic communication with learners in the classroom. Earlier discussions have stressed the need for practitioners to be both highly skilled pedagogically with sound content knowledge, and also having a view to their vocation as a life-long engagement between a synthesis of theoretical research and practice. If our classroom research has to date indicated the opposite of this crucial relationship, then how can we expect teaching assistants, with fewer opportunities, to engage with theory and methodology in any given discipline and to apply them in their teaching/ interactions with pupils? Do school leaders and practitioners, therefore, have different pedagogical expectations for the TAs and, by implication, different, meaning 'lower', expectations for the groups of pupils being taught by the TAs? Indeed, a walk around many schools today will present a permanent model of small groups of pupils (usually identified as 'weaker' students needing support) working outside the main classroom with a teaching assistant. Setting aside for a moment the dialogic implications of this growing practice, what messages are being sent to those 'supported groups' in relation to their self-esteem, learner identities and locked-in levels of expectation? If these pupils are to be 'locked-in' to this pedagogical divide and level of segregation, one which happens on a daily basis, if teachers are consciously selecting groups to teach based on their cognitive abilities, then Bernstein's (1996) prophetic statement of 'privileging texts' needs careful attention. Research by Radford et al.

(2011) originated from the 'Deployment and Impact of Support Staff' (DISS) project designed to obtain reliable data on the deployment and characteristics of support staff and the impact of support staff on pupil outcomes and teacher workloads over a five-year period (2003–08). The study covered primary, secondary and special schools in England and Wales and involved responses from 6,079 schools, 4,091 teachers and 7,667 support staff (DISS). This study also recognised the quality of TAs' oral skills as being crucial for learning and has been rarely researched. Radford's study compared teacher talk and TA talk in terms of turn allocation, topic generation and repair; from 130 recordings, transcripts of mathematics teaching in four lessons were analysed in depth: 'We found that teachers open up students whilst TAs close down talk, teachers with whole classes, adopt inclusive strategies to ensure oral participation whereas TAs working with individuals emphasise task completion' (Radford et al. 2011, p. 625).

The Radford et al. study also found that the children who received most support from TAs made significantly less progress in mathematics, English and science than similar children with less TA support, even when controlling for pupil characteristics likely to be the reason for TA support (p. 3). These findings strongly suggest that the most vulnerable of learners who are in need of a carefully differentiated, layered and sequenced set of strategies are being misunderstood as pupils who require a separate pedagogical intervention by a non-teacher. However, the main findings from the case studies reveal many of the TAs' viewpoints, for example:

- Many TAs were not involved with lesson planning and felt underprepared for tasks they supported pupils with.
- TAs picked up subject and pedagogical knowledge by 'tuning in' to teachers' delivery to the whole class.
- TAs felt frustrated that information fed back to teachers was not used (e.g. integrated into future lesson planning) (DISS – Project briefing note 2, p. 2).

This has two consequences '...since time is at a premium what counts as appropriate talk, in both length and form, will reduce pupil speech and increase teacher talk' (Eke & Lee 2004, p. 220). Myhill's (2006) research found that:

> contrary to the advocacy of the National Literacy and Numeracy Strategies much whole class teaching involved relatively little interaction which supported and scaffolded children in their learning. Teacher talk dominated whole class teaching ... the child's answer served to end an interaction sequence and rarely to begin or initiate it' (p. 24).

Despite evidence that the teachers had a strong sense of cognitive concepts and skills 'which they hoped would be addressed through their teaching' (p. 34), this cognitive and conceptual understanding in principle was not realised in the practicalities of the classroom learning situation, and what emerged from the data was:

> The low percentage of questions making links between prior knowledge and present learning and the relative paucity of process questions giving children opportunities to reflect and articulate their learning points to whole class discourse more oriented to teachers' curriculum delivery goals than to guiding pupils towards greater understanding. (p. 35)

Teacher:　as a writer, how did he [Roald Dahl] get across the significance of that [the event]? [The children put their hands up and the teacher pointed to different children to answer].

Child 1:　He said he was hungry and went to the sweet shop.

Teacher:　Yes [though really meaning 'No'], so what was he using?

Child 2:　Similes

Teacher:　Yes [though really meaning 'No'] and?

Child 3:　Metaphors.

Teacher:　[Gives the kind of answer she was looking for] well, he was really building up a description .... (Myhill 2006, p. 28)

Further, Eke & Lee's (2004) research revealed that in one class of 30 children 'over half of pupil utterances were less than six words' (p. 222). This unbalanced relationship is even recognised in current government policy statements: 'Teacher talk continues to dominate pupil talk despite efforts to the contrary' (DCSF 2008, p. 9).

Inevitably the individual is diminished as the focus for teaching and learning and pedagogy sits within a contradiction: the 'closed recitation script' (Alexander 2004).

If asked the question regarding the importance of talk in classrooms and its development, many practitioners would positively agree that they actively encourage talk with and amongst their pupils; alongside some understanding of its social and cognitive benefits. However, this paints a simplistic view of talk and dialogue and suggests that they are equivalent in complexity, status and purpose.

In the classroom example below pupils were consciously or subconsciously connecting prior learning to a present theme and they were re-drafting openly and orally their developing conceptualisation of counting in tens in a non-rigidly controlled classroom environment.

This is an example, rare in our observations, of co-construction between the teacher and the pupil enabling the pupils' dialogue to expand by non-intervention from the teacher at the point of the first pupil's question, thus enabling the pupils to 'drive' the learning direction.

Case study   Mathematics lesson Year 1 children

Learning focus: counting in tens (10 more/10 less)

Context: The previous week the pupils had explored the concept of odd and even numbers. In this lesson the whole class was on the carpet exploring counting. The teacher recorded the following dialogue which took place as the pupils worked on grouping as part of the process of understanding the concept.

Teacher:	Let's count to 100 in tens.
Burhan:	Three sets of ten make 30 but it is an odd number.
Mohammed:	Is it an odd number?
Burhan:	Yes, it is odd.
Teacher:	Well is it an odd number?
Burhan:	If you had three people, one would get 10, one would get 10 and one would get 10.
Teacher:	What about two people?
Reem:	One person would get 5, 5 and 5.
Teacher:	How many is that?
Reem:	15.
Teacher:	What is that doubled?
Reem:	30.
Teacher:	Burhan, you can share 30 as 15 and 15.

Analysis

In this formative classroom situation the children were demonstrating the following: they were consciously or sub-consciously connecting prior learning to the present theme and they were re-drafting orally and collaboratively their developing conceptualisation of 'counting in tens' in an open classroom culture. This is a genuine example of co-construction between the teacher and the group of pupils (through enabling the pupils' dialogue to expand and by non-intervention at the pupil's question) and of divergence from a planned format to enable the children to 'drive' the learning direction.

The misconception, that the digit 3 makes 30 into an odd number, is explored and rectified in group discussion. The teacher, by not closing the learning agenda by responding with a definitive answer to the first pupil's question, has enabled the pupils to orally explore and work through two concepts, that is multiples of 10 and odds and evens.

In conversation the teacher reflectively observed 'I should have given Burhan, Reem and Mohammed a task outside the main group to explore their own numbers'.

However, unlike the above example the norm of many teachers' pedagogy is that, far from the formative principles of involving pupils in their own learning, teachers are controlling the learning agenda even more firmly.

> Many schools give the impression of having implemented AfL when in reality the change in pedagogy that it requires has not taken place. This may happen when teachers feel constrained by external tests over which they have no control. As a result they are unlikely to give pupils a greater role in directing their (own) learning. (Assessment Reform Group 2006, p. 9)

Alexander (2008b) delineates a clear distinction between conversation and dialogue: 'Where conversation often consists of a sequence of unchained two-part exchanges as participants talk at or past each other (though it *can* be very different), classroom dialogue explicitly seeks to make attention and engagement mandatory and to chain exchanges into a meaningful sequence' (p. 104).

It is the latter dialogic teaching that is the most absent form in classrooms, and this view is evidenced by international research (Alexander 2001; Scott et al. 2007; Wells 1999) which supports the notion that teachers may actually discourage such active verbal contributions. The seminal international discourse data by Alexander (2001) which began in the early 1990s focused on a close-grounded analysis of videotapes and transcripts of classroom talk in France, India, Russia, England and the United States. Detailed quantitative and qualitative cross-cultural analysis of classroom talk included substantial extracts from linguistic and paralinguistic aspects of classroom talk. This research highlighted two overarching themes between:

> those questions and responses which were chained into meaningful and cognitively demanding sequences and those which were blocked. Whether by the repetitive initiation response (IR) exchange of rote (as in many of the Indian classrooms); by the ambiguities and vagaries of quasi-conversation (as frequently in the United States); by an emphasis on participation at the expense of engagement and thematic continuity. (Alexander 2008b, p. 105)

Types of talk

The paradigms of teaching talk comprise five aspects typically found in most classrooms as follows:

- Rote: the drilling of facts, ideas and routines through constant repetition
- Recitation: the accumulation of knowledge and understanding through questions designed to test or stimulate recall of what has previously been encountered or to cue pupils to work out the answer from clues provided in the question
- Instruction/exposition: telling the pupil what to do and/or imparting information, and/or explaining facts, principles or procedures
- Discussion: the exchange of ideas with a view to sharing information and solving problems
- Dialogue: achieving common understanding through structured, cumulative questioning and discussion which guide and prompt, reduce choices, minimise risk and error and expedite the 'handover' of concepts and principles. (Alexander 2005, p. 12).

The cumulative aspect of dialogic teaching

Alexander (2008b, p. 118) stated that 'cumulation is possibly the toughest of the five principles to achieve in the classroom'. The origins of dialogic teaching build upon and work within the frameworks of co-constructed and self-regulatory identities. The teacher is the facilitator of the chains of ideas which emanate from deregulated pupils in an open cultured classroom situation – enabled by teacher understanding of the integration of the conative, cognitive and affective domains in learning. Classroom talk is not always dialogic in form. There are many occasions when the teacher is not interested in exploring children's ideas and taking account of them in the development of the lesson. Here the teacher (see below) is likely to focus on the science point of view, and if ideas or questions which do not contribute to the development of the school science story are raised by pupils they are likely to be re-shaped or ignored by the teacher. This kind of talk is 'authoritative' in nature (Scott et al. 2007) and importantly has a place in teachers' pedagogical repertoires, but it is one of balance and judicious decision-making.

Below is an example of the current stage of 'dialogue' in many classroom settings in England. The teacher is clearly controlling every aspect of the 'conversation', which is a manifestation of initiation, response and feedback (IRF) in action (Tharp & Gallimore 1991). We have called this the 'starting point' or the baseline for a development from an emerging authoritative dialogue into a more interactive/dialogic mode of talk.

Case study   The starting point: closing down dialogue, closing down learning

Context: Teacher with four pupils talking about 'settings'.

Teacher:	Can someone give me an idea of what a setting is?
Iqbal:	A football ground.
Teacher:	Yes, a football ground, anything else?
Jean:	A church.
Teacher:	Yes, anything else?
Iqbal:	A football team.
Teacher:	Is a football team a setting? The football team would be in the ground which is a setting, yes? Do we have any more settings?
Iqbal:	A football ground.
Teacher:	Let's get my football ground out [flicks through photographs and shows all the children the stadium]. So we've got the football ground, fantastic. [Continues to show different pictures of settings.]
Jean:	A church.
Teacher:	Yes, a church, let's have a look for a church, let's see if we have a church ...
Iqbal:	A dig.
Teacher:	Have we got a church, have we?
Jean:	Yeah.
Teacher:	[Picks up a picture] Is it a church? What is it?
Jean:	Another football ...
Teacher:	It's a mosque isn't it? Where is this mosque?
Tommy:	The outside.
Teacher:	Is this in the mosque?
Tommy:	The outside.
Teacher:	So we've got a mosque [picks up another picture]. Where is this setting?
Jean:	The home.
Teacher:	Where is this in the home? What room do you think this is?

Iqbal:	Front room.
Teacher:	What do you think those people are doing?
Jean:	Laughing.
Teacher:	Laughing and joking, OK what setting is this? [Jean picks up another picture.] Is it inside the school or outside?
Jean:	Outside.
Teacher:	Ooh, now this is my favourite.
Tommy:	A castle.
Teacher:	A spooky castle, it has a moon, ooh I like this one too, what sounds can you hear in this one? [No response from the group] What is this setting?
Tommy:	Outside.
Teacher:	[Reminds Iqbal to sit down as he is attempting to look at the other pictures.]
Iqbal:	There are horses …
Bobby:	There are … I wish that I could go there …
Teacher:	Well that might be a little bit of a surprise that you have told everyone, because we are hoping that we are going to a castle on a visit.
Iqbal:	You know my grandma? She took me to a castle …
Teacher:	You know the scary castle? You will know all of these sounds then when we visit, fantastic. [Reminds Iqbal to sit down.]

[Children are then given small pieces of A4 paper to stick down their chosen setting and write the sounds present within each setting. Teacher has not provided any modelling, scribing or how to write a mind map.]

Teacher:	We are going to do our own mind map about the football ground [talking to Jean] so we need to think about all of these different sounds that we can hear at the football ground. [Jean nods].
Teacher:	Do you think you will be able to write some down here [points to Jean's picture, Jean nods again].
Teacher:	What do you think?
Jean:	[nods] Heading the ball.

(Continued)

(Continued)

Teacher:	Good heading from the crowd, what other sounds do you think you could hear? [Jean holds arms up as if cheering at a goal.] Good idea, fantastic.
Teacher:	You've got enough glue on that [to Jean]. Can I just put that pencil over there? Ok thank you.
Teacher:	[asks Iqbal] can you please move your chair over there? [Tells Bobby] I think you've got enough glue on that now.
Iqbal:	Thank you Iqbal [winds down glue stick for him]. Right, now you need to think about your settings, now Tommy, what is your setting?
Tommy:	It's a spooky castle.
Teacher:	How do you know it's a spooky castle?
Tommy:	Because it's very dark.
Teacher:	We need to write down on our mind map what kind of spooky sounds you can hear, do you think you'll be OK with that?
Tommy:	[Nods].
Teacher:	Thumbs up if you know what you are doing?
Children:	[all put two thumbs up.]

Analysis

This form of talk is highly formulaic (IRF: initiation, response, feedback) in form, content and purpose. This transcript also revealed many of the aspects of Alexander's (2005) international research in which:

> The heuristic device of mainly open-questions coupled with the genial paralinguistic features of chatty conversation masked an essentially closed agenda, for only certain answers were accepted and teachers would go on asking or paraphrasing their questions and cueing or even mouthing the required answers until these at last emerged. (p. 8)

We also note from the above classroom transcript that many detrimental aspects emerge and become evident:

- The children's responses are exclusively monosyllabic and they are never allowed at any point, to develop into 'chained responses' with their peers or with the teacher.

- Communication in this context is not viewed by the teacher as a valuable tool both in cognition and its social mediating effects. 'Language not only manifests thinking but also structures it and speech shapes the higher mental processes necessary for so much learning ... which ought to take place in schools' (Alexander 2005, p. 2).
- The children's affective domains are virtually ignored as their potential contributions as valued reciprocators are never explored or developed as they remain in the role of passive legatee.
- The dominance of an 'authoritative' type of talk strongly suggests that the teacher does not have a repertoire of pedagogical tools to draw upon. 'Pedagogy is not a mere matter of teaching technique, it is a purposive cultural intervention in individual human development' (Alexander 2008b, p. 92).

Our classroom research strongly suggests that many practitioners view communication and its intellectual capacity as separate from the self and the learners' identity. Wells (2001) argues that this 'separation' is largely due to the 'transmission' model of knowing in which IRF modes of communication dominate, the teacher is the originator of discourse patterns in the classroom with monologic uses of language as a high priority. In short, the teacher controls all aspects of dialogue. Reddy (1975) perceptively referred to this separation as the 'Conduit metaphor of communication – in which language carries thoughts as trains carry goods with no interaction' (in Wells 2001, p. 4).

As discussed earlier, we have advocated several precepts linked to communication through the social mediation of learning (Vygotsky 1978), in that knowledge is socially constructed and not perceived as a fixed entity (as intelligence so often is) but rather in terms of an incremental view of learning, experiences and information gathering. The socio-linguist Bakhtin (1986) is particularly important in this context for his theory on the social genesis of language and its development:

> Every utterance is a link in a very complexly organised chain of other utterances ... multi-voicedness is a recognition that in any utterance there is more than one voice speaking ... in learning to speak we do not take words from the dictionary but from the utterances of other speakers. In both these ways, our utterances are inevitably filled with dialogic overtones. (Bakhtin 1986, p. 29)

The social acts of 'knowing and coming to know' (Wells 2001) present knowledge building (Scardamalia & Bereiter 1992) within the framework of co-construction and self-regulation. In a formative classroom, one in which the roles of teacher and student have been de-regulated (Perrenoud 1998), there is the potential for real dialogic teaching as an embedded aspect of a teacher's pedagogy. Conversely, 'knowledge building' within an asymmetrical discourse which sees the practitioner generating, initiating, directing and concluding much of the classroom communication will inevitably negate much of the learners' social, cognitive and conative learning gains. Classroom research by Kirby (1996) explored the nature and operation of teacher questioning over a nine-month period during storybook reading using propositional analysis (i) to identify the complexity of teacher questions and (ii) to consider the levels of demand made upon children by both 'low'- and 'high'-level questions (p. 12). His findings strongly suggest that neither of the teachers 'used questions to develop and build upon the children's story knowledge' (p. 13) and 'the children's responses tended to be via communal ritualized responses' (p. 11). This small-scale study cannot claim to be representative or generalisable in its findings, however the 'take home' message in which 157 questions from one teacher during six lessons (two of which were generated by the children) and 129 questions during three lessons (11 of which were generated by the children' p. 12) cannot be ignored and remain unchallenged and defended as 'normal classroom practice'.

This necessity (remaking authority – Shor & Freire 1987) creates a huge demand not only on a practitioner's ability to constantly reflect but also on adaptation, planning, interaction and implementing the necessary strategies for genuine reciprocal communication which is located within a teaching framework. It cannot happen, for example, at whim or by chance as a 'hit or miss' strategy which forces every learner to speak; indeed, Shor and Freire (1987) caution against this overly simplistic perception of dialogue:

> For them to feel pressured to speak even when they have nothing to add creates a false democracy, a fake moment of discussion. In a way, this is an imposition on the students by a teacher who has made dialogue into a dogma, a technique instead of into a genuine open exchange. (p. 16)

Dialogic teaching has at its core a guiding principle of valuing every learner's capacity to communicate as a true measure of a humanising process.

Dialogue: A democratic character

In 1970 the Brazilian educator Paulo Freire published his book *Pedagogy of the Oppressed* which introduced expressions such as 'humanising pedagogy' and the 'banking model' of education. Over 20 years have passed since the National Curriculum and its assessment was implemented in England, followed by the introduction of international testing and performance league tables. These events have produced a dehumanising of the taught curriculum, with the pupil as a recipient of a delivery model measured by coverage and the banking of facts. Freire's humanistic principles for an enlightened education system have been submerged internationally by 'one-size-fits-all' government-issue pedagogy; fast tracked in basic teacher training in 'delivery' for teachers based on the model of pupil as producer of performance data rather than as an individual with a stake in his or her own learning journey. For Shor and Freire (1987) dialogue ' … rejects narrative lecturing where teacher talk silences and alienates students. In a problem-posing participatory format, the teacher and the students transform learning into a collaborative process to illuminate and act on reality' (p. 11). Dialogue is so wrapped up in what essentially makes us human that it is deepened further when our utterances are allowed to find the space to be heard, respected and developed. Authentic dialogue demands a conceptual shift towards the critical question of 'knowledge and becoming to know', particularly in relation to knowledge building in the classroom. Who is the authority on knowledge construction? Is knowledge, and by implication intelligence, perceived as fixed? Stable? Or finite?

> Dialogue is the sealing together of the teacher and the students in the joint act of knowing and re-knowing the object of the study. Then instead of transforming the knowledge statically, as a fixed possession of the teacher, dialogue demands a dynamic approximation towards the object. (Shor & Freire 1987, p. 14)

Case study   Emerging authoritative/dialogic (Stage 1)

Sequence 1 provides an example of a whole class session in an English primary school in which the pupils had been discussing a set of statements about the solar system to decide if they were true or false.

Teacher:	Keighley, would you read out number 9 for us.
Keighley [reads]:	The moon changes shape because it is in the shadow of the earth.
Teacher:	Right, now what does your group think about that?
Keighley:	True.
Teacher:	What? Why do you think that?
Keighley:	Because it is when earth is dark then, not quite sure but we think it was true.

(Continued)

(Continued)

Teacher: Right, people with hands up [to Keighley]. Who would you want to contribute?

Keighley: Sadie.

Sadie: I think it is false because when the sun moves round the earth it shines on the moon which projects down to the earth.

Teacher [to Sadie]: Do you want to choose somebody else? That sounds good.

Sadie: Matthew.

Matthew: We weren't actually sure because we were thinking the actual moon changes, which it never does or if it is our point of view from earth which would put us in a shadow.

Teacher: that is a good point isn't it. It doesn't actually change. It looks as if it changes shape to us. That's a really good point (Mercer 2008, p. 11).

To us this example is a tentative first step from exclusive teacher control towards an emerging authoritative/dialogic mode. Mercer however states that 'this is archetypal classroom dialogue but the questions are not the usual closed 'tests'; the teacher does not make a critical assessment of these ideas as right or wrong, making only one evaluative comment at the end' (p. 11).

Case study   Emerging authoritative/dialogic (Stage 2)

To take this to the next level of authoritative/dialogic teaching, the following is an extract from a discussion on the question: Why does light travel at the speed of 300,000km per second?

Ian: I have thought. I don't know if it is true. Maybe light will go slower if it were underwater or faster or maybe …

Erin: But Ian, no, do you know how light travels? It goes through the molecules of the water.

Ray: But what about in outer space? Maybe the molecule structure is different. Maybe it is just one big molecule?

Erin:	It goes through a vacuum I know that.
Steve:	Erin, I think it was Nicky said up there [points to the notes on the classroom wall] that if you shine a light through a glass it slows down.
Erin:	Yes, I know [thoughtfully].
Ian:	Maybe light would go faster in a black hole because there is nothing in it ... maybe if there is something in it then that is not good.
Erin.	I am not really sure.
Ian:	Maybe there was this alien planet and a black hole and we are on the other side of the black hole ... well I don't know [in response to quizzical glances from Erin and Steve].
Erin:	That would be very possible to trace and even if it were...
Steve:	Are you saying that on the other side of black holes, there is an alien planet? (Wells 1995, p. 248).

Analysis

The above Stage 2 example demonstrates Alexander's definition of 'achieving common understanding through structured, cumulative questioning and discussion which guide and prompt, reduce choices, minimise risk and error and expedite the "handover" of concepts and principles' (2005, p. 12). Note that the teacher is absent in the dialogic sequence. This absence has been enabled through the teacher having established a culture of the negotiation of ideas and exploration in his/her 'handover' to the pupils as the norm of classroom conversation and research as part of the learning process. It is Vygotsky's claim that

> the true direction of the development of thinking is not from the individual to the socialised but from the social to the individual ... this development of thinking and dialogue proves a potent form of peer intervention as the learner progresses across the zone of next or potential development. (Alexander 2008b, p. 107)

It is equally important to understand that learning across, in, next to and within the ZPD includes practitioners too as it becomes a rich learning experience for all participants (Wells 2001).

Learning through 'rich' classroom dialogue.

Developing a classroom culture of dialogue is important as a means of communication so that children become accustomed to reflecting on teacher questions, posing their own questions and engaging in task-related conversations with their peers. This replaces the culture of pupils feeling pressured (affective domain) to supply an 'instant' response (answer) to a teacher question.

Think about a framework of teacher observations to help measure the impact on learning of improved class dialogue:

- Do pupils supply longer/more detailed responses if you open the dialogue with a 'how' or 'why' type question?
- Do more pupils voluntarily contribute responses (across socio-economic/ ability strata) in teaching sessions?
- Do pupils collaborate (on their own initiative) in discussion with peers in thinking/collective responses to questions/problem solving?
- Do pupils start to originate questions in teaching sessions?

Analyse strategies used by teachers to develop this collaborative, sharing culture and increased dialogue: 'no hands up', 'wait time', targeting of children for questions, non-judgemental response from teacher to pupil contribution, no response from teacher to child contribution as an indication that peers should be responding/continuing the dialogue, 'no wrong answers', are challenging questions from the pupils encouraged by the teacher? Use a strategy of 'key questions' to start off a discussion amongst the pupils.

10

Ways Forward

> In this chapter we consider the various paradigms of assessment and their impact on pedagogy.

Assessment now has three paradigms and one result. Paradigm one is the accountancy model, beloved of policy makers and at the core of the school effectiveness debate (Gorard 2010). It is best defined as 'teach to be measured', in which the sole purpose of teaching is to deliver or cover material that will later be tested; there is no involvement of the pupil in that learning process. Paradigm two is the banking model (Freire 1970) in which the teacher teaches and the pupils are taught and those are the fixed and immutable roles; there is no deregulation of the role (Allal & Ducrey 2000; Perrenoud 1998; Zimmerman 2000). In 'olden days' this was known as the 'topping up' model in which the child was the empty vessel and was topped up or filled up with knowledge, which she recited back to the teacher to prove that learning had taken place (Alexander 2005, 2008; Tharp & Gallimore 1991 in Smith et al. 2004). Paradigm three is the 'testocracy' in which the metric is laid down and the teaching and learning process conforms to that testing metric. Its limitations and the humanistic and social implications (as follows) are not even considered as flaws in the system: 'test scores correlate with parental income (and even grandparents' socio-economic status) rather than actual student performance …' (Guinier & Torres, 2003, p. 68). The fact that the testocracy reduces merit and a meritocracy to a meaningless pre-destined ordination is ignored. 'Test-centred techniques are used to ration access to elite higher education as appropriate measures of merit' (Guinier & Torres 2003, p. 69) and '… at no point was any attempt made to reconcile this with an elitist rationing process'

(p. 69). Guinier and Torres assert that alongside the testocracy even the vagaries and lack of standardisation of teacher assessment stand out like a beacon of fairness and equity: 'reliance on teacher ratings excludes fewer people from lower socio-economic backgrounds than does reliance on test scores' (2003, p. 71). The testocracy knows no boundaries but income; it even, as Guinier and Torres found in their research in the USA, redefines merit: 'it moved from an assumption that tests are meritocratic for everyone except people of colour to a larger critique of the way in which the conventional testocracy denies opportunity to many deserving white applicants as well. It changed the definition of merit.' (2003, p. 72).

The three paradigms of assessment as outlined above have contrived to produce one result: a reduced pedagogy so that the complexity of the individual learner is ignored through the insistence of the system that the learner conforms to the (narrow) norms of the metric (Guinier & Torres 2003) as defined by political intervention, which soon became centralised control of a minimum competency 'standards'-based account-ancy and accountability system.

Our research has highlighted the following five issues: differentiation, divergence, definition, depth and demythology. Teachers for pedagogi-cal or philosophical, legacy or conceptual reasons clearly have problems with understanding differentiation. Differentiation has been evidenced as equating with setting and labelling children in static inflexible groups that remain constant throughout the time that child remains in the year group (usually based on the sole evidence of test scores from the previous year). 'Differentiation implies the imposition of different curricula for different groups of pupils – or it means nothing' (Simon 1985, p. 6). The following of a formulaic whole class 'lesson plan' seems to be the sole pedagogical model so there is no 'divergence'. The under-standing of formative assessment (or its synonym, AfL) and its practical operation is poor so there is no clarity of definition. Pedagogy is driven by 'coverage' and 'pace' which have precedence over depth and security in learning; as Myhill described it, the 'Coverage and elicitation of facts rather than the creation and co-construction of interconnected learn-ing' (2006, p. 34). The associated gimmicks camouflage what is the simple truth of formative teaching, that is the child's learning needs at the centre of a teacher's planning, and therefore the concept of formative assessment needs demythologising.

These discussions about formative assessment have centred on teach-ers' awareness in order that they can make teaching adjustments that respond to pupils' reasoning, conceptions and participation. We have raised concerns over teachers' preparedness and readiness to analyse pupil thinking beyond the level of checking on responses as correct information. Effective assessment in education should extend attention to the substance of pupil reasoning. Teachers should elicit (see Chapter 5, Analysis and Feedback), afford value to and pay 'persistent attention' (Strike and Posner 1992) to children's arguments. What reasons do children have for answering as they have? What evidence and logic are they using? In this way, teachers are not only becoming more informed about pupil reasoning but are modelling for those pupils how they should be focusing their efforts within the lesson/theme/concept. They are assessing pupil reasoning in ways that are consistent with how pupils should learn to assess ideas as participants in a learning situation. In essence this is posing the question, does formative assessment involve awareness of how pupils are involved in learning? Are students reasoning about an equation or a scientific experiment, or are they saying 'what they are supposed to say', playing the classroom 'game' (Lemke 1990) of telling the teacher what s/he has made clear that s/he wants to hear? (Coffey et al. 2011, p. 1122).

We believe that formative assessment should be understood as a matter of attention to disciplinary substance and in this sense it should be inherent through classroom activity, not restricted to specifically designated 'assessment activities'. While we have heard this sentiment or aspiration aired and read it in the rhetoric of literature definitions, it is seldom achieved (Boyle and Charles 2010).

The fusion or dissolution of formative assessment into a larger conception of the mechanisms of regulation suggests new approaches for analysing even the most commonplace aspects of the classroom. Rather than being solely concerned with the formative assessment practices of teachers, why not conceptualise and observe more widely the process of regulation at work in classroom situations and the classroom organisation that underlies them? Using this method, the work on situated learning (Allal) and the organisation of differentiation could provide the instruments for comparative analysis.

The task is not just to describe and compare situations and the organisation practised by various teachers but to observe more closely the mechanisms for regulating the learning process within each case. If formative assessment becomes an established element in teaching practice, one cannot limit its analysis to the intentional acts of teachers; it is necessary to address the effective regulation of the processes to the underlying situations and organisation. 'From formative assessment (evaluation) to a controlled regulation of learning processes', as a formula remains ambiguous. The first hypothesis is that the more the assessment is integrated into situations, becomes interactive and lasts, the further it distances itself from normative and summative assessment, the province of tests and examinations and their consequences. The role of the teacher as initiator and conductor of regulation remains central even if, and especially if, s/he does not intervene in person but puts in place a metacognitive culture, mutual forms of teaching and the organisation of the regulation of learning processes run by technologies or incorporated into classroom organisation and management. 'Perhaps it would be more appropriate to talk about "formative intention" and observation as elements of regulatory intervention, as resources for the orchestration of regulation' (Perrenoud, 1991, 1996, 1998 p. 553).

Key areas of professional education/development

There are four key areas in which focused professional development would enable teachers to use assessment in support of teaching and learning.

Key area 1: Active in their own learning

We currently hear a lot about pupils being 'active' in their own learning. One of the official suggestions of ways to achieve this is sharing objectives and success criteria. It has become almost a mantra. However, this strategy is a complex process; it encapsulates the whole culture and interaction of the classroom context and the teacher's complex role as a manager of learners. All the official publications about assessment for learning (see AfL website www.assessmentforlearning.edu/au/) list sharing learning objectives with the pupil, but they do not spell out clearly that learning objectives:

- Are not lists of tasks to be covered during the lesson
- Need to be differentiated to take account of learning styles and learning pace
- Require that the teacher makes a decision as to when the pupils understand the learning objective(s) and are ready to start the task
- Require that the teacher be constantly observant of and alert to pupil progress against the learning objectives and that in some cases this may mean re-defining or consolidating against those objectives.

Quite a learning agenda in its own right! The verb 'sharing' implies not just 'telling' pupils what the objectives are, but regularly checking out their understanding of the learning objectives, for example by asking layered strategic questions that lead the pupils to deeper understanding such as: 'Do you know what we are learning here?' 'Why are we learning it now?' 'How can you show me what we have been learning?' 'Where do you go next in your learning?'

Key area 2: Involved in their own learning

'Involving pupils in their own learning' is an indication of whether assessment in support of learning has taken place if pupils are 'involved'. You can achieve this involvement by making sure that the pupils are included in discussing and sharing planning of all aspects of the learning process, that is, by asking 'What am I doing?' 'Why am I doing it?' Over time pupils will become more confident as independent learners and will feel secure in taking responsibility for their own learning. This requires sustained inputs and commitment by the teacher, creating a culture of fluidity of roles, collegiality and collaboration.

In a recent teaching situation I observed the teacher introducing pupils to writing problems for their working partners to solve, involving the concept of 'distractors' (surplus and therefore distracting information which obscured the solutions). They had to self-assess the level of difficulty of the problems. When have you used an activity which actively involved pupils in their own learning in this way?

Key area 3: More collaborative learning

The third key area is that of making learning more collaborative. It is probably safe to say that we all subscribe to the notion that learning is a collaborative social process in which pupils work together sharing knowledge with their peers (Vygotsky 1978). So, in harmony with that description of learning, teachers need to be aware that the learning process is a dialogue. Through that dialogue, teacher and student access richer information to support their teaching and learning. Through support children will develop their own confidence and competence in learning. The use of learning partners is a first step to encouraging the sharing and talking through of learning issues. Teachers, therefore, have to be modelling collaborative learning behaviours and strategies consistently – not as 'one off' ideas which then are simply ignored.

Key area 4: 'Peer' and 'self assessment'

The fourth key area is potentially the most rewarding for learning but it is also the most difficult and is fraught with risks. If understood and operationalised formatively, 'self' and 'peer-assessment' are the crucial central planks upon which teaching, learning and assessment should be built. A teacher will know if 'peer' and 'self-assessment' are working if the learner rather than the teacher becomes the central point of the teaching and learning process. There has to be an element of challenge in the teaching, learning and assessment process. Enabling 'peer' and 'self-assessment' to take place in the class does not mean that the teacher is losing control of the learning process. The teacher has the opportunity to plan his/her interventions to focus and support pupil learning.

Exploring these four areas will offer teachers a rate to develop firstly a formative classroom culture (which is essential for learner-centred teaching) and then gradually to achieve the 'changing of the roles' which brings both teacher and student into the 'learning cycle'.

References

Adams, S., Alexander, E., Drummond, M.J. & Moyles, J. (2004) *Inside the Foundation Stage: Recreating the Reception Year*. Final Report. Commissioned and published by the Association of Teachers and Lecturers.

Alexander, R.J., Willcocks, J., Kinder, K. & Nelson, N. (1995) *Versions of Primary Education*. London & New York: Routledge.

Alexander R.J. (1997a) *Policy and Practice in Primary Education: Local initiative, National agenda*. London: Routledge.

Alexander, R.J. (2001) *Culture and Pedagogy: International Comparisons in Primary Education*. Oxford: Blackwell.

Alexander, R.J. (2004) Still no pedagogy? Principle, pragmatism and compliance in primary education. *Cambridge Journal of Education*, 34(1), pp. 7–33.

Alexander, R.J. (2008a) *Education for All: The Quality Imperative and the Problem of Pedagogy*. Consortium for Research on Educational Access, Transitions and Equity. April.

Alexander, R.J. (2008b) *Essays on pedagogy*. London: Routledge.

Alexander, R.J. (2010) Speaking but not listening? Accountable talk in an unaccountable context. *Literacy*, 44(3), pp. 103–11.

Allal, L. (1988) Vers un elargissement de la pedagogie de maîtrise: processus de regulation interactive, retroactive et proactive. In M. Huberman (ed.) *Assurer la réussite des apprentissages scolaires? Les propositions de la pédagogie de maîtrise*. Neuchatel: Delachaux et Niestlé, pp. 86–126.

Allal, L. & Saada-Robert, M. (1992) La Métacognition: Cadre conceptual pour l'étude des régulations en situation scolaire. *Archive de psychologie*, 60, pp. 265–96.

Allal, L. (1993) Regulations metacognitives. In L. Allal, D. Bain & P. Perrenoud (eds) *L'evaluation formative et didactique du francais*. Neuchatel: Delachaux et Niestlé, pp. 81–98.

Allal, L. & Ducrey, G.P. (2000) Assessment of – or in – the zone of proximal development. *Learning and Instruction*, 10(2), pp. 137–52.

Allal, L. (2001) Situated cognition and learning: from conceptual frameworks to classroom investigations. *Schweizerische Zeitschrift fur Bildungs wissenschaften*, 23(3) pp. 407–22.

Allal, L. & Lopez, M. (2005) *Formative Assessment of Learning: A Review of Publications in French*. Paris: OECD.

Applebee, A. (1978) *The Child's Concept of Story: Ages Two to Seventeen*. Chicago, IL: The University of Chicago Press.

Assessment Reform Group (ARG) (2003) *Assessment for Learning: 10 Principles*. London: Assessment Reform Group.

Assessment Reform Group (ARG) (2006) *The Role of Teachers in the Assessment of Learning*. ARG – supported by the Nuffield Foundation. Newcastle Document Services.

Ash, D. & Levitt, K. (2003) Working within the zone of proximal development: Formative assessment as a professional development. *Journal of Science Teacher Education*, 14(1), pp. 23–48.

Astolfi, J.P. (1997) *L'erreur, un outil pour enseigner*. Paris: ESF Editeur.

Audibert, S. (1980) En d'autres mots ... l'evaluation des apprentissages!, *Mesure et evaluation en education*, 3, pp. 59–64.

Ayers, W.C. (2008) *Handbook of Social Justice in Education*. New York: Routledge.

Bain, D. (1988) L'evaluation formative faut fausse route, *Mesure et evaluation en education*, 10, pp. 23–32.

Bakhtin, M.N. (1986) *Speech Genres and Other Late Essays*. Austin: University of Texas Press.

Ball, S.J. (1994) *Education Reform: A Critical and Post-Structural Approach*. Buckingham: Open University Press.

Ball, D.L., Thames, M. & Phelps, G. (2008) Content knowledge for teaching: What makes it special? *Journal of Teacher Education*, 59(5), pp. 389–407.

Ball, D.L. & Forzani, F.M. (2011) Teaching skillful teaching. *The Effective Educator*, 68(4): pp. 40–46.

Barber, M. (2001) The very big picture. *School Effectiveness and Improvement*, 12(2), pp. 213–28.

Barber, M. (2002) *From Good to Great: Large-scale Reform in England*. Paper presented at Futures of Education Conference, 23 April, Zurich, Switzerland.

Barkam, J., Sharpe, R. & Miller, J. (2008) *The National Strategies: Support or Straitjacket?* New Redland Papers.

Beard, R. (2000) Research and the national literacy strategy. *Oxford Review of Education*, 26(3&4), pp. 421–36.

Bell, B. & Cowie, B. (2001) The characteristics of formative assessment in science education. *Science Education*, 85, pp. 536–53.

Becker, H.S. (1963) *Outsiders: Studies in the Sociology of Deviance*. London: Free Press of Glencoe.

Becker, H.J. & Epstein, J.L. (1982) Parent involvement: A survey of teacher practices. *Elementary School Journal*, 83(2), pp. 85–102.

Bennett, R.E. (2011) Formative assessment: A critical review. *Assessment in Education*, 18(1), pp. 5–25.

Berninger, V., Abbott, R. & Jones, J. (2006) Early development of language by hand: Composing, reading, listening and speaking connections; three letter-writing modes and fast mapping in spelling. *Developmental Neuropsychology*, 29(1), pp. 61–92.

Bernstein, B. (1962a) Linguistic codes, hesitation phenomena and intelligence. *Journal of Language & Speech*, 5(1), pp. 31–46.

Bernstein, B. (1962b) Social Class, linguistic codes and grammatical elements. *Language and Speech*, 5(4), pp 221–40.

Bernstein, B. (1973) *Class, Codes and Control*. London: Routledge & Kegan Paul.

Bernstein, B. (1996) *Pedgogy, Symbolic Control and Identity: Theory, Research, Critique*. London: Taylor & Francis.

Birdwhistell, R.L. (1970) *Kinesics and Context: Essays on Body Motion Communication*. Philadelphia: University of Pennsylvania.

Blatchford, P., Baines, E., Kutnick, P. & Martin, C. (2001) Classroom Contexts: Connections between class size and within class grouping. *British Journal of Educational Psychology*, 71, pp. 283–302.

Blatchford, P., Bassett, P., Brown, P., Martin, C., Russell, A. & Webster, R. (2009) Deployment and Impact of Support Staff Project (DISS). Research Brief Department for Children, Schools & Families, August, RB 148.

Blatchford, P., Bassett, P., Brown, P., Martin, C., Russell, A. & Webster, R. (2010) *The Characteristics of Support Staff and Preparedness.* DISS project briefing note 2. Department for Education (SRF 11/2010).

Blatchford., P., Kutnick, P., & Baines, E. (2007) *Pupil Grouping for Learning in Classrooms: Results from the UK SPRinG study.* Paper presented at Symposium 'International Perspectives on Effective Groupwork: Theory, Evidence & Implications', AERA Annual Meeting, Chicago.

Blair, T. (1997) BBC news: http://news.bbc.co.uk/go/pr/fr/-/l/hi/education/6564933.stm.

Bloom, A. (2006) Children's progress to dictate lessons. *Times Educational Supplement,* 20 October, p. 8.

Bloom, B.S. (1988) Helping all children learn in elementary school and beyond. *Principal,* 67(4), pp. 12–17.

Blote, A.W. (1995) Students' self-concept in relation to perceived differential teacher treatment. *Learning and Instruction,* 5(3), pp. 221–36.

Boaler, J. (2005) The 'psychological prison' from which they never escaped: The role of ability grouping in reproducing social class inequities. *Forum,* 47(2&3), pp. 135–44.

Bond, L., Smith, R., Baker, W.K. & Hattie, J.A. (2000) *Certification System of the National Board for Professional Teaching Standards:* A Construct and Consequential Validity Study. Washington, DC: National Board for Professional Teaching Standards.

Bourdieu, P. (1966) Condition de classe et position de classe. *Archives européennes de sociologie,* VII(2), pp. 201–23.

Bourdieu, P. & Passeron, J.C. (1970a) *Reproduction in Education, Society and Culture.* London: Sage Publications.

Bourdieu, P. & Passeron, J.C. (1970b) *La reproduction: éléments pour un théorie du système d'enseignement.* Paris: Minuit.

Bourke, L. & Adams, A.M. (2010) Cognitive constraints and the early learning goals in writing. *Journal of Research in Reading,* 33(1), pp. 94–110.

Boyle, B. (2008) Testing to the limits – a very 'accountable' 20-year period in primary education in England. *Primary Leadership Today,* 2(13), pp. 20–23.

Boyle, B. & Bragg, J. (2006), A curriculum without foundation. *British Educational Research Journal,* 32(4), pp. 569–82.

Boyle, B. & Charles, M. (2007) Taking bricks from the wall: how the revised framework is influencing planning across the globe. *Primary Leadership Today,* 2(9) pp. 26–8.

Boyle, B. and Charles, M. (2008) Are we doing it right? A review of the Assessment for Learning Strategy. *Primary Leadership Today,* 2(14), pp. 20–4.

Boyle, B. & Charles, M. (2009) Formative assessment of teaching and learning in primary classrooms. *International Journal of Learner Diversity,* 1(1), pp. 17–34.

Boyle, B. & Charles, M. (2010) Leading learning through assessment for learning. *School Leadership & Management,* 30(3), pp. 285–300.

Boyle, B. & Charles, M. (2011) Re-defining assessment: The struggle to ensure a balance between accountability and comparability based on a 'testocracy' and the development of humanistic individuals through assessment. Special issue of *CADMO: An International Journal of Educational Research,* 19(1), pp. 55–65.

Boyle, B. & Charles, M. (2012) David, Mr Bear and Bernstein: Searching for an equitable pedagogy through guided group work. *The Curriculum Journal*, 23(1), pp. 117–33.

Boyle, B., Lamprianou, I. & Boyle, T. (2005) A longitudinal study of teacher change: What makes professional development effective? Report of the second year of the study. *Journal of School Improvement and School Effectiveness*, 16(1), pp. 1–27.

Bradbury, A. (2011) Rethinking assessment and inequality: The production of disparities in attainment in early years education. *Journal of Education Policy*, 26(5), pp. 655–75.

Breakwell, G.M. (1983) Formulation and searches. In G.M. Breakwell (ed.) *Threatened Identities*. Chichester, UK: Wiley, pp. 3–26.

Brehony, K.J. (2005) Primary schooling under New Labour. *Oxford Review of Education*, 31(1), pp. 29–46.

Brockner, J. (1979) The effects of self-esteem, success–failure, and self-consciousness on task performance. *Journal of Personality and Social Psychology*, 37(10), pp. 1732–41.

Brown, M., Askew, M., Baker, D., Denvir, H. & Millet, A. (1998) Is the National Numeracy Strategy Research-based. *British Journal of Educational Studies*, 46(4), pp. 362–85.

Burkard, T. (2004) *After the Literacy Hour. May the Best Plan Win!* Centre for Policy Studies, March.

Butler, D.L. & Winne, P.H. (1995) Feedback and self-regulated learning: A theoretical synthesis. *Review of Educational Research*, 65(3), pp. 245–81.

Butler, R. (1988) Enhancing and undermining intrinsic motivation. The effects of task-involving and ego involving evaluation on interest and performance. *British Journal of Educational Psychology*, 58, pp. 1–14.

Cardinet, J. (1986) *Evaluation scolaire et pratique*. Bruxelles: De Boeck.

Carlisle, O. and Jordan, A. (2008) It works practice but will it work in theory. The theoretical underplanning of pedagogy. Web: www.aishe.org/carlisle/jordan/IT

Carr, M. (2001) Assessment in Early Childhood Settings: Learning Stories. London: Paul Chapman Publishing.

Chevallard, Y. (1986) Vers une analyse didactique des faits d'evaluation. In J-M de Ketel (ed.) *Evaluation: approche descriptif ou perscriptif?* Bruxels: De Boeck, pp. 31–59.

Children and their Primary Schools. A report of the Central Advisory Council for Education (England – The Plowden Report) Volume 1, HMSO (1967).

Christie, T. & Boyle, B. (1991) *A Guide to Teacher Assessment Packs A, B & C*. London: Heinemann.

Clariana, R.B., Wagner, D. & Roher Murphy, L.C. (2000) Applying a connectionist description of feedback timing. *Educational Technology Research & Development*, 48, pp. 5–11.

Coffey, J., Hammer, D., Levin, D.M. & Grant, T. (2011) The missing disciplinary substance of formative assessment. *Journal of Research in Science Teaching*, 48(10), pp. 1109–36.

Corno, L. (1993) The best laid plans. *Educational Researcher*, 22(2) pp. 14–22.

Covington, M.V. (2000) Goal theory, motivation, and school achievement: An integrative review. *Annual Review Psychology*, 51, pp. 171–200.

Cowie, B. (2005) Pupil commentary on assessment for learning. *The Curriculum Journal*, 16(2), pp. 137–51.

Cowie, J. & Ruddock, H. (1988) *Co-operative Group Work: An Overview*. Volume 1. BP Educational Service: UK.

Creswell, J.W. (2003) *Research Design: Qualitative, Quantitative and Mixed Methods Approaches*, 2nd edn. Thousand Oaks, CA: Sage.

Crooks, T. (1988) The impact of classroom evaluation practice on students. *Review of Educational Research*, 48, pp. 438–81.

Curtis, A. & Bailey, K.M. (2001) Picture your students talking: Using pictures in the language classroom. *ESL Magazine*, 4(4), pp. 10–11.

Dadds, M. (2001) The politics of pedagogy. *Teachers and Teaching: Theory and Practice*, 7(1), pp. 43–58.

Danzig, A. (1995) Applications and distortions of Basil Bernstein's code. In A.R. Sadovnik (ed.) *Knowledge and Pedagogy: The Sociology of Basil Bernstein*. Norwood, NJ: Ablex Publishing, pp. 145–70.

Dearing, R. (1994) *The National Curriculum and its Assessment*. School Curriculum & Assessment Association.

Deci, E.L., Koestner, R. & Ryan, R.M. (1999) A meta-analytic review of experiments examining the effects of extrinsic rewards on intrinsic motivation. *Psychological Bulletin*, 125, pp. 627–68.

De Waal A. (2006). *Times Educational Supplement.*

Department for Children, Schools and Families (DCSF) (2007) *Improving Writing with a Focus on Guided Writing*. London: DCSF.

Department for Children, Schools and Families (2008) *The Early Years Foundation Stage. Setting the Standard for Learning, Development and Care for Children from Birth to Five*. London: DCSF.

Department for Education and Employment (1998a) *The Implementation of the National Literacy Strategy: The Final Report of the Literacy Task Force*. London: DfEE.

Department for Education and Employment (1998b) *The Implementation of the National Numeracy Strategy: The Final Report of the Numeracy Task Force*. London: DfEE.

Department for Education and Employment (1998c) *The National Literacy Strategy: Framework for Teaching*. London: DfEE.

Department for Education and Employment (1999) *The National Numeracy Strategy: Framework for Teaching Mathematics from Reception to Year 6*. London: DfEE.

Department for Education and Science (DES) (1975) *A Language for Life. (The Bullock Report.)* London: HMSO.

Department for Education and Science (DES) Task Group on Assessment and Testing (1988) *National Curriculum Task Group on Assessment and Testing: Three Supplementary Reports*. London: DES.

Department for Education and Science (1988b) *Education Reform Act*. London: HMSO.

Department for Education and Skills (2003) *Excellence and Enjoyment: A Strategy for Primary Schools*. London: DfES.

Department for Education and Skills (2005) *KEEP: Key Elements of Effective Practice*. London: DfES.

Department for Education and Skills (2006) *Revised Primary Framework*. London: DfES.

Deployment and Impact of Support Staff (DISS) (2003–2008) The Characteristics of Support Staff and Preparedness. DISS briefing note 2. Blatchford, P., Bassett, P., Brown, P., Martin, C., Russell, A. & Webster, R. (2009) DCSF – RB 148.

Depree, H. & Iversen, S. (1994) *Early Literacy in the Classroom*. Desoto, TX: Wright Group Publishing.

Dewey, J. (1933) *How we Think: A Restatement of the Relation of Reflective Thinking to the Educative Process*. Boston: D.C. Health.

Douglas, M. (1992) *Risk and Blame: Essays in Cultural Theory*. Abingdon: Routledge.

Duke, N.K. & Kays, J. (1998) 'Can I say once upon a time'? Kindergarten children developing knowledge of information book language. *Early Childhood Research Quarterly*, 13(2), pp. 295–318.

Dunn, K.E. & Mulvenon, S.W. (2009) A Critical Review of Research on FA: The Limited scientific Evidence of the impact of FA in Education. *Practical Assessment, Research & Evaluation*, 14(7), pp. 1–11.

Dunphy, L. (2008) Developing pedagogy in infant classes in primary schools in Ireland. *Learning from Research*, 27(1), pp. 55–70.

Dweck, C.S., Davidson, W., Nelson, S. & Enna, B. (1978) Sex differences in learned helplessness. II. The contingencies of evaluative feedback in the classroom and III. An experimental analysis. *Developmental Psychology*, 14(3), pp. 268–76.

Edwards, A. (2001) Researching Pedagogy: A Socio-cultural agenda. *Pedagogy, Culture and Society*, 9, pp. 161–86.

Eisner, E.W. (1985) *Educational Imagination: On the Design and Evaluation of School Programs*. New York: Macmillan.

Eke, R. & Lee, J. (2004) Pace and differentiation in the literacy hour: Some outcomes of an analysis of transcripts. *The Curriculum Journal*, 15(3), pp. 219–31.

Englert, C.S., Berry, R. & Dunsmore, K.L. (2001) A case study of the apprenticeship process: Another perspective on the apprentice and the scaffolding metaphor. *Journal of Learning Disabilities*, 34(2), pp. 152–71.

Englert, C.S., Mariage, T.B. & Dunsmore, K. (2006) *Tenets of Sociological Theory in Writing Instruction Research*, pp. 208–21.

Eraut, M. (1994) *Developing Professional Knowledge and Competence*. London: Falmer Press.

Erickson, F. (1986) Qualitative methods on research on teaching. In M.C. Wittrock (ed.) *Handbook of Research on Teaching*. New York: Macmillan, pp. 119–61.

Fisher, R. & Williams, M. (2000) *Unlocking Literacy: A Guide for Teachers*. London: David Fulton.

Flower, L., Hayes, J.R., Carey, L., Shriver, K. & Stratman, J. (1986) Detection diagnosis and the strategies of revision. *College Composition & Communication*, 37 (1), pp. 16–53.

Fook, J., White, S. & Gardner, F. (2006) *Critical Reflection in Health & Social Care*. Maidenhead: Open University Press.

Foucault, M. (1975) *Surveillir et punir: naissance de la prison*. Paris: Gallimard.

Freire, P. (1970) *Pedagogy of the Oppressed*. New York: Continuum.

Galton, M., & Hargreaves, L. (2009) Group Work: still a neglected art? *Cambridge Journal of Education* (39), pp. 1–6.

Galton, M., Hargreaves, L., Comber, C., Wall, D. & Pell, T. (1999) Changes in patterns of teacher interaction in primary classrooms: 1976–1996. *British Educational Research Journal*, 25(1), pp. 23–37.

Galton, M., Simon, B. & Croll, P. (1980) *Inside the Primary Classroom*. London: Routledge & Kegan Paul.

Gammage, P. (1986) *Primary Education: Structure and Context*. London: Harper and Row.

Gerson, H. & Bateman, E. (2010) Authority in an agency-centred, inquiry-based university calculus classroom. *Journal of Mathematical Behavior*, 29(4), pp 195–206.

Giddens, A. (1987) *The Constitution of Society: Outline of the Theory of Structuration*. Berkeley, CA: University of California Press.

Gipps, C. (1994) *Beyond Testing: Towards a Theory of Educational Assessment*. London: Falmer Press.

Gipps, C., Brown, M., McCallun, B., & McAllister, S. (1995) Intuition or Evidence. Buckinghamshire: Open University Press.

Good, R. (2011) Formative use of assessment: it's a process, so let's say what we mean. *Practical Assessment, Research & Evaluation*, 16(3).

Goouch, K. (2008) Understanding playful pedagogies, play narratives and play spaces. *Journal of Early Years Education*, 28(1), pp. 93–102.

Gorard, S. (2010) Semius doubts about school effectiveness. *British Educational Research Journal*, 36(5), pp. 745–66.

Gould, J.S. (1981) *Mismeasure of Man*. New York: W.W. Norton.

Graham, S. & Harris, K.R. (1989) Improving learning disabled students' skills at composing essays: Self-instructional strategy training. *Exceptional Children*, 56, pp. 201–31.

Graham, S., Harris, K.R. & Mason, L. (2005). Improving the writing performance, knowledge, and self-efficacy of struggling young writers: The effects of self-regulated strategy development. *Contemporary Educational Psychology*, 30, pp. 207–41.

Graziano, K.G. (2008) Walk the Talk: Connecting critical pedagogy and practice in teacher education. *Teaching Education*, 19(2), pp. 153–63.

Green, S. & Oates, T. (2007) *How to Promote Educational Quality Through National Assessment Systems*. Paper presented at the International Association for Educational Assessment, Annual Conference, Baku, Azerbaijan, September. University of Cambridge.

Greeno, J. & Goldman, S. (eds) (1998) Thinking Practices in Mathematics and Science Learning. Mahwah, NJ: Lawrence Erlbaum Associates Inc.

Guinier, L. (2003) The Supreme Court, 2002 Term: Comment: Admissions Rituals as Political Acts: Guardians at the Gates of Our Democratic Ideals. *Harvard Law Review*, November 2003.

Guinier, L. & Torres, G. (2003) *The Miner's Canary: Enlisting Race, Resisting Power, Transforming Democracy*. Cambridge, MA: Harvard University Press.

Guthrie, J.T. & Wigfield, A. (2000) Engagement and Motivation in Reading. In M.L. Kamil, P.B. Mosenthal, P.D. Pearson & R. Barr (eds) *Handbook of Reading Research*, Vol 3, pp. 403–22.

Haberman, M. (1991) The pedagogy of poverty versus good teaching. *Phi Delta Kappan*, 73(4), pp. 290–294.

Hager, P. & Hodgkinson, P. (2009) Moving beyond the metaphor of transfer of learning. *BERJ*, 35(4), pp. 619–38.

Hall, K., Collins, J., Benjamin, S., Nind, M. & Sheehy, K. (2004) Saturated models of pupildom: Assessment and inclusion/exclusion. *British Educational Research Journal*, 30(6), pp. 801–17.

Hall, K. & Harding, A. (2002) Level descriptions and teacher assessment in England: Towards a community of practice. *Educational Research*, 44(1), pp. 1–15.

Hallam, S. & Ireson, J. (2003) Secondary school teachers' attitudes to and beliefs about ability grouping. *British Journal of Educational Psychology*, 73, pp. 343–56.

Hallam, S., Ireson, J. & Davies, J. (2004) Primary pupils' experiences of different types of grouping in school. *British Journal of Educational Research*, 30, pp. 515–33.

Hamm, J.V. & Perry, M. (2002) Learning mathematics in first-grade classrooms: on whose authority? *Journal of Educational Psychology*, 94(1), pp. 126–37.

Harris, E.L. (1995) Toward a grid and group interpretation of school culture. *Journal of School Leadership*, 56(6), pp. 617–46.

Hartley, D. (1993) *Understanding the Nursery School.* London: Cassell.

Hartley, D. (2002) Global influences on teacher education. *Journal of Education for Teaching*, 28(3), pp. 78–105.

Hartley, D. (2003) New economy, new pedagogy? *Oxford Review of Education*, 29(1), pp. 81–94.

Hattie, J.A. (1992) *Self-concept.* Hillsdale, NJ: Lawrence Erlbaum.

Hattie, J.A., Biggs, J. & Purdie, N. (1996) Effects of learning skills intervention on student learning. A meta-analysis. *Review of Research in Education*, 66, pp. 99–136.

Hattie, J. & Timperley, H. (2007) The power of feedback. *Review of Educational Research*, 77(1), pp. 81–112.

Hayes, J. & Flower, L. (1986) Writing research and the writer. *American Psychologist*, 41, pp. 1106–13.

Hayes, N. (2008) Teaching matters in early educational practice: The case for a nurturing pedagogy. *Early Education and Development*, 19(3), pp. 430–40.

Heritage, M. (2011) Knowing what to do next: The hard part of formative assessment? Special issue of *CADMO: An International Journal of Education Research*, 19(1), pp. 67–84.

Hodges, H. (2001) Overcoming a pedagogy of poverty. In R.W. Cole (ed) *More Strategies for Educating Everybody's Children*, pp. 1–9. Alexandria, VA: Association for Supervision and Curriculum Development.

Hopkins, D. (1993) *A Teacher's Guide to Classroom Research.* Buckingham: Open University.

Howard, S.K. (2007) Teacher change: A preliminary exploration of teachers' risk-taking in the context of ICT integration. *Journal of Australian Association for Research in Education*, pp. 1–13.

Howie, E., Sy, S., Ford, L. & Vincente, K.J. (2000) Human-computer interface design can reduce misperceptions of feedback. *System Dynamics Review*, 16(3), pp. 151–71.

Hudson, J.A. & Shapiro, L.R. (1991) From knowing to telling … In A. McCabe & C. Peterson (eds) *Developing Narrative Structure* (Chapter 3). Hillsdale, NJ: Laurence Erlbaum Associates.

Huitt, W.G. & Cain, S.C. (2005) An overview of the conative domain. *Educational Psychology Interactive.* Available at: http://www.edpsycinteractive.org/brilstar/chapters/conative.pdf

Hunter, J. (2009) Developing a Productive Discourse Community in the Mathematics Classroom. In Hunter, R., Bicknell, B. & Burgess, T. (eds) Crossing divides: Proceedings of the 32nd Annual Conference of the Mathematics Education Research group of Australasia (Vol 1) Palmerston, North NZ: MEDGA.

Jiaoqian, B.M. (2004) Application of the skills of non-verbal communication in classroom teaching. www.1.open.edu.cn/elt/8/5.htm.

Jolliffe, W. (2004) *The National Literacy Strategy: Not Prescriptive Enough?* Paper presented at the British Educational Research Association Annual Conference, University of Manchester, 16–18 September.

Kazemi, E., Franke, M. & Lampert, M. (2009) Developing pedagogies in teacher education to support novice teachers' ability to enact ambitious instruction. In R. Hunter, B. Bicknell & T. Burgess (eds) *Crossing Divides: Proceedings of the 32nd Annual Conference of the Mathematics Education Research Group of Australasia, Vol. 1.* Palmerston North, New Zealand: Mathematics Education Research Group of Australasia, pp. 11–29.

Kirby, P. (1996) Teacher questions during story-book reading: Who's building whose building. *Literacy*, 30(1), pp. 8–15.

Kluger, A.N. & DeNisi, A. (1996) The effects of feedback interventions on performance: A historical review, a meta-analysis and a preliminary feedback intervention theory. *Psychological Bulletin*, 119(2), pp. 254–84.

Kulhavey, R.W. & Wagner, W. (1993) Feedback in programmed instruction: Historical context and implication for practice. In J.V. Dempsey & G.C. Sales (eds), *Interactive Instruction and Feedback*. Englewood Cliffs: Education Technology.

Kulvaney, R.W., White, M.T., Topp, B.W., Chan, A.L. & Adams, J. (1985) Feedback complexity and corrective efficiency. *Contemporary Educational Psychology*, 10, pp. 285–91.

Kutnick, P., Blatchford, P. & Baines, E. (2002) Pupil grouping in primary school classrooms: Sites for learning and social pedagogy? *British Educational Research Journal*, 28(2), pp. 189–208.

Lave, J. (1991) Situating learning in communities of practice. In L.B. Resnick, J.M. Levine & S.D. Teasley (eds) *Perspectives on Socially Shared Cognition*. Washington, DC: American Psychological Association, pp. 63–82.

Lemke, J. (1990) *Talking Science: Language Learning and Values*. Norwood, NJ: Ablex Publishing Corporation.

Lopez, G.M. & Allal, L. (2007) *Regulation des apprentissages en situation scolaire et en formation*. Bruxelles: De Boeck.

Lupton, D. (1999) Introduction: Risk and socio-cultural theory. In D. Lupton (ed.) *Risk and Socio-cultural Theory: New Directions and Perspectives*. Cambridge: Cambridge University Press, pp. 1–11.

Macleod, F. & Golby, M. (2003) Theories of learning and pedagogy: Issues for teacher development. *Teacher Development*, 7(3), pp. 345–61.

McAdamis, S. (2001) Teachers tailor their instruction to meet a variety of student needs. *Journal of Staff Development*, 22(2) pp. 1–5.

McCombs, B.L. & Marzano, R.J. (1990) Putting the self in self-regulated learning: The self as agent in integrating skill and will. *Educational Psychologist*, 25(6), pp. 51–69.

McGee, L.M. & Schickendanz, J.A. (2007) Repeated read-alouds in preschool and kindergarten. *The Reading Teacher*, 60(8), pp. 742–51.

Mahoney, J.L., Hextall, I. & Menter, I. (2004) Threshold assessment and performance management: Modernizing or masculinising teaching in England. *Gender and Education*, 16(2), pp. 131–44.

Makin, L. & Whiteman, P. (2006) Young children as active participants in the investigation of teaching and learning. *European Early Childhood Education Research Journal*, 14(1), pp. 33–41.

Marsh, J. & Millard, E. (2001) Words with pictures: The role of visual literacy in writing and its implications for schooling. *Reading Literacy and Language*, 35(92), pp. 55–61.

Martin L.E., Segraves, S., Thacker, M. and Young, L. (2005) The writing process: Three first grade teachers and their students refresh on what was learned. *Reading Psychology*, 26, pp. 235–49.

Mason, R.A. & Just, M.A. (2011) *Differential Cortical Networks for Inferences Concerning People's Intentions Versus Physical Causality*. Department of Psychology, Paper 416. Dietrich College of Humanities, USA.

Matthews (1999) *The Art of Childhood and Adolescence: The Construction of Meaning*. London: The Falmer Press.

Mehan, H.B. (1971) Accomplished understanding in educational settings. Doctoral dissertation, University of California, USA.

Mercer, N. (2008) Talk and the development of reasoning and understanding. *Human Development*, 51(1), pp. 90–100.

Mercer, N. & Dawes, L. (2008) The value of exploratory talk. In N. Mercer & S. Hodgkinson (eds) *Exploring Talk in School*. London: Sage.

Meyer, D.K. & Turner, J.C. (2002) Discovering emotion in classroom motivation research. *Educational Psychologist*, 37(2), pp. 107–14.

Meyer, L., Wardrop, J., Stahl, S. & Linn, R. (1994) Effects of reading storybooks aloud to children. *Journal of Educational Research*, 88, pp. 69–85.

Ministry of Education (1996) Te Whãriki Matauranga mo nga O Aotearoa. Early Childhood Curriculum. Wellington, New Zealand: Learning Media Ltd.

Minstrell, J. & Van Zee, E.H. (2003) Using questioning to assess and foster student thinking. In J.M Atkin & J.E. Coffey (eds) *Everyday Assessment in the Science Classroom*. Arlington, VA: National Science Teachers Association Press.

Monteil, J.M. & Huguet, P. (1999) *Social Context and Cognitive Performance: Towards a Social Psychology of Cognition*. Hove, East Sussex: Psychology Press.

Monteil, J.M. & Huguet, P. (2001) The social regulation of classroom performances: A theoretical outline. *Social Psychology of Education*, 4, pp. 359–72.

Morrissette, J. (2011) Formative assessment: Revisiting the territory from the point of view of teachers. *McGill Journal of Education*, 46(2), pp. 247–64.

Moss, G. (2007) *Lessons from the National Literacy Strategy*. Paper presented at the Annual Conference of the British Educational Research Association, September.

Mottier Lopez, L. & Allal, L. (2007) Socio-mathematical norms and the regulation of problem solving in the classroom. *International Journal of Educational Research*, 46, pp. 252–65.

Moyles, J. Adams, S. & Musgrove, A. (2002) *SPEEL: Study of Pedagogical Effectiveness in Early Years Learning*. Department for Education & Skills. Research Report RR363.

Murphy, J. (1980) *Peace At Last*. London: Walker Books.

Myhill, D. (2006) Talk, talk, talk: Teaching and learning in whole class discourse. *Research Papers in Education*, 21(1), pp. 19–41.

Newman, D., Griffin, P. & Cole, M. (1989) *The Construction Zone: Working for cognitive change in school*. New York: Cambridge University Press.

Nobes, G., Moore, D., Martin, A., Clifford, B., Butterworth, G., Panayiotaki, G. & Siegal, M. (2003) Children's understanding of the earth in a multicultural community: Mental modes or fragments of knowledge? *Developmental Science*, 6(1), pp. 72–85.

Nystrand, M. (1997) Dialogic instruction: When recitation becomes conversation. In M. Nystrand, A. Gamoran, R. Kachur & C. Prendergast (1997) *Opening Dialogue: Understanding the Dynamics of Language and Learning in the English Classroom*. New York: Teachers College Press, pp. 1–29.

Nystrand, M., Gamoran, A., Kachur, R. & Prendergast, C. (1997) *Opening Dialogue: Understanding the Dynamics of Language and Learning in the English Classroom*. New York: Teachers College Press.

Office for Standards in Education (2004) *Annual Report of Her Majesty's Chief Inspector of Schools*. Ofsted: London.

Organisation for Economic Co-operation and Development (OECD) (2004) *Lifelong Learning*. Policy Brief, February. Paris: OECD.

Organisation for Economic Co-operation and Development (OECD) (2005) *Formative assessment: Improving learning in secondary classrooms*. Policy Brief, November. Paris: OECD.

Osborn, M., McNess, E. & Broadfoot, P., with Pollard, A. & Triggs, P. (2000) *What Teachers Do: Changing Policy and Practice in Primary Education, Findings from the PACE Project*. London: Continuum.

Paris, S.G., Wixson, K.K. & Palincsar, A.M. (1986) Instructional approaches to reading comprehension. In E. Rothkopt (ed). *Review of Research in Education*. Wahington, DC: American Educational Research Association, pp. 91–128.

Paris, S.G. & Cunningham, A. (1996) Children become students. In D. Berliner & R. Calfee (eds) *Handbook of Educational Psychology*. New York: Macmillan, pp. 117–47.

Paris, S.G. & Winograd, P. (1999) *The Role of Self-regulated Learning in Contextual Teaching: Principles and Practices for Teacher Preparation. Contextual Teaching and Learning: Preparing Teachers to Enhance Student Success in the Workplace and Beyond*. (Information Series no 376), Columbus, OH.

Paris, S.G. & Paris, A.H. (2001) Classroom applications of research on self-regulated learning. *Educational Psychologist*, 36(2), pp. 89–101.

Patrick, F., Forde, C. & McPhee, A. (2003) Challenging the 'New Professionalism': From managerialism to pedagogy? *Journal of In-service Education*, 29(2), pp. 237–53.

Perrenoud, P. (1991) Towards a pragmatic approach to formative evaluation. In P. Weston (ed.) *Assessment of Pupils' Achievement: Motivation and school success*. Amsterdam: Swets & Zeitlinger, pp. 79–101.

Perrenoud, P. (1996) The teaching profession between proletarianism and professionalization: two models of change. *Outlook* XXVI, pp. 543–62.

Perrenoud, P. (1997) Pedagogie differenciee: Des intentions a l'action. Issy-les-Moulineaux: EFS Editeur.

Perrenoud, P. (1998) From a formative evaluation to a controlled regulation of learning processes towards a wider conceptual field. *Assessment in Education: Principles, Policy and Practice,* 5(1), pp. 85–102.

Perrenoud, P. (2004) Métier d'élève et sens du travail scolaire. Paris: Editions Sociales Françaises.

Perry, N.E., Hutchinson, L. & Thauberger, C. (2007) Mentoring student teachers to design and implement literacy tasks that support self-regulated reading and writing. *Reading & Writing Quarterly*, 23, pp. 27–50.

Piazza, C.L. (2003) *Journeys: The Teaching of Writing in Elementary Classrooms*. Upper Saddle River, NJ: Pearson Education.

Pollard, A., with Anderson, J., Maddock, M., Swaffield, S., Warin, J. & Warwick, P. (2008) *Reflective Teaching: Evidence-informed Professional Practice*, 3rd edn. London: Continuum.

Pollard, A. & Tann, S. (1995) *Reflective Teaching in the Primary School: A Handbook for the Classroom*. London: Cassell.

Popham, W.J. (2006) Phony formative assessments: Buyer beware! *Educational Leadership*. 64(3) pp. 86–87.

Popham, W.J. (2008) *Transformative Assessment*. Alexandria, VA: Association of Supervision & Curriculum Development.

Powell, A. (2001) Notes on the origins of meritocracy in American schooling. *History of Education Quarterly*, 41(1) pp. 73–80.

Pradl, G. (1979) *Expectation and Cohesion*. Bay Area Writing Project, University of California, USA.

Pressley, M., Harris, K.R. & Marks, M.B. (1992) But good strategy instructors are constructivists! *Educational Psychology Review*, 4, pp. 3–31.

Primary Framework for literacy and mathematics. A Summary of the DFES Framework – Ref. 0211–2206 BOK-EN, October 2006.

Protheroe, N. (2010) *Principal's Playbook: Tackling School Improvement*. Alexandria, VA: Educational Research Service.

Pryor, J. & Crossouard, B. (2008) A Socio-cultural Theorisation of FA. *Oxford Review of Education* 34(10), pp. 1–20.

Purcell-Gates, V., McIntyre, E. & Freppon, P. (1995) Learning written storybook language in school: A comparison of low SES children in skills-based and whole language classrooms. *American Educational Research Journal*, 32, pp. 659–85.

Radford, J., Blatchford, P. & Webster, R. (2011) Opening up and closing down: How teachers and TAs manage turn-taking, topic and repair in mathematics lessons. *Learning and Instruction*, 21(5), pp. 625–35.

Ramaprasad, A. (1983) On the definition of feedback. *Behavioural Science*, 28(1) pp. 4–13.

Randi, J. & Corno, L. (1997) Teachers as innovators. International Handbook of Teachers & Teaching. Vol 1. pp. 1163–1221. Netherlands: Kluwer Academic.

Randi, J. & Corno, L. (2000) Teacher innovations in self-regulated learning. In M. Bockaerts, P.R. Pintrich & M. Zeidner, (eds) *Handbook of Self-regulation*, pp. 651–85. San Diego, CA: Academic Press.

Raveaud, M. (2005) Hares, tortoises and the social construction of the pupil: Differentiated learning in French and English primary schools. *British Educational Research Journal*, 31(4), pp. 459–79.

Reeves, D., Boyle, B. & Christie, T. (2001) The relationship between teacher assessments and pupil attainments in standard tests/tasks at key stage 2, 1996–98. *British Educational Research Journal*, 27(2), pp. 141–60.

Rijlaarsdam, G., Braaksma, M., Couzijn, M., Janssen, T., Raedts, M., Steendam, E.V., Toorenaar, A. & Van Den Bergh, H. (2008) Observation of peers in learning to write: Practise and research. *Journal of Writing Research*, 1(1), pp. 53–63.

Rist, R.C. (1977) On understanding the process of schooling: The contributions of labelling theory. In J. Karabel & A.H. Halsey (eds) *Power and Ideology in Education*. New York: Oxford University Press, pp. 292–305.

Robbins, C. & Ehri, L.C. (1994) Reading storybooks to kindergarteners help them to learn new vocabulary words. *Journal of Educational Psychology*, 86(1), pp. 54–64.

Rogoff, B. (1990) *Apprerticeship in Thinking*. New York: OUP.

Rogoff, B., Baker-Sennett, J., Lacasa, P. & Goldsmith, D. (1995) Development through participation in sociocultural activity. In J.J. Goodnow, P.J. Miller & F. Kessel (eds) *Cultural Practices as Contexts for Development*. San Francisco: Jossey-Bass, pp. 45–65.

Rohrmann, B. & Renn, O. (2000) Risk perception research – an introduction. In O. Renn and B. Rohrmann (eds) *Cross-cultural Risk Preceptions: A Survey of Empirical Studies*. Dordrecht: Kluwer Academic Publishers, Vol. 13, pp. 11–54.

Rosenthal, R. & Jacobson, L. (1968) *Pygmalion in the Classroom: Teacher Expectations and Student Intellectual Development*. New York: Holt.

Rowsell, J., Kosnik, C. & Beck, C. (2008) Fostering multiliteracies pedagogy through pre-service teacher education. *Teaching Education*, 19(2), pp. 109–22.

Ruthven, K., Hofmann, R. & Mercer, N. (2011) A dialogic approach to plenary problem synthesis. Proceedings of the 35th Conference of the International Group for the Psychology of Mathematics Education, 4, pp. 81–8.

Ruttle, K. (2004) What goes on inside my head when I'm writing? A case study of 8–9 year old boys. *Literacy*, July, pp. 71–7.

Sadler, D.R. (1989) *Formative Assessment and the Design of Instructional Systems*. Boston, MA: Kluwer Academic Press.

Salvetti, E.P. (2001) Project story boost: Read-alouds for student at risk. *The Reading Teacher*, 55(1), pp. 76–83.

Scardamalia, M. & Bereiter, C. (1992) Text-based and knowledge-based questioning by children. *Cognition and Instruction*, 9(3), pp. 177–99.

Schön, D.A. (1983) *The Reflective Practitioner*. Farnham, UK: Ashgate Publishing.

Schunk, D.H. & Zimmerman, B.J. (1997) Social origins of self-regulatory competence. *Educationalist Psychologist*, 32(4), pp. 195–208.

Schunk, D.H. & Zimmerman, B.J. (2007) Influencing children's self-efficacy and self-regulation of reading and writing through modelling. *Reading & Writing Quarterly*, 23, pp. 7–25.

Scott, P., Ametller, J., Dawes, L., Mercer, N. & Kleine-Staarman, J. (2007) *An Investigation of Dialogic Teaching in Science Classrooms*. Paper presented at NARST, New Orleans, April.

Senechal, M. & Young, L. (2008) The effect of family literacy intervention on children's acquisition of reading from kindergarten to Grade 3: A meta-analytic review. *Review of Educational Research*, 78, pp. 880–907.

Shepard, L.A. (2000) The role of assessment in a learning culture. *Educational Researcher*, 29(7), pp. 4–14.

Shepard, L.A. (2005) Linking formative assessment to scaffolding. *Educational Leadership*, 63(3), pp. 66–70.

Shor, I. & Freire, P. (1987) *A Pedagogy for Liberation: Dialogues on Transforming Education*. South Hadley, MA: Bergin & Garvey Publishers.

Silverman, D. (2000) *Doing Qualitative Research*. London: Sage.

Simon, B. (1985) Why no pedagogy in England? In B. Simon & W. Tayor (eds) *Education in the Eighties: The Central Issues*. London: Batsford, pp. 124–45.

Simmons, V. & Gebhardt, A. (2009) Concept of story. (Summer 2008.) Available at: http://red6747.pbwiki.com/Concept%20of%20Story.

Siraj-Blatchford, I., Sylva, K., Muttock, S., Gilden, R. & Bell, D. (2002) *Researching Effective Pedagogy in the Early Years*. DfES Research Report 365.

Siraj-Blatchford, I. & Manni, L. (2008) Would you like to tidy up now? An analysis of adult questioning in the English Foundation Stage. *Early Years Journal*, 28(1), pp. 5–22.

Sjoberg, L., Koaroa, D., Rucai, A. & Bernstorm, M. (2000) Risk perception in Bulgaria and Romania. In O. Renn & B. Rohrmann (eds) *Cross-cultural Risk Perception: A Survey of Empirical Studies*. Dordrecht: Kluwer Academic Publishers, Vol. 13, pp. 145–84.

Smith, A.B. (1996) The early Child Curriculum from a Sociological Perspective. *Journal of Early Child Development & Care*. 115(1) pp. 51–64.

Smith, F., Hardman, F., Wall, K. & Mroz, M. (2004) Interactive whole class teaching in the national literacy and numeracy strategies. *British Educational Research Journal*, 30(3), pp. 295–411.

Soler, J. & Miller, L. (2003) The struggle for early childhood curricula: A comparison of the English Foundation Stage Curriculum, 'Te Whariki' and Reggio Emilia. *International Journal of Early Years Education*, 11(1), pp. 57–67.

Solity, J.E. (2003) *Teaching phonics in context: A Critique of the National Literacy Strategy. Playing with Sounds*. London: DfES.

Spitzer, D.R. (1975) Effect of discussion on teachers' attitudes toward risk taking in educational situations. *Journal of Educational Research*, 68(10), pp. 371–4.

Strathern, M. (2002) Abstraction and decontextualisation – an anthropological comment. In S. Woolgar (ed.) *Virtual Society? Get Real! The Sociological Science of Electronic Technologies*. Oxford: Oxford University Press.

Strike, K.A. & Posner, G.J. (1992) A revisionist theory of conceptual change. In R. Duschl & R. Hamilton (eds) *Philosophy of Science, Cognitive Psychology, and Educational Theory and Practice*. Albany, NY: SUNY Press, pp. 147–76.

Sylva, K., Melhuish, E., Sammons, P. & Siraj-Blatchford, I. (2004) The Effective provision of the pre-school education (EPPE) project: Findings from pre-school to end of key stage 1. epp.ioe.ac.uk/eppe/eppe pdfs/R&Tec 1223 sept 0412.pdf

Taber, K.S. (2000) Exploring conceptual integration in student thinking: Evidence from a case study. *International Journal of Science Education*, 30(14), pp. 1915–43.

Task Group on Assessment and Testing (TGAT) (1998) *National Curriculum Task Group on Assessment and Testing: Three Supplementary Reports*. London: Department for Education and Science.

Tharp, R.G. & Gallimore, R. (1991) *Rousing Minds to Life: Teaching, Learning and Schooling in a Social Context*. Cambridge: Cambridge University Press.

Tizard, B., Hughes, M., Carmichael, H. & Pinkerton, G. (1983) Language and social class: Is verbal deprivation a myth? *Journal of Child Psychology*, 24(4), pp. 533–42.

Tochon, F.W. (1986) Rappel stimuli, objectivation Clinique, reflexion Partagee. Fondements methodologiques et applications pratiques de la retroaction video en recherché et en formation. *Revue des Science de l'education*, 22(3), pp. 467–502.

Tochon, F. (2008) A brief history of video feedback and its role in foreign language education. *CALICO Journal*, 25(3), pp. 420–35.

Tomlinson, C.A. (2001) *How to Differentiate Instruction in Mixed-ability Classrooms.* 2nd edn. Alexandria, VA: ASCD.

Topping, K. (2001) *Thinking, Reading, Writing: A practical Guide to Paired Learning with Peers, Parents & Volunteers.* London and New York: Continuum.

Torrance, H. & Pryor, J. (1998) Investigating FA: teaching, learning & assessment in the classroom. Buckingham: Open University Press

Torrance, H. & Pryor, J. (2007) Developing FA in the classroom: using action-research to explore and modify theory. *BERJ*, 26(5), 615–31.

Troman, G., Jeffrey, B. & Raggl, A. (2007) *Performative Policies and Primary Teacher Commitment and Identity: Continuity and Change. ESRC End of Award Report: RES-000-23-0748.* Swindon: ESRC.

Twing, J., Boyle, B. & Charles, M. (2010) *Integrated Assessment Systems for Improved Learning.* Paper presented at the 36th Annual Conference of the International Association of Educational Assessment (IAEA), Bangkok, Thailand, 22–27 August.

Vanderburg, R.M. (2006) Reviewing research on teaching writing based on Vygotsky's theories: What we can learn. *Reading & Writing Quarterly*, 22, pp. 375–93.

Vygotsky, L. (1962) *Thought and Language.* Cambridge, MA: MIT Press.

Vygotsky, L. (1978) *Mind in Society.* Cambridge, MA: Harvard.

Vygotsky, L. (1986) *Thought and Language.* Cambridge, MA: MIT Press.

Webb, R. & Vulliamy, G. (2006) *Coming Full Circle: The Impact of New Labour's Education Policies on Primary School Teachers' Work.* London: Association of Teachers and Lecturers.

Webb, R. & Vulliamy, G. (2007) Changing classroom practice at Key Stage 2: The impact of New Labour's national strategies. *Oxford Review of Education,* 33 (5), pp. 561–80.

Wells, G. (1995) Language and the inquiry-oriented curriculum. *Curriculum and Inquiry,* 25(3), pp. 233–269.

Wells, G. (1999) Dialogic Enquiry: Towards a Socio-cultural Practice & Theory of Education. Cambridge: Cambridge University Press.

Wells, G. (2001) Action, talk, and text: The case for dialogic inquiry. In *Learning and Teaching Through Inquiry.* Williston, VT: Teachers College Press.

Whitehurst, G.J. & Lonigan, C.J. (1998) Child development and emergent literacy. *Child Development*, 69(3), pp. 848–72.

Williams, P. (2008) *Independent Review of Mathematics Teaching in Early Years Settings and Primary Schools. Final Report.* London: Department for Children, Schools and Families.

Wiggins, A. & Tymms, P. (2002) Dysfunctional effects of league tables: A comparison between English and Scottish primary schools. *Public Money and Management,* January–March, pp. 43–8.

Winterbottom, M., Brindley, S., Taber, K., Fisher, L.G., Finney, J. & Riga, F. (2008) Concepts of assessment: trainee teachers practice and values. *The Curriculum Journal* 19(3), pp. 193–213.

Woods, P. (2006) *Qualitative Research. Education Research in Action E835*, section 6 study guide. Open University.

Wyse, D., McCreery, E. & Torrance, H. (2007) *The Trajectory and Impact of National Reform: Curriculum and Assessment in English Primary Schools. Primary Review Interim Report.* Cambridge University.

Yackel, E. & Cobb, P. (1996) Socio-mathematical norms, argumentation and autonomy in mathematics. *Journal for Research in Mathematical Education* 27(4), pp. 458–77.

Yarrow, F. & Topping, K.J. (2001) Collaborative writing: The effect of meta-cognitive prompting and structured peer interaction. *British Journal of Educational Psychology*, 71(2), pp. 261–82.

Zakhartchouk, J.M. (2001) Pedagogie différenciée: Une indispensable clarification. *Les langues modernes*, 95(4), pp. 32–7.

Zimmerman, B.J. (2000) Attaining self-regulation: A social-cognitive perspective. In M. Boekarts, P.R. Pintich & M. Zeidner (eds) *Handbook of self-regulation*. San Diego: Academic Press, pp. 13–39.

Index